Our Street

By the Same Author

NON-FICTION

Pull No More Bines: An Oral History of East London Women Hop Pickers

A Night Out with the Girls: Women Having Fun

My East End: A History of Cockney London

FICTION

The Cockney Girl

Whitechapel Girl

The Bells of Bow

Just Around the Corner

Cissie Flowers

Dream On

The Lights of London

Playing Around

Getting There

The Sins of Their Fathers

Our Street

East End Life in the Second World War

Gilda O'Neill

VIKING
an imprint of
PENGUIN BOOKS

VIKING

Published by the Penguin Group
Penguin Books Ltd, 80 Strand, London WC2R 0RL, England
Penguin Putnam Inc., 375 Hudson Street, New York, New York 10014, USA
Penguin Books Australia Ltd, 250 Camberwell Road, Camberwell, Victoria 3124, Australia
Penguin Books Canada Ltd, 10 Alcorn Avenue, Toronto, Ontario, Canada M4V 3B2
Penguin Books India (P) Ltd, 11 Community Centre, Panchsheel Park, New Delhi – 110 017, India
Penguin Books (NZ) Ltd, Cnr Rosedale and Airborne Roads, Albany, Auckland, New Zealand
Penguin Books (South Africa) (Pty) Ltd, 24 Sturdee Avenue, Rosebank 2196, South Africa

Penguin Books Ltd, Registered Offices: 80 Strand, London WC2R 0RL, England

www.penguin.com

First published 2003
1

Set in 12/15 pt Minion
Typeset by Rowland Phototypesetting Ltd, Bury St Edmunds, Suffolk
Printed in Great Britain by Clays Ltd, St Ives plc

A CIP catalogue record for this book is available from the British Library

ISBN 0–670–91511–4

With my thanks, as always, to Eleo Gordon, and, of course, to Lesley Levene

When a man dies, a book dies with him.
Caribbean saying

Contents

List of Illustrations xi
Preface 1
Introduction: The Build-up to War 9

1 ARP, the Blackout and Sheltering 19
2 Coping with the Bombing 43
3 Childhood 67
4 Evacuation 85
5 Rationing, Shortages, Making-do and Mending 113
6 Joining Up and Doing Your Bit 140
7 Work 154
8 Needing the Doctor 173
9 Courting and Weddings 186
10 Family Separation and Loss 206
11 Community Spirit 217
12 Breaking the Rules 227
13 Leisure Time 246
14 The Aftermath: It's All Over, or is It? 265

Chronology 283
Acknowledgements 294
Sources of Information and Suggestions for Further Reading 299

List of Illustrations

Section One

1. Blitz damage to Whitman House on the Cornwall Estate, Bethnal Green.
2. ARP Warden King, accompanied by his dog Rip, begins his nightly duties along Southill Street during a London peasouper.
3. The railway arches, Arnold Road, Bow, showing the sandbagged entrance to the shelter belonging to J. O'Connor, the cooper and barrel merchants.
4. Bedtime stories in the shelter.
5. East Enders experience nightly overcrowding and lack of privacy as they shelter in the underground.
6. Devastation in Poplar.
7. GIs lend Londoners a hand to clear up after a raid.
8. Searching through the debris of a house in Cyprus Street, Old Ford.
9. An ARP warden helping homeless East End mothers and their babies move to a place of greater safety.

10–13. Ordinary domestic life still had to go on.

14. The postman does his best to deliver the mail.
15. A family with nowhere left to receive their letters. All that remains of their home is piled up on the handcart.

Section Two

16. Young Peter Hodgson sitting among the blitzed ruins of Single Street School, Stepney.
17. London families waiting for transport to evacuate the women and children from the bombing.
18. Little ones evacuated from Columbia Market Nursery to

Alwalton Hall, near Peterborough, wave goodbye to their parents.
19. Older London lads, evacuated to Devon, being taught how to plough.
20. London evacuees and Italian prisoners of war in the West Country.
21. A young Londoner 'doing her bit' by adding scraps to the pig bin.
22. A housewife 'doing her bit' by sorting tin and paper for salvage.
23. Queen Elizabeth pays a visit to the Sewardstone Road piggery in June 1943.
24. Models demonstrating the new Utility underwear.
25. Cancelling the coupons for a customer's weekly ration, comprising tea, sugar, butter, cooking fat, bacon and 'special margarine'.
26. Goods such as tobacco, cigarettes and especially matches were not rationed, but they were still hard to come by.
27. Children in Russia Lane, Bethnal Green, clearing a bomb site to create allotments for growing vegetables.
28. Part of the astonishing 100 tons of scrap collected at Northumberland Wharf in Poplar after the mayor made an appeal for salvage in July 1940.
29. Exhausted and dirty but safe, a childhood victim of war is given what limited comfort is available.
30. An adult casualty being tended until medical help arrives.
31. Nurses at St Peter's Hospital, Stepney, recover what they can from the debris, April 1941.

Section Three

32. Damage to Spiller's Flour Mills, Royal Victoria Dock, following the first mass daylight raid on London on 7 September 1940.

33. A 1939 appeal for civil defence volunteers from the stage of the 'Ipp' – the Poplar Hippodrome, East India Dock Road.
34. Protecting the docks, November 1941. A detachment of the Port of London's Home Guard, originally known as Local Defence Volunteers, march with fixed bayonets.
35. Tin hats, buckets and stirrup pumps were used by fire watchers such as these men on duty on the roof of the Troxy Cinema, Commercial Road.
36. The London Fire Brigade battles with blazing warehouses in the Eastern Basin, St Katherine Dock, 8 September 1940.
37. Salvaging what was left of the tens of thousands of tons of sugar that went up in flames in the West India Dock, 8 September 1940.
38. Members of the Women's Legion preparing cheese rolls for London dockers.
39–40. Enjoying their work – women showing off newly found skills on the railways and the factory floor.
41. Taking care of homeless East End youngsters.
42. Elaborate use of gummed paper to protect the window of the Victoria Wine Company in East India Dock Road.
43. London families settling down to enjoy their Sunday dinner.
44. Londoners enjoying their special day, despite the sandbags, tin helmets and gas masks, and the lack of a traditional wedding gown.
45. Even 'down the shelter' – in this case a section of uncompleted underground line between Liverpool Street and Bethnal Green – Londoners could still enjoy a knees-up.
46. King George V Dock, March 1946. The war is over and young Peter Stewart is somewhat dubious as he inspects tins of honey and dried fruits.
47. It's 1946, and yes, we have some bananas! A stall in Bethnal Green proudly displays the much-missed fruit and also has beetroot for sale at 5d a pound.

Endpaper: Detail from a clothing ration book, 1949–50.

Illustration Acknowledgements
Associated Press: 9, 13, 17, 26, 31; Camera Press: 4, 24, 45; Hulton Archive/Getty Images: 44; Imperial War Museum: 12, 19, 20, 21, 22, 25; Mirrorpix: 29; Museum in Docklands PLA Collection: 32, 34, 36, 37, 38, 46; Museum of London: 5; News International Syndication: 11, 16, 41; Press Association: 7, 10, 47; Public Record Office: 30, 39, 40, endpaper, pages 15, 23, 87, 126, 156, 208, 258; Science and Society Picture Library, Science Museum: 14, 15, 43; Tower Hamlets Local History Library: 1, 2, 3, 6, 8, 18, 23, 27, 28,
33, 35, 42.

Preface

One day, while I was watching the news on television, I saw a reporter interviewing members of the public about their sightings of an escaped vulture that had, for some reason, taken a fancy to roosting in their street. What interested me, apart from the presence of such an exotic creature, was the predominant response of the people being interviewed – one not of fear or surprise, but of pleasure. Not only was it an unusual and exciting event – visiting vultures must surely rank right up there with the remarkable – but it was also something that, in the words of one elderly man, 'brought us all together, and that doesn't happen very often nowadays'. For those few days, that street had been drawn back into being a community, and people in the neighbourhood were actually talking to one another.

I wanted to write about a time and a place when living in such a street – or rather a community – would have been part of so-called ordinary working people's everyday experience, but when the circumstances couldn't exactly be described as normal. So, in this book, 'our street' is a place in the East End of London during the Second World War.

It is any average little turning in the area nowadays geographically defined by the London boroughs of Tower Hamlets and Newham, the borders of which also blur and leak into Hackney to the north and urbanized Essex to the east, and are, as always, halted by the Thames to the south and the City to the west. But it might just as easily have been situated anywhere that working people have thought of as home. It is most definitely a neighbourhood where you were part of a community, where you knew people by name and where you would notice if something untoward happened – such as if someone was 'bothering' the local kids. Because our street was a place where you looked out for one another, and you and your children probably lived just a few doors along from your mum and dad, if not in a few rooms in the same house where you were born.

In my own post-war childhood – in Grove Road, Bow, in the early 1950s, and later, because of the so-called slum clearances, on the Becontree housing estate in Dagenham – when one gang of kids said to another, 'Come and play down our street,' they weren't talking about a game of dodge the traffic. Nor were they likely to have been intimidated by bigger kids making threats, either to them or to terrified elderly residents. The difference in my experience – and in the experiences of many of those who contributed their testimonies to this book – was that our street, like your street, was a communal public space. Children would 'play out' together; adults would pass the time of day with one another, and maybe even have their place of work there. But most importantly, it was a place for people, a place where there was a sense of belonging, and not just a thoroughfare for speeding cars to use as a rush-hour rat run.

Our Street looks at what went on in that world when, despite the backdrop of the tribulations and horrors of the Second World War, and the lack of even quite basic domestic facilities such as hot water, people didn't live as isolated strangers. They were part of something that, while often very far from perfect, still gave them the chance to enjoy a way of life that has, for many people, all but vanished. Judging by the many letters I received from readers of *My East End*, a previous history book of mine, that way of life meant more to them than being able to afford the latest electronic goods or a week's break to the Costas. Obviously, even the most nostalgic among us would agree that material comfort beats discomfort hands down, and that a nice holiday isn't something many people would refuse if given the opportunity. But there are other things that, on reflection, we should perhaps prize more highly, and, based on the experiences of the people I spoke to, I believe sharing a sense of community certainly has to be one of them. That is why this book is not so much about the 'big picture' of history but is concerned with everyday experiences. While we are living them they might seem commonplace, but as they disappear into the past they become events and incidents and emotions that we begin to recognize as being worth remembering, recording and treasuring. The supposedly ordinary lives of ordinary people are all too easily forgotten, especially in our modern world, where everything is changing so rapidly, and new practices, beliefs and habits become the norm between each bewildered blink of the eye.

While these are Londoners' stories, they will, I hope, have meaning and resonance for anyone interested in how communities of working people lived through wartime – either because they have shared similar experiences or because they want to learn more about an all but vanished way of life. The stories themselves have inspired and dictated the shape and concerns of the book: because they are personal memories, told in the words of the people themselves, it is their views that are expressed and their emphases that are respected. This book is most definitely not concerned with the opinions of outsiders as they pass judgement on the people who lived in our street during the war – although that was absolutely the case with some of the histories I consulted while doing the background research. There were appallingly condescending assumptions made, for example, about cinemagoers, which went something along the lines of 'the cheaper the seats, the more emotional the viewers'. And even a usually admirable historian, when writing about what he called the East End's 'ugly streets', was baffled by the Cockney inhabitants' keenness to return to their homes and communities once the bomb damage had been repaired.

But why the period of the Second World War? Well, because in many respects life in our street had remained the same for generations, but so much was set to change.

It wasn't only huge swathes of the physical topography that were destroyed for ever; the social and psychological expectations of those who remembered living and working in the pre-war East End would never be the same again. And yet, as so many people said, with simple, stoical logic, even when bombs were crashing around them, 'life still had to go on'.

How could it? How did people manage in those six long years between 1939 and 1945? That was a major question I wanted to address in this book, and I did so by combining traditional research with original testimonies, as I had done in *My East End*. In fact, I actually decided to start this project after the overwhelming response I received to that earlier book. So many people generously bothered to contact me after they had read it. They sent letters, poems and cards, some saying how glad they were to have 'their' history written down somewhere, and others that they'd learned about an area they weren't familiar with other than through cartoonish stereotypes of Cockney London. It was this response, and the many other recollections of the Second World War I heard, that inspired me to write this book.

I believe, passionately, that all our lives are worth recording and that all our stories are important. There is no such thing as an unimportant or 'ordinary' person. But lives lived out against the backdrop of such dramatic and cataclysmic world events, and that are still within living memory, seem to me to have both a personal importance and a wider significance that people who did not experience those times can barely begin to imagine. And so, despite the daunting prospect – remembering how long it took me to complete my previous East End history, and how difficult it had been to carry on when my much-loved mother died – I knew it was a story I wanted to write – these were the testimonies I wanted to do justice to. Because if I didn't record them, what would happen to them? They might not be taken seriously, would maybe be misinterpreted or, perhaps, worst of all, simply lost. Sadly, several people who contributed their testimonies to the book died during the time of its writing, so I had a very real sense of the increasing urgency to get it finished. These are real people's stories, not fictional accounts that could be picked up and put down at will. This also explains why the book is not conventionally structured, with chapters of neatly equal length. There were some things that people wanted to speak about at length and others that, while they were still important, could be dealt with in a passing comment.

People were speaking of times in which monumental world events were happening and yet their memories were often of the small domestic detail, tiny moments which illuminated the bigger picture: the everyday life of their family, neighbourhood and workplace. As I was told on more than one occasion, just because bombs were falling in the street outside, or even on your roof, it didn't stop your child from becoming sick or demanding to be fed or getting up to mischief, or your old woman from carrying on with a bloke while your back was turned. In short, this book is about intimate events taking place against the staggering backdrop of international conflict. And that is why I have included a brief chronology at the back of the book – a time line outlining not only the events that people were experiencing in our street on the home front, but also those that were literally exploding and igniting the world around them. And it is this contrast that leads me to my other motivation for recording these stories. The world of *Our Street* has, on the whole, disappeared; or rather it has been destroyed, whether smashed by enemy bombs and fires, or bulldozed by the muddle-headed, ill-thought-out, post-war housing clearances that flattened so much of what was left. It might have been an often dangerous, poor, slum-ridden world, but many still regret its passing.

As I concluded in *My East End*, people are often mourning when they tell their stories, mourning the loss of a way of life in which they were part of a community that had grown organically over the generations. Unlike the planners and architects who moved them around as if they were pawns in a chess game, they understand that communities are not created by ordering removal vans to simply transplant people from one location to another – not if they are to have a cohesiveness that makes sense to those who live within them. But that said, communities change: they develop, flourish and die, and new ones grow up in their place – just as with any other living organism. And it is the recording of the once vibrant communities of wartime east London with which this book is concerned.

As promised, all contributors who wished to be are listed in the acknowledgements, but, for reasons of confidentiality, they are not identified within the text. Also as promised, I have not edited the material – in the sense that I have not changed its meaning or the way language is used – but I have removed repetition and anything that might compromise confidentiality.

Finally, before the book begins, I would like to add a dedication. It is said that one death is a tragedy and that a thousand deaths are a statistic, but as we know from viewing events in more modern times – be it in Belfast or New York, Afghanistan or Rwanda – that really isn't so. Admittedly, electronic mass communication has meant that we are privy to the stories of individuals in a way that would have been rare some sixty years ago, and people who die are not the complete strangers they might once have been as we read about them in the papers and hear about them on the news. But in the Second World War those people came from my street and your street – we knew them, loved them, argued with them, worked with them, laughed with them, danced with them, had children, lives and dreams with them, and we miss them still.

This book is dedicated to every one of them.

Introduction: The Build-up to War

In the First World War of 1914–18, the majority of casualties had been troops fighting at the front and in the trenches, but the 1939–45 conflict would see a different type of warfare in which civilians – those remaining on the home front and living in our street – would be as much a target as those on the battlefield. Knowing this, I was amazed as I talked to people who had lived in the East End through those hard, often terrifying times, by how many of them managed to make their experiences sound like little more than just a bit of a laugh, or perhaps a bothersome inconvenience. And I soon came to realize that this attitude was neither chest-beating bravado nor whistling in the dark. It sprang from a pragmatic acceptance of the fact that there were things to be done – important, vital things – and that everyday life had to be lived despite the extraordinary circumstances. In the words of one woman from Canning Town, 'You bloody well had to get on with it. You had a purpose. It was a good feeling.'

What choice did most working people have anyway? Unless you were in one of the categories earmarked for evacuation, going off on an extended trip to a safer locale wasn't exactly on the cards, as it was for more privileged individuals. And even if there was an opportunity to leave London, many families still chose to stay put – and together – the very thought of the pain of separation being more powerful than any fears of the dangers to come.

Having come to understand that attitude, I was surprised yet again – this time when reading through the local east London newspapers that were being published little more than a month before war was declared. I had not expected to see how 'ordinary' much of the news coverage seemed to be, and how nonchalant were the references to what was brewing across the Channel – despite the ever increasing possibility of war breaking out. Headlines concerned themselves with Stepney council's response to the district auditor, who had criticized the inappropriate use of the mayoral car and an expense claim that had been put in for a trip to Paris. It wasn't until page 4 that there was any mention of matters that would prove to have such a profound impact on the area's entire population for the next six terrible years.

This was in a report on arrangements for shelters. Stepney Borough Council's ARP Committee had discussed the matter, but they were not exactly cracking on with the arrangements, and overall there was no particular sense of urgency.

Whether or not the lightness of tone in the papers was adopted or imposed as a matter of national policy, it reads today as being either remarkably composed or incredibly gung-ho.

By the following week, there was, almost incidentally, a little piece announcing, 'Black out. Lights go out at 12.30 a.m. next Thursday morning. The streets of Poplar and Stepney will be darker than they have been since the war . . .' – the 'war', of course, being a reference to 1914–18. But inside the same edition is a far bigger piece, accompanied by a large map, showing Bank Holiday tours of Kent and East Sussex as recommended by the Automobile Association, and an item celebrating the joys of a Belgian camping holiday to be enjoyed by 500 lucky East End children. The choice of venue might, with hindsight, seem a little curious, not to say positively dangerous.

News of the council's progress regarding shelters was slipped in between stories about IRA threats to the mainland, supplies of continental sugar candy to be found in the West India Dock, the dental care of Bethnal Green toddlers and personal ads offering the services of 'psycho-analysis' for those 'in trouble' and euphemistically described 'medical samples and advice', which were 'free to the married'.

A few weeks later and it wasn't until page 6 – in a piece about the imminent hop-picking season – that the possibility of war was even mentioned. At the end of the item, pickers were told that they should take their own gas masks with them when they left for Kent at the beginning of September, as Tonbridge Rural District Council did not have sufficient reserves for the temporary incomers. Other than that, the rest of the inside of the paper had a regular diet of late-summer weddings, sports reports and short pieces on petty crime, including, in this edition, a story about a rag and bone man having been fined five shillings for giving children goldfish and inflatable balls in exchange for rags (the offence he had committed was putting the children in danger of infection, though whether from the rags, the fish or the balls was not made clear). However, the back page did have a letter from the No-Conscription League, and a very positive item about the effectiveness of the blackout in the docks.

Astonishingly, even as late as Saturday 26 August the headlines were still not looking to Europe, but were dedicated to a very sad but parochial story about the drowning of a young lighterman. In retrospect, despite the numbers who would die in the conflict to come, it reminds us that every death is a tragedy for someone. Inside the paper, there were two full columns devoted to a picturesque cycling route for those wishing to visit friends during the coming hop harvest, alongside a far briefer appeal from County Hall for volunteers to assist mothers with under-fives, should there be a need for mass evacuation in the event of a 'national emergency'.

That same edition carried an article about 'our friend the dog' and an ad for a Stimo dog food that 'wags tails' at just 4½d a pop – the same doggy friends, presumably, who would, in just a few weeks' time, be destroyed in their tens of thousands in a patriotic gesture to save food.

But the possibility of that national emergency was not enough of a threat to prevent a complaining note on the back page following the traffic chaos that resulted from troops returning to London through the Blackwall Tunnel after manoeuvres.

It isn't until 2 September 1939 – the day before the declaration of war – that the tone eventually changed.

What was it actually like to live during the build-up to war? This is the experience of a seven-year-old girl living in the East End, a small child out by herself in the street – a street that wasn't then seen as a place of danger but as a playground, even at a time when, despite the comforting tone of stories in the newspapers, talk of war was most definitely in the air.

The first time I was aware that there was a war was on a Sunday in September. A big gun was pulled to the end of the street by six soldiers. It seemed like any other Sunday: my nan had whitened the two steps to the front door – a ritual carried out every day, as was black-leading the kitchen range. 'Get off that step and let it dry!' I was ordered as I went off to look for my friends. Joanie lived at number 8, I lived at number 12, and Rosie lived at the last house, number 20. I knocked for Joan first. She was willing to come out and play hopscotch, but 'not if you knock for that Rosie'. Joan didn't like Rosie, because she was always scruffy, whereas Joan was always kept tidy and spotless by her mum. I suppose I came somewhere in between the two as they both played with me. I could turn on the little madam to Joanie's mum and play dolls games with her, or become a tomboy like Rosie – climbing and fighting – whatever the mood or friend present.

'G–, come and get your tea!' Nan's voice called down the street. Tea on Sunday was always the same: shrimps and winkles bought off the winkle man, who pushed his handcart round the streets on

Sunday mornings. To me, it was the best tea of the week – even though it was a slow job picking out the winkles with a pin one by one, and taking the tops and tails off the shrimps. We had real butter on our bread on Sundays and maybe jelly and custard to follow or maybe cake.

The summer Sunday nights were always the same. The chairs were put outside by the doorstep for Dad and Nan – anyone else had to sit on the step – and until it got dark or chilly there they sat, Nan doing her knitting, Dad reading the paper, and conversation called up and down the street to the neighbours also sitting on their fronts. I was curious. I wanted to know about the gun and the war everyone was talking about. 'Children should be seen and not heard,' was what I was told, which meant, 'Don't ask, you're not going to be told,' so I decided to seek out Rosie and ask her. Rosie knew everything [even about where babies came from, and] she had a big sister, Queenie, who was twelve, to tell her anything she didn't know. The war and the gun was something Rosie knew about. 'We've got to have that gun to shoot down the Germans 'cause they're going to bomb us and the bombs have got gas in that will choke us if we don't.' She made the 'us' and 'they' sound very personal. I couldn't understand why the Germans would want to do that to us – me and my dad and nan. I didn't even know any Germans – at least, I don't think I did. They must have lived even further away than Chrisp* Street, I thought.

AQQS2703, that number was drummed into me – 'Don't forget it' – and I remember it today. This was my identity number. We were all issued with identity cards with numbers and also gas masks. 'See,' said Rosie, 'I told you they were coming to gas us.' Everyone had to go to St John's Church to collect their masks and be shown how to put them on. To me, they were very frightening. They covered your face, and the end looked like a half a tin can with holes in. When on, they smelt of the rubber they were made of, and you had to get the eyepiece just right or you couldn't see. My sister's baby was just a few

* Always pronounced Chris.

months old and was issued with a black cocoon that had a face visor and a pump at the end for air once the baby was sealed inside. This was standard for all babies. Children up to five got a 'Mickey Mouse' mask, which was nothing like Mickey Mouse. It was put over the face like the adult masks, but it was blue with a floppy red rubber nose. Along with the gas masks we were given a cardboard box with a string shoulder strap [and] told these were our gas-mask cases and to carry them with us at all times; not to lose them, as they were not replaceable; and [to] make sure our name and address was in the case along with our gas mask. Children going to school, mothers with their babies out shopping, people going to work – all walking along with our cardboard boxes over our shoulder. We were also given a demonstration of the air-raid warning and the all-clear sound – a wavy, up-and-down sound for the warning, one long steady note for all clear – then told to go home and practise the sounds so there would be no mistakes when the time came for the real thing.

It was because 'the real thing' was getting ever closer that organizing shelters had become a priority, and people were now focusing on what arrangements they could make. But preparing a shelter was obviously easier for people with their own back yards or gardens than it was for those living in multi-occupancy houses or high above the ground in tenement blocks.

We had a nice house with a nice back garden [on the Isle of Dogs] that was my dad's pride and joy. An arched trellis had roses growing over it, ducks and chickens in a pen at the bottom of the garden, but most of all I remember the hollyhocks. Our garden backed on to the park, a small square of concrete with three swings and a roundabout. The dividing wall between the garden and the park was not very high, so the tall sticks with hollyhocks growing up them gave us some privacy. It was a great shock to me when I came home from school for lunch to find men digging the biggest, deepest hole I had ever

seen at the bottom of the garden. Looking over the walls to the right and left, I could see everyone had these big holes. They were for our Anderson shelters. [These were] made of corrugated iron. The lower half went into the ground, and the top, dome-shaped bit was bolted together, then covered with the dirt that was from the hole . . . a hole for a door was left at the front. Looking from an upstairs window, the gardens looked like they all had giant molehills in them. I wondered if these would fool 'Hitler' – who had now become a household name – that it was not people taking shelter in them, but some kind of animal cage. My father planted flowers in the earth on top of the shelter and made a wooden effigy of Hitler hanging from a gallows that swung above the shelter doorway. 'If we've got to spend time in this thing, it might as well be as comfortable as we can make it,' my nan said. So in went an old piece of carpet, a small table and some chairs. Candles were placed around the sides in tin lids for some light and an old oil stove found a new home there.

Despite all their best efforts, however, when the bombing finally got under way, there would be little comfort to be had in those shelters.

The nights of Saturday 2 and Sunday 3 September 1939 saw violent storms pounding the country, but Sunday dawned bright and fresh – the weather completely at odds with the dark message that was to come in Prime Minister Chamberlain's wireless address to the nation. But as these East Enders' memories show, the first experience of 'the real thing' was to prove to be a bit of an anticlimax, although after the long build-up and the dire warnings about gas attacks, it was taken very seriously indeed.

I was a six-year-old boy pedalling on my tricycle over an iron bridge in Canning Town, known to us locally as 'Peg O'Leggy Steps'. The siren sounded for the first air raid of the war, which, fortunately, never came to anything. But Mother never knew this at the time and came screaming at full throttle. 'Where's my boy? Bloody Hitler, leave us alone!' She found me, gathered me up under one arm and the tricycle under the other, and ran for home.

When the war started it was Sunday 3 September. It was 11 a.m. and I was in church. The siren went and we had to leave and go home, because the wardens asked us to. The streets were cleared of all people, because no one knew what would happen.

Well, it finally happened, this Hitler had marched into Poland, and it was on everyone's lips – here we were, with war at our door. My H– used to joke about it, that it wouldn't last long, not now he and [his best mate] L– were in the army. But when it did come, it took six years of one's life, plus all the horrors it brought with it. Gossip and preaching had stopped and fear had begun. Everyone's plans were dashed, our boys were being conscripted and our whole world was in turmoil. Fathers and sons drilling in the streets with brooms in place of guns, gas masks being dished out to our children, and here they were taking your railings from your front, and your pots and pans, anything to help with munitions. Oh, God, what next? The school had become the ARP station and on the other side of H–'s there was a fire station. Everyone was so busy.

I was on holiday in Norwich on the Sunday that war was declared, staying with an aunt and uncle, and my immediate reaction was panic to get home to Mum and Dad. I had travelled from London by coach, and on enquiring at Norwich for my return home, I was informed that there were no coaches leaving Norwich, I would have to pick one up at Yarmouth at 8.30 a.m. So the next morning I was up at the crack of dawn to catch a train to get there. It was full of early-morning fishermen returning home after their catch and, believe me, the smell in the coach was no 'ashes of violets'. So I arrive at Yarmouth and have the dilemma of trying to find out exactly where the coach will pick me up. Yarmouth was deserted, so I took potluck and, of course, I was completely the wrong side of the road. So I'm waving frantically to the driver and thankfully he sees me, but here comes the problem. I was dressed to kill: I had my cocky hat with a feather – all the rage – perched on the side of my head, high heels, white kid gloves, handbag and suitcase, also a large carrier bag that my dear relatives had filled with potatoes, carrots, onions, cucumber, tomatoes and apples, and just as I reached the coach, the bottom fell out of the carrier. There was veg and fruit rolling everywhere, and me frantically trying to retrieve it. By the time I eventually got on the coach, my gloves were filthy and my hat skewwhiff. It was a case of Nellie Wallace* eat your heart out, which was made even worse because everyone was sniggering when I got on. Anyway, I got home, and what pandemonium. Everybody was filling sandbags to pile up in front of their houses, taping all the windows with brown sticky tape, yet everybody was laughing and joking about it, not realizing what was in store for us . . .

Once it began in earnest, the laughter stopped – for a while, at least – as people became all too well aware of what Cockneys were going through.

One of my most vivid memories is standing in the road watching the dogfights overhead with the words, 'It's the East End,' or, 'They've hit the docks,' sounding in my ears.

And as Mrs Smith, not a Cockney herself, put it when she wrote to me: 'I think every Londoner has a tale to tell.'

* A famous music-hall artiste, who was one of the first female pantomime dames.

[1] *ARP, the Blackout and Sheltering*

Put that light out in number 6!

Air-raid precautions (ARP) were being discussed in a government subcommittee from as early as 1924. Following the experiences of the First World War, during which there had been unprecedented air attacks on British civilian targets, resulting in a total of 1,413 deaths, there was official concern that arrangements should be in place for civil defence. The population would be guided as to what they should and shouldn't do in the event of enemy action, and there would be plans to ensure that services were maintained both during and after any bombing raids and gas attacks.

In 1935, local authorities were approached with guidelines about what they would be expected to do, and then, in 1937, an act followed these initial propositions, setting out exactly what was required of them. But with little conviction that anything would actually happen – 'Surely "they" wouldn't let us go to war again, not after the last lot' being a commonly held view – ARP weren't given any sort of priority, especially as they required local authorities to come up with the funding. Eventually, however, matters could no longer be ignored and ARP *had* to be taken seriously. Wardens were recruited, windows taped against blasts, gas masks distributed and evacuation plans pushed up into top gear – all just in time for when the first air-raid warning went off in London at 11.27 a.m. on Sunday 3 September 1939, just minutes after the Prime Minister had informed the nation that we were at war.

Reportedly there was a mixture of alarm and curiosity on that sunny Sunday morning, with gas attacks being particularly feared. But this was soon to dissipate into something closer to a mixture of boredom and impatience as the air raids didn't materialize – the first bombs were not to fall on central London until August 1940. Despite the introduction of further precautions, such as the conducting of the census on which the National Registration Scheme for the distribution of identity cards would be based, Britain was lulled into a false sense of calm – maybe even into a certain degree of complacency. This was the period initially known as the Bore War, but it would soon be called by its now more familiar, Americanized name, the Phoney War.

Ironically, during this time it was ARP, in the form of the blackout, that caused most of the war's early casualties, not the enemy bombing from which they were supposed to be protecting British citizens. Most people had stories of some mishap or other.

You were forever falling up and down steps, and off the pavement, and bashing into things.

My poor dad came in from a hard day's work with a terrible black eye. He had met a lamppost on the way home and the lamppost won.

With every source of light being either extinguished or shielded, the blackout wasn't simply a minor inconvenience, along the lines of, 'How did you know when your bus is coming?' It was more, 'How did you cross the road without walking out in front of it?'

In the blackout there were white lines everywhere . . . it was said that if you stood still long enough, you would end up with the inevitable white lines painted round your legs!

Despite those white lines – painted along kerbs, in the middle of the road, and round the base of lampposts and other street obstacles and furniture – serious accidents were just waiting to happen. And when the numbers of casualties, and even fatalities, began to grow, it was decided that, for the sake of civilian safety, a certain amount of light had to be allowed in the streets. Slight relaxations were made, but even though it soon became apparent that this did not result in enemy bombers immediately being flagged straight towards unsuspecting targets, the regulations remained stringent and fines were rigorously imposed for failure to comply.

Tape was put on windows – criss-crossed – to stop the glass falling in after a blast. Blackout curtains were draped over windows and doors so we could not be seen by enemy planes. The warden was told to warn of any chinks of light and would call out, 'Put that light out!'

And it wasn't just a matter of pulling the curtains. If you weren't to be fined for violation of the rules, there was a meticulous routine to be carried out, just adding – apparently for no reason – to the general feeling of weariness with everything.

The blackout was awful. We liked it when there was a full moon – but so did the enemy. The wardens walked the streets to see if anyone was not pulling their blackout curtains or blinds properly. In the winter, when it got dark early, everything was in complete darkness. Sometimes you could see searchlights in the sky, but other times, nothing, and you could lose your way, which was very frightening.

At the beginning of the war my sister and I went to the pictures, as we called it in those days, and on coming out we experienced the complete blackout for the first time. What a shock! It was very, very black, a low-cloud night. We were terrified, as we had a long walk home and could hear footsteps behind us. Very frightening. We ran most of the way. My sister was quite stout, after having had a baby, so we were two very exhausted people when we got home. That was the last time we went to the pictures at night until the war ended.

It was hard. We hated being outside our own district – the place we knew. Getting lost was a problem.

The blackout – what a time! You could see more when there was a full moon, but that was a 'bomber's moon' and there was a real chance of a raid. Then, when there was no moon, or [it was] extremely cloudy, well, you often could not see a hand in front of you. Then there were times when it was both very dark and foggy. I know one night, I left my grandmother's house at the end of the road – it went through another road, which went in a complete circle. It was foggy and dark and somehow I turned into the circle and could not find my way out. I walked around and around. In the end I knocked at someone's door to see where I was. It was a really frightening feeling. My mother wondered where on earth I had got to because I had said I would only be a few minutes.

The blackout was a nightmare, especially in the winter, when we got bad fogs. My mother had been out one evening and, coming home, she got lost and ended up falling down a manhole, but, being Mum, she crawled out and eventually found her way home.

To help prevent such accidents, close to home at least, Cardinal polish – beloved of step-polishers throughout the East End – was being advertised in a white version that would ensure safety during the blackout and would not wash off in the rain. So at least there was less danger of tripping up your own front step – although venturing out any further, whether to the street corner or beyond, could become something of an adventure.

You had to have a torch with you, and it had to be just a slip of light [pointed downwards]. Between air raids, I used to run to the chip

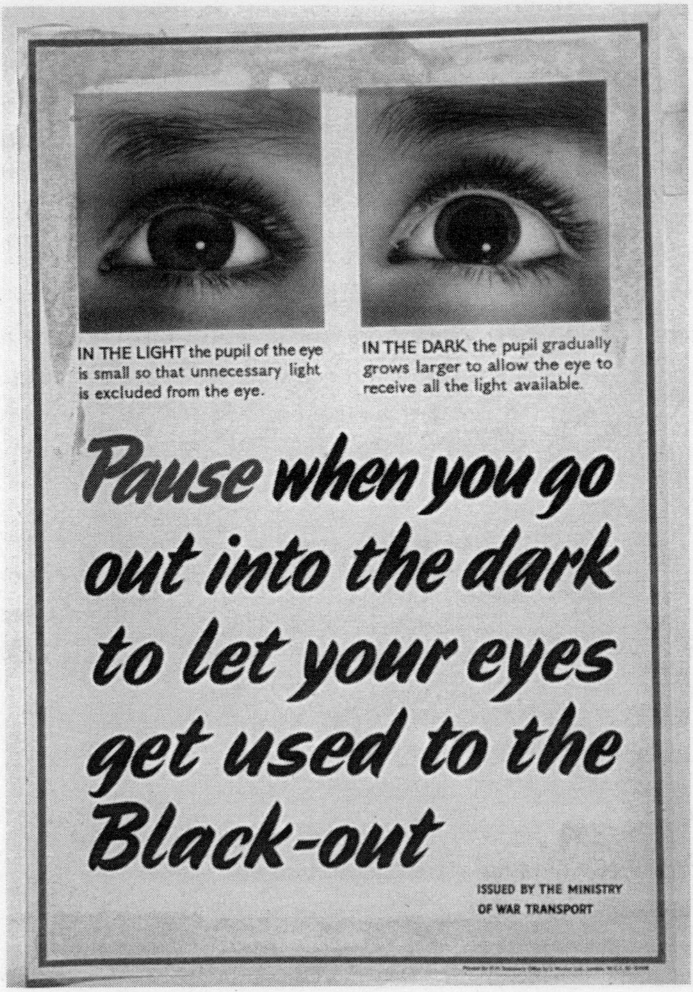

shop on the corner for our supper. Everyone talked to each other, although you could not see them . . . You had to be quick going in and out of the shops, so as not to let out any light.

The blackout did have a plus side, because we could do a bit of canoodling without being seen, but there were quite a few accidents at first with people tripping and falling . . . We all ate plenty of carrots, so we could see better in the dark!

My mother told me about walking home from work in the blackout and suddenly realizing she was being followed. She could hear heavy breathing getting closer and closer, and the sound of steps of more than one person behind her. She stopped and pressed herself against the wall – hoping she wouldn't be attacked in the pitch darkness – only to be faced by a bewildered horse that had wandered out of a nearby haulier's stable yard.

Meanwhile, there were still no bombs, and with apparently no immediate threat – other than that from stray animals and lampposts – ARP wardens were mocked and their existence begrudged. They were even accused of cowardice. The question being asked was, 'Why don't they join up?' Opinion would soon change with the coming of the raids, but for the time being it was as if they were employed to do nothing other than to harass an increasingly irritable public. And still the Phoney War continued. The once genuine fear of gas attacks somehow slipped from the forefront of public consciousness, and gas masks, which had been diligently distributed and demonstrated, were increasingly rarely spotted hanging from people's shoulders, despite the fact that it was an offence not to carry one at all times. Those that were carried were often in what would nowadays be described as 'designer' cases – either customized by the owner or bought specially for the purpose – and were seen more as fashion accessories than as pieces of life-saving safety equipment.

If anyone took the carrying of masks seriously, it was the wardens – after all, this was part of their job.

I was hop picking in Kent, when war was declared, with my mum and my little boy, who was nearly three years old. We stayed to finish harvesting the hop fields. My husband was an ARP warden at that time and when I arrived home from hopping – to the two rooms we rented from the lady downstairs – the bedroom was packed full of gas masks. People in the neighbourhood had to come round to collect them from him. Things were quiet – for a time. Then the raids started.

Once they did, the general public had no choice but to take things far more seriously, and sheltering from raids became a major preoccupation.

Shelters took various forms: an Anderson in the back yard; a mattress in the cupboard under the stairs; a Morrison in the living room that doubled as a table during the day; public, communal brick and cement efforts; maybe going each night into informally – even illegally – commandeered places under railway arches, down on tube platforms and even on the actual lines, having to drag your bedding and any necessities, whether a flask, deck chair, lavatory paper or the children's teddy bears, with you each time; or even taking potluck and just staying in bed with the attitude that you might as well 'all go together, if the bomb's got your name on it'.

In the shelters, apart from the fear of being killed or losing your home and even your loved ones, there was the great slog of boredom, lack of sleep and minimal, unpleasant facilities.

Our shelter was damp, dark, no lights, no heating, and just a bucket in the corner which served as a toilet.

The shelters were made as comfortable as possible. I know our [Anderson] shelter had a couple of bunks in it . . . they were not very wide, so the top one was used as a shelf, and we laid down on the floor on something soft. There we would be, night after night. If it was a bit quieter – thank goodness – sometimes there was time to have an hour or so in bed, and then a lot of people took a chance and stayed in their bed [a bit longer], but there wasn't much sleep, because of the bombs and the bombardment of our guns. I know one night, when my father was at home, it was fairly quiet in the shelter, when a bomb dropped extremely close, and we got a lot of the blast. He sat up and shouted, 'Those ****ing B*******!' Well, was his face red! He just could not stop apologizing. I had never heard my father swear before.

*

Before retiring to bed under the Morrison, my mother would replace the single forty-watt light bulb with a ten-watt bulb that remained on all night, [giving] an eerie glow around the room with just enough light to avoid the furniture if one had to get up in the middle of the night.

My lasting memory of that time was the noise – absolute bedlam. After the siren came the guns. We lived a stone's throw from Victoria Park, where they had a gun battery. I was absolutely terrified as they blasted skywards. My mum always left it late going to the shelter. My dad, who was in the ARP rescue squad, used to rush over from his depot, put his tin hat on my baby brother, then run with us to the shelter, where we stayed until morning. Dawn came and we were taken back to our flat and told to get dressed for school.

The communal shelters were disliked not only for the conditions in which people were expected to try and rest for the night; there was also the difficult business of the private becoming very much public.

Our shelter was made of brick and housed a lot of people, so it had a nasty smell. It was very crowded and damp, and the toilet had sacking draped round it. You depended on all the people who shared it keeping it clean. There were bunks – you got one if you were lucky – better than the floor. The older people hardly slept and there always seemed to be a baby crying. It wasn't lit very well, but you just tried to make the most of it, knitting and that. We had a tea bar run by volunteers, with the milk, sugar and tea given by everyone who could spare it. Even in the shelter you could still hear the bombs exploding and you'd pray that you would still have a home when it was all over for the night. Our flat *was* hit, and we lost most of what we had, but we were lucky – we were in the shelter. Some were not.

*

When the raids started we had to run down the street to a brick surface shelter which had been built for people with no shelter of their own. They weren't nearly as good as the Andersons, which were sunk into the ground. So when my husband was called up in 1940, my mum took me to stay with her as she had an Anderson in the back yard. But the raids were very bad [because of the nearby docks] and we never went to bed at night – the shelter was our bed. A factory at the back of us, where they allowed a lot of people to shelter, was hit. A whole family of twelve was killed – all except one boy, who had been called up as a soldier. We went out the next morning and there were dead people lying all along the street. The demolition crews were there all day digging it out.

The efficacy of the shelters differed too. The widespread use of the phrase 'London can take it!' – with even a short, very chipper film on the theme being shown at the cinema – must have sometimes rung hollow with those who lived there, and never more so than following the loss of life when mass shelters were hit in Stoke Newington, Stepney and Bermondsey. Even the Anderson shelters had a mixed reputation. The first memory was quite jolly, but the ones which follow are anything but.

When Dad and I dived down the Anderson shelter, he would always say, 'We're in, Meredith, we're in!' To this day I don't know where that saying originated.*

During the heavy bombing of the London docks, our place in Bow was destroyed by a direct hit. Good fortune had it that my mother was away convalescing after an operation, and my father was on night work at the gas company, and my older brother was away in the army

* According to Eric Partridge's *Dictionary of Catchphrases*, the reference comes from a music-hall sketch first performed by Fred Karno's company in 1907.

in France. The raid started in the evening, after I had got home from work. I took my brother's wife and baby, who lived with us, with all their bedding etc. to the shelter. This was in the wine cellars of Halls Wine, the makers of Wincarnis, the tonic wine. Halls was behind our houses and actually owned them – it was to them that we paid our rent. I intended leaving, but because of the intensity of the raid the warden refused to allow me to leave the shelter. Had he let me, I would have followed my usual pattern: cycled into Stratford to a public house there and then returned home to sleep. My sister-in-law always claimed she saved my life by insisting I went over to the shelter with her, a practice I'd always rejected. When inspecting the crater that was once our home, I saw that the next-door neighbours' Anderson shelter was completely full of house bricks. It was lucky they were away at the time. People placed little faith in the Andersons, and although they built them, many remained unused and waterlogged.

I had to go to the loo and was let out of the door of the shelter. Mum held on to my shirt-tail in case I ran away. As I looked up at the house, it was wrecked. I later saw . . . people sitting near wrecked houses and shelters with bloodstained bandages round their heads. The shelters had twisted metal edges where the bombs had torn them apart.

It was an October night in 1940. We lived in Plaistow and were struck by a bomb when we were in our Anderson shelter. We were all buried alive. I felt my hand was free and managed to pull myself out. I saw my mother's legs and began pulling her. I was calling out for help. There was a massive crater where my father and fiancé had been sleeping. My father was blown three houses away and my fiancé was in a nearby garden. My father was dead. I never knew what parts were in the coffin. My fiancé was screaming in pain. He, my two brothers, my sister, myself and Mum were all taken to hospital. My fiancé died. I went to Dad's funeral, but Mum was away in another part of town in hospital, having operations on both of her legs. My fiancé was buried the next day. I went to that.

My earliest memories are of being in the shelter one night with Mum and Dad and brother Alfie. I recall quite vividly my mother lying on top of both Alfie and me when the bombs were exploding outside. Someone came into the shelter while it was dark and had a type of large pack on his back. He administered oxygen or something similar to Dad. I have since learned that a German land mine had landed nearby and buried us in the shelter. We were saved by my mother's cries for help. She had lain on top of us and probably saved our lives. I never knew until after Mum's death that she had put her own life at risk to save ours. Dad was injured and had to spend time in hospital. We went and stayed with relatives . . . but were bombed out again, which is when Mum called it a day and decided to remove us to the safety of the country . . . My parents had a nice house before it was bombed, and it had contained many articles of furniture and fine china that they had collected over the years. All this was destroyed in that one night. How badly Mum must have felt. Can you imagine losing your home, your eldest children living with strangers far away [his three older sisters had already been evacuated], being buried alive with your youngest children and then having to emerge from the rubble to find food and shelter for your family?

If you were 'lucky', like the person speaking below, you might take refuge in a workplace or warehouse. Members of my family used the basement of Spratt's animal food factory, where my grandfather had worked.

When the bombing was really rough, we would take our bedding palliasses filled with straw, Primus stove, loaves of bread and make the daily trek to the docks, usually before the start of the raids. The place we went to was the Free Trade Wharf. The authorities allowed the dockers' families to seek sanctuary there in the warehouse. We seemed to spend half our lives there, as everywhere outside was being bombed and everything was alight. Hitler was looking for fresh warehouses to bomb every night . . . In general, the people were a jolly bunch, taking what was being thrown at them, with the adults trying to calm the young ones. We had singsongs with our neighbours, who had joined us until the all clear was sounded. I remember Grandad standing looking through the Dickensian windows, saying that they had dropped another lot of incendiary bombs on a warehouse over the other side of the Thames and that it was well alight. We didn't know until later on, from an observation made by my uncle, that we were sheltering well below the waterline in the warehouse, and if it took a bomb at a slight angle we would all have drowned. Considering the amount of time we spent down there, we [were very lucky], thank God!

Those incendiaries could, in fact, cause more problems than high-explosive bombs, as they not only lit up the targets to guide enemy planes but also started the fires that caused so many casualties and widespread damage to property. The solution was for individuals to be enlisted as fire watchers, the idea being that they could disable the bombs by smothering them with sand or soaking them with water from stirrup pumps. This was a vital safety measure, because if a street's occupants were all in the shelters or a workplace was deserted for the night, the buildings were more or less left open to attack.

If you had small children, though, taking care of them in the shelter was where you wanted to be, not standing up on the roof, waiting for bombs.

At night, when the sirens would sound, my mother would tell me to stand on my bed, and she would scoop me up in the coat which always covered my bed to keep me warm, and hurry me down to the shelter.

*

Every night when Dad went on duty [in the Home Guard], Mum and I would go to our shelter . . . Dad had built up the doorway with sandbags to form a porch. He painted the walls with distemper, rigged up a battery wireless set, and we slept on canvas hammocks until later in the war, when we were issued with bunks. We had a Tilley lamp for light and a Valor paraffin stove for warmth. Mum would put a coffee percolator on the paraffin stove at 7 p.m. and the coffee would be ready for about 10.30 p.m. Dad made it very cosy, despite the condensation, which ran down the walls. Weather permitting, Mum used to hang the bedding on the washing line every morning to dry out. I loved living in the air-raid shelter. To a young child, it was a great adventure.

Contemporary newspaper pieces certainly tell of East Enders battling on, as in the quote above, and such stories were undoubtedly good for public morale, but considering how hard it was to boil that drop of water for a hot drink shows how tough even simple everyday tasks had become. Words used by older contributors when talking about their experiences of keeping things together on the home front for their children included 'nerve-racking', 'unending' and 'totally exhausting'.

Commercial organizations soon caught on to this. Whether it was getting a decent night's sleep despite the raids – thanks to a cup of soothing Bournvita – or treating yourself to a restorative pick-me-up which enabled the female in the newspaper advertisement to 'keep calm and banish depression' despite 'tired, worn-out nerves' – thanks to a glass of Phosferine tonic wine – companies cashed in on the situation. And it was no wonder that consumers at least tried their products if, while they were still trying to clear up from the previous night's raids, the next lot of bombers, complete with fighter escorts, were on their way yet again.

Later on in the war, the council built brick shelters in the road outside our houses, so we used them. They had bunks built into them, but they were not very nice for a long stay. There were some ferocious air raids and Grandfather would not join us, but would stand on the doorstep in his bare feet. He would rush over from time to time and shout, 'I think they've copped a land mine over Mile End way.' And Gran would shout back, 'Get some shoes on your feet, you old sod.' But he never did. The pavement was peppered with shrapnel after a raid, red hot and very dangerous to anyone without shoes . . . After a while, we never used these brick shelters, as people used them as toilets and they stank to high heaven, and rats were seen in them after the raids eating any rubbish that was left behind. And later, as we got used to it and the raids decreased, we all felt a bit easier in our own beds at home.

Even if you did persist with nightly sheltering, a certain degree of initiative was needed to find your way around the difficulties, inconvenience and discomfort.

One old lady in our communal shelter always stayed fully dressed all night, including her hat, with her feet firmly placed on two upturned flowerpots with candles inside [to] keep her feet warm.

If my dad and my uncle were off duty from the ARP and Home Guard, they'd just go next door to shelter. You see, the house had been bombed out, but there was still the Anderson shelter in the garden, so they went and used that, leaving our shelter to the four of us – me and my brother, Mum and Nan.

If the sheltering arrangements were not properly organized, they could cause more problems than staying put indoors, with modesty – or rather the lack of it – being a constant concern for those using the public or communal shelters.

We'd had air raids all the afternoon and in the evening my husband said, 'Come to have a drink.' [The pub] was only round the corner, so I said, 'All right.' So I went round there with him. We'd just got a drink and someone called in the door, 'Bombs are dropping everywhere.' It was the night they dropped that Molotov [basket], just like a big basket of bombs.

'Hurry up,' someone said to me, 'one's [dropped] around where you live.' I came running out and my husband ran after me, but he had his pint in his hand. 'I'm not leaving that. I've only just got it.'

Anyway, when we got home, the house was alight, like the third storey, and next door was alight in their kitchen and all. All around, they were falling like starlights. And . . . the water supply was very poor – in those days we only had the one tap downstairs. We didn't have water upstairs or anything like that. [But] we managed to get those fires out, and I've still got that pint glass. [Then] we were all back in the air-raid shelter and my mum said, 'I can hear somebody saying we've all got to get out . . .' All of a sudden a policeman put his head in the shelter: 'Come on, out, all out!'

So there was my sister heavily pregnant, my dad ill, and a couple of other people we were sharing the shelter with for the night, and we all had to go around to the . . . church. There was a big tree and there was a land mine hanging from it. [So] we all had to go around the corner to the school, and I mean it was only just around the corner, no further away than what our houses were. It was so stupid. Next door there was a house full mainly of girls – hardly any fellers about then – and they were all running along, and one had a bag. There was a bra hanging out and her knickers and everything, and her father was saying, 'Look at your bag, you're showing your knickers!' She said, 'It don't matter about me knickers, come on!'

. . . we used to go to bed as normal, then, if the siren went, we got dressed [ready for the shelter]. My dear old mum was always in trouble, trying to find her bloomers. Dad used to get so exasperated with her, and used to call out, 'For Christ's sake, he's coming to bomb you, not to rape you!' but she insisted on her bloomers.

My husband's family used to go to the arches by the Salmon and Ball.* I went down there once to sing to the people sheltering. There was a makeshift canteen, and people lying head to toe with young children. It was sad to see.

It was the presence of children, and the need to keep them calm, that saw adults putting on a brave face and even risking their lives to ensure their youngsters' safety.

To get out of the building meant me jumping with my baby in my arms down a complete flight of stairs.

We went to visit my Aunt M– and when it was time to go home there were no buses, so Aunt M– [said she'd walk] back with us. On the way there was an air-raid warning. Auntie carried me with her coat over her head, and Mum had my little brother with a blanket over his head. London was burning. Everywhere was on fire. They ran, carrying us children, to a building at the top end of the road where there was a shelter in the basement. I cannot remember ever being afraid. That, I think, must have been due to my mum's attitude to the whole thing.

As schoolchildren we were told, 'If the siren starts and you are nearer the school – run back. If closer to home – run there.' Invariably, people, even when you didn't know them and you were in a street that wasn't your own, would call out, 'Come in here, love, quick, get out the back.' And they would take you through their home down into their shelter till the all clear went.

*

* The pub in Bethnal Green.

Once we got into the shelter it wasn't too bad, once you got used to the musty smell. We wrapped up in a blanket and climbed on to our bunk. Someone would put a doorstep of bread and dripping in your fist and that kept your mind off the raid a bit.

In a block of flats at the top end of our street there was a young mum who had had polio and she had both her legs in irons. Her husband was away and she was caring for the baby by herself. The baby slept in a suitcase tucked under her bed. Then when the siren went, she didn't have to wake up the infant, but closed down the lid that had all air holes in it, and carried the case down the outside steps of the flats to the communal shelter.

In our living room we had a table [Morrison] shelter. It was like an iron cage with mesh sides, and Mum put blankets all around the edge. Then, I thought it was to make it cosy to go to bed in, but since I realized it was to deflect the debris in the event of a bomb blast – which is exactly what it did when two streets away got a direct hit. The blast tore the roof right off our house and one wall came down. We were trapped in our shelter until some Americans dug us out. The wardens were so busy that night that the Americans were helping out. I remember them giving us chocolate, and I remember seeing our poor chickens lying dead, and all the beans that Mum had grown drooping from their poles. We lost a lot of our belongings, but at least we were all alive and unhurt.

Those chickens must have been a real loss, as their eggs and meat were such a useful supplement to any household's rations, but just as London Zoo had to be realistic in the extraordinary circumstances, so the public had to consider what they would do with less productive animals – their pets. One option was to have the animals put down, either to prevent them suffering or in a patriotic desire to save the food they would consume – or both. This was a choice made by many families and the zoo alike. Poisonous snakes would be an obvious risk in the event of a hit on Regent's Park; likewise the damage that would be done by the gallons of water contained in the massive tanks of the aquarium. A risk that hadn't been taken into account, however, when loyal Londoners had their domestic cats and dogs destroyed in the tens of thousands, was the subsequent increase in vermin – a significant if temporary cause for concern until the domestic and wild animal population became more balanced again. If animals were spared, however, there were difficulties, and not only because of the struggle to find sufficient food that was palatable. Officially, pets were not allowed into public shelters – not that the British public has ever been known for kowtowing to what they consider to be the petty rules of bureaucrats, as was happily pointed out to me by someone at the Public Record Office, and as was seen when they defied all official warnings and threats and proceeded to go down into the underground system to shelter.

But arrangements did have to be made for their animals.

My mum used to have to go to work at Ford's. She was one of 'Mr Bevin's young ladies' [people conscripted for essential industries rather than armed or other national service] and, before she went out, she used to make sure that the flap was up in the shelter and the back door open so that when the warning went, Tess, our dog, could go down into the shelter. She would stop there until the all clear went. One day, my mum forgot to lift the flap and Tess stood outside the shelter and cried and cried. Our next-door neighbour tried to get Tess to go in her shelter, but she wouldn't, so the neighbour, who had the key, had to chance it and come round and let Tess into our shelter.

We never had to wait for the siren as our dog used to run around and bark before it went, so we were well on the way by the time the official warning was heard. I don't know how she knew – obviously some animal instinct of danger. We would always be on our way to the shelter before the siren sounded. One time, we received our early doggy call when my mum and I were about to sit down for dinner. My mum said to me, 'Pick up your plate and take it with you,' and so we took our food down the shelter. She said that the last time we had come back from the shelter, we had found ceiling plaster in our food where the blast from a bomb had shaken the house. She wasn't about to have that happen again . . . We emerged from the shelter to an eerie silence and all the windows of the upstairs rooms of our house were broken.

Pets weren't the only unofficial shelterers.

We were all in the communal shelter when a bomb hit the corner of our flats and a German plane was brought down. A young German airman – I don't know whether he was a pilot or a gunner – was brought into the shelter by some of the men. He was in shock, shaking. So they found him a drop of brandy and kept him there with us until the authorities came and took him away.

But there were some who disliked the shelters so much that, regardless of who or what was in there, they chose to take their chance with fate and not go into them at all.

When it rained, the mud steps down into the shelter turned into a slide, and the water went into the carpet – so a regular mop-up and carpet drying was necessary. For all the so-called comfort [introduced by Nan] we didn't spend many nights in there. [My sister] and her baby were staying with us now, as we were getting raids and bombs most nights. So we all doubled up in our beds, listening for the warning, listening to the bombs falling, wondering where they had fallen, wondering what would behold our eyes next day, and hoping none of our relations had 'caught it'.

We had shelters at work underneath the buildings, but we never used to use them much. It was a nasty feeling. You'd got a three-storey building and you'd got a shelter all underneath the footings. It was no wider than this room, with seats all down there [in the dark], right down the whole length of the building – perhaps 200 or 300 feet – very claustrophobic. Not very nice. I didn't like it, a lot of us didn't, [so] we never used to go there.

1940 started uneventfully and we got confident that not much would happen. How wrong can you be? The bombing started and we then knew that we really were at war. We were living about 200 yards from Hackney Marshes and they had large ack-ack guns and searchlights, and, believe me, once the Blitz started it was hell. We lived on the ground floor of a large block of flats, and the only shelters we had were the brick-built huts. My mum said we stood more chance of survival in our flat, so there we stayed. My dad wouldn't stay there. He always went to Liverpool Street underground. We went just once with him, but it was hell, so we stayed indoors and took our chance. Some of the upstairs neighbours asked if they could come down and stay with [us]. We had quite a long passage – no posh 'halls' in those days – so we used to sit facing each other on the floor and sing our hearts out, trying to lessen the noise of guns and bombs. One particular night, we were having a very, very heavy raid, then suddenly all was quiet. No all clear had gone, but it had been quiet for quite a long time, so we were lulled into a sense of false security and decided we would go to bed and get an hour's sleep. Everybody drifted upstairs to their respective flats except one couple, who asked if they could stay. I only had a three-foot bed, but the lady was very slim, and so was I. We didn't undress, but got under the bedclothes as we were. Her husband was going to sleep on the floor in the front room, so Mum gets out clean sheets and a white quilt, and made him up a bed. Suddenly we were woken by a loud explosion. The windows were blown out, and the front door off its hinges. I'm trying to find the bedroom door and found myself in the wardrobe. Eventually I found a torch but couldn't put any lights on as the blackout curtains had blown down. I secured the curtains in the front room and put the light on. What a sight. You couldn't see our poor neighbour for soot. He was sitting up, dazed, with soot all over him and no sign of the *white* quilt and sheets. How we laughed. But the next morning wasn't so funny when we saw the devastation. The church had been blasted, but behind the church was a row of eight little terraced houses – the two-up, two-down type – and they had got a direct hit. Most of the people were killed, as they had also returned to their beds. One of the most strange things was that the end one of the terrace was flattened except for the outside end wall, and on this wall was a dresser. No sign of plates or crockery left on it, except on one shelf with six eggcups, each containing an egg, and not one egg was broken. It was really uncanny.

There were some who proved to have ulterior motives for refusing to go to the shelter.

B–'s Aunt Nell had had a sad love life. Her boyfriend had been killed in the First World War and she remained single up until her death. When there was a raid she would cross herself and say three Hail Marys and bury herself under the table in the basement kitchen. We couldn't understand why Aunt Nell wouldn't come to the shelter with all of us but preferred to spend the night under the kitchen table. We found out at our wedding. She'd been supping B–'s whisky while we were in the shelter and topping the bottle up with tap water!

Sadly, though, staying put wasn't always the right decision.

The bombers' aim was not too good and most of the bombs missed the docks and fell on to houses, killing thousands of people and destroying their homes . . . My mother's father was defiant to the end and would not be scared from his bed by those 'no good Germans'. He would not sleep in the shelter and one night he was killed, along with his faithful dog, when a bomb destroyed his house.

It really was very much a matter of chance, as on other occasions experience would prove that going to the shelters was a more dangerous option than staying put in your own home.

We used to use a shelter in Stratford High Street – it was under the shops and workplaces – but we all had to get out when the businesses above caught light and the industrial sewing machines started falling through the floors.

There has been much speculation about the materials and building methods used for the brick public shelters in east London. Some people have suggested that the mix of cement employed in their construction was inadequate and others that someone somewhere messed up the measurements and quantities required to make them strong enough to resist bomb blasts – which, if true, meant that those places were little more than potential death traps. But even the best designed of structures might be expected to fail when under direct bombardment from high explosives.

Mum worked in a laundry by day and was a warden by night. A bomb dropped right by her shelter, killing her father and her fiancé. She had her three brothers and sisters – aged six, seven and nine – to look after, and had to visit her mum in hospital. She wasn't allowed to tell her mum that her father had died.

It was their doubts about the safety of the air-raid shelters that resulted in thousands of East Enders heading for what they hoped was the protection – albeit illicit – of the underground, so much so that it became the preferred place of safety for Londoners, who believed they genuinely had no other choice. Despite official concerns about morale being destroyed if the people who used them were to develop a 'deep-shelter' mentality, refusing to surface and get on with their vital war work,

Londoners carried on going down there – apparently oblivious of the threat of the tube being flooded if a bomb cracked one of the many river tunnels that threaded their way below the capital.

I got myself a bunk down the underground because of my little girl. The rest slept on the floor. Well, what stories can be told about that like the American soldiers used to bring their ladies of the night down there and they used to say to us, 'We don't know how you put up with this!' And there was one family at the other end of the platform – thank goodness – and the man used to come 'home' on the very late train full of drink. They used to fight as if they were in their own home, with her throwing cups and all sorts at him and swearing and shouting. It was quite amazing.

Tragically, it was the tube itself that was to become a death trap on more than one occasion. Probably the most famous of the incidents was what became known as the Bethnal Green tube disaster.

I lived in Bethnal Green in a flat with my baby son. When the warning sounded we would go down the tube to shelter, which was about 400 yards away. With a baby, you still had to get your cooking, washing and other jobs done in between the bombings, and then that terrible blaring noise of the warning again, so back down the tube. We took our blankets and flasks of tea and something to eat. We slept on the railway platforms, neck to neck with other people, and, as there were no trains at that time, we even slept on the tracks, while the German bombers went overhead, heavily loaded with bombs to attack the docks and the rest of London. I was there on the night when that dreadful accident happened. I had just got down the stairs to the station when an ack-ack gun was fired above ground at an enemy plane that had tried to get below the metallic barrage balloons that were up in the air to stop the Germans from flying too low. A woman was alarmed and stumbled down the stairs and many others tumbled down on top of her and were crushed to death on the stairway. Luckily for me, I was already down and escaped the horror.

While the majority of people I spoke to agreed with this version of events on the evening of 3 March 1943 – which proved to be the worst civilian disaster of the Second World War, with 173 dead, including sixty-two children, and a further sixty-two injured severely enough to be detained in hospital – there were other opinions as to what actually happened. Partly because of the rumours that were spreading, the War Cabinet ordered an inquiry into the incident, the report on which was marked 'Most Secret' and 'To Be Kept Under Lock and Key'. It was decided that civilian confidence would be damaged if the full report were to be made public, and might even encourage further 'nuisance raids' by the enemy, so a short statement was made in the House of Commons instead.

In the report itself, two of the main allegations circulating at the time about the cause of the deaths – that it was either a panic induced by Fascists or criminals, or a 'Jewish panic' – were considered. This second 'canard', as the report put it, had even been supported in a broadcast by someone referred to as a 'renegade traitor' from Germany and was aimed at fuelling anti-Semitic sentiment in the East End. Both rumours were dismissed as having no foundation whatsoever, although it has to be said that the first was thought the most likely cause by some of the people who spoke of the event, their belief being that a shouted alert about a pickpocket 'dipping' as people made their way down the stairs caused the initial stumble, which resulted in that terrible tragedy.

[2] *Coping with the Bombing*

It was amazing what people would and did get used to.

People took great care to explain to me that it wasn't only the fact that you might surface from your shelter to find the very fabric of your home reduced to rubble, with all your worldly goods scattered and scorched by the blast and draped all over the surrounding devastation – there, on full view, for everyone to see; or that the water, gas and sewage mains were fractured and you couldn't even make yourself a cup of tea. No, it was the fact that life became a seemingly never-ending round, day in day out, of having to cope.

And, as always in life, some coped better than others.

Home on leave from the army, I got a glimpse of what they had to put up with at home, the bombing and the sheltering in the crypt of the church every night. They were the real soldiers.

I remember the matter-of-fact way we got on with things, the sense of humour. We could laugh at so many things, even at the ridiculous Lord Haw-Haw.* The Germans thought they could frighten us with the stupid things he would say. Mind you, sometimes he got near the mark and it would be a bit frightening, especially when he would say about a certain ship going down.

*

* The nickname of William Joyce, an American-born Nazi propagandist who broadcast on Radio Hamburg throughout the Second World War.

. . . everyone helped everyone else clear up, and, in typical East End fashion, insinuated that Hitler's mother was never married!

My husband's family's next-door neighbour used to run around in a panic with a saucepan over her head, shouting, 'The bombers are coming! The bombers are coming!' every time a plane went over.

One evening, our three guests [a friend of my mother and her two children], deciding that they would just be able to catch the next bus at the top of the road, left clutching their shaded torches and scuttled off into the darkness. We had just settled down to our evening routine [me going to bed in the Morrison shelter] when the air-raid warning sounded and the distant rumble of anti-aircraft guns began. It became evident that things were a bit closer than usual when the heavy 'bong' of the four-and-a-half-inch guns on Wanstead Flats started to join in and the familiar throb of unsynchronized aircraft engines signalled that the enemy was about. The crump of bombs dropping in the distance prompted my mother and grandmother to join me under the [Morrison] shelter, [when there was] a frantic knocking at the front door. [It was] our three recent guests, breathless and begging for shelter, having been caught in the open in the middle of a raid . . . We all huddled together under the shelter. This was not a place for anyone suffering from claustrophobia . . . My mother's friend pointed out that my grandmother still had her rear end poking out into the room, offering a ripe target to flying glass and other debris. An argument was about to develop when the unmistakable sound of an approaching bomb drowned everything out . . . The noise increased to a crescendo . . . The banshee-like scream increased in pitch as well as amplitude until it was unbearable. [Then] the screaming suddenly stopped and for a split second there was complete silence . . . The carpet started to ripple and dust rose from the floor in a kind of miniature fog. Then the house shook. The windows rattled as in a sudden gust of wind, followed by the sound of breaking glass. Then the only sound, apart from the whistles of air-raid wardens and the approach of the rescue services, was the collective sighs of relief. My grandmother [went] to investigate [and] soon returned and announced that the bomb had fallen at the end of the road . . . Next morning [we] went to see the extent of the damage . . . The street now lacked its familiar symmetry. It was like a smile with a missing tooth, the first assault on my own little world . . . It was probably the first time I realized that people got hurt in this war.

. . . we were sort of prepared for being in air raids. Lots of older people were being critical about [the reactions to] 11 September, talking about what they had gone through in the war, but I think it was entirely different, because their whole being was not prepared for what was to come when the terrorists struck. Nevertheless, the raids were not something I would ever want to experience again. The very sound of an air-raid warning really gets to me and the fireworks these days are so loud and violent, I hate them, they sound so much like gunfire. At first the air raids were interspersed [with calm], but then they were regular every night and it became a routine to get home from work as best I could, get changed into my shelter gear, maybe have my tea at the table, but very often the warning would go before I had eaten it, then down to the shelter we would go. We had my paternal grandmother living with us. She walked with a stick and was supposed to be quite infirm, but as soon as the warning went there used to be a race between Granny and the dog as to who got there first. We used to have a laugh over it . . .

It was when the raids became regular and insistent that the period that became known as the Blitz began.

When the Luftwaffe dropped bombs over central London on 24 August 1940, the Royal Air Force flew a retaliation raid on Berlin, and this, in turn, prompted a response by the Luftwaffe. For Londoners, this was to be the precursor of the Blitzkrieg –

the Lightning War – and the onslaught that would begin in earnest on a fine Saturday in September 1940.

Although the Royal Air Force had been fighting the Battle of Britain since 10 July – and would continue to do so for four long months (see Chronology for details) – it is the day the docks were set on fire, Black Saturday, that is remembered by East Enders.

Not only were the docks a major target for the enemy because of the importance to the country's survival of the goods they received, but those precious cargoes also served to fuel the conflagration, adding to the terrible fire and smoke hazards for the rescue services.

The existence of the enemy was now all too real for those living in what had become the direct firing line.

My childhood was too good to be true – the bloody war was to alter this. That first Black Saturday of the Blitz was to find the Germans bombing us non-stop throughout the day and night. I was twelve years old and I was working part-time in a shoe repair shop. I would deliver the shoes on a Saturday afternoon after the all clear sounded, I would go back to the shop for the evening deliveries. It was ironic that, after three hours' bombing, the guv'nor wanted me to go back to his home near the docks to see if his house was still standing. When I think back – I am in awe to think – how did this sort of person carry on repairing shoes when all [that] mayhem was around him? Come to think of it, what was I doing at twelve years of age riding my bike amongst the firemen's hoses and dangerous building debris?

Back to London [from being evacuated], and back to the Blitz, with night after night taking our bedding back down the underground station as soon as possible after we arrived home from school that we attended only half a day . . . These were not happy days.

*

We were living in Bethnal Green and, during that first big air raid when they attacked the docks, Mother put me in a cupboard. The house was shaking and I was petrified.

I was born and continued to live in Bow during the Blitz. I shall never forget the ocean of flames surrounding my home and the docks and nearby factories blazed, the bomb explosions, the rain of falling shrapnel from anti-aircraft guns, the death of friends and neighbours – digging their bodies out from the ruins of their houses . . . In 1940, being on statutory fire-watch duties on the roof of my office near St Paul's Cathedral, the immediate area was hit by thousands of incendiary bombs. Many buildings, including my offices, which we were trying to protect, went up in flames. One could only gaze in utter disbelief and despair that we were witnessing yet gain another Great Fire of London on the very same site. Some of my colleagues died that night.

History books may tell you that the Great Fire of London happened in 1666. But some of us know better. For we saw the big one: 1940. And nobody who witnessed that ever forgot it for the rest of their lives. Air raids were noisy affairs at the best of times, carried out with typical Teutonic efficiency. They nearly always began at five or six in the evening. Only occasionally would this time vary. Then, when Jerry was a few minutes late in arriving, it tended to spark off grim gallows humour: 'Hello! Six o'clock and no Jerry? Here, hope nothing's happened to him!' But he would arrive, every night, without fail, for months on end, and not leave until eight the following morning. Fourteen hours of battering that took heavy toll of life and real estate. I can still remember the way those calm, cultured, unemotional BBC announcers would give us the grim details the next morning: 'Five firemen, four policemen and 186 civilians are known to have lost their lives.' Always that formula, always separated into groups like that. It was then that I first learned what this word 'civilian' meant. And those few words on the radio, plus a few lines in the papers, would be the only mention they'd get. No papers filled with grief and woe for months about them. Nobody strewing flowers all over the place. No time, no point. Everybody knew that the next night was going to see about 200 more killed. Dangerous times, at least for adults. Kids, insulated by youthful stupidity, found it all pretty exciting. But that night, the night of the fire, that was special. In its own somewhat unfriendly fashion, the Germans' plan was a shrewd one. They chose a time when the Thames was low, making fire fighting difficult. The London docks . . . were stuffed with things that would burn nicely. And so over came daylight raiders just to get the ball rolling. Even during the day these fires became colossal, covering miles . . . A convenient beacon to guide in the night bombers, which proceeded to fill in any gaps with fires of their own, linking everything into one vast whole. Which duly made that memorable night. My brothers were off in the RAF, Dad was Home-Guarding somewhere, leaving just the three of us – my mother, sister and me – at an upstairs window, doing what thousands of others must have been doing, gazing out upon a scene which, quite simply, defies adequate description. In every direction, an unbroken circle, one great bonfire. Flames leaping 100 feet into the air, as yet a mile or more from us but seemingly bent upon advancing everywhere until every square inch of London would be mere ashes. I can honestly say that I wasn't afraid. Not that this denotes any great courage on my part. It doesn't. I have been afraid plenty of times since then . . . But then, no. To a seven-year-old this was simply a terrific sight. Really was. Horrible but still terrific . . . Terror was coming from Mum in tangible waves, impinging even upon my dull perception. Now I can understand and sympathize with what she must have been feeling, lumbered with one adolescent daughter and one idiot ankle-biter, and apparently doomed to see both them and herself consumed by an inescapable inferno. But we weren't. Performing miracles, staying in place for days, the firemen did finally get the fires beaten. Whole [parts] of London had ceased to exist . . . Yeah, I'll never forget it. Since then I have seen other memorable sights, even on occasion a few that could be called awesome, but never one more awesome.

It was during the week of my birthday in September 1940 that I invited two friends to be my guests and attend an afternoon matinée at a local cinema – the Grand, near Blackwall Tunnel. The film had been on for about half an hour when suddenly, instead of being on the screen, it was up on the ceiling, and then suddenly stopped. The cinema manager ordered everyone – about sixty people – to vacate the place, because German aeroplanes were overhead dropping bombs. We came out of the cinema and were astonished. The docks were ablaze. Planes overhead were firing guns to shoot each other down. Bombs were being dropped and exploding, and the ground anti-aircraft guns were firing up to shoot down the bombers. We made our way home with shell shrapnel from the anti-aircraft guns falling on the roads and rooftops of houses. My friends lived in a house which had a corrugated-iron Anderson shelter with sandbags covering it. My family lived in flats so had a communal brick shelter with no windows, built three feet below ground level and six feet above. The walls were eighteen inches thick, with a heavy wooden door. When we arrived home, my father and mother were in the shelter with about thirty others, and we joined them. We were still in there about an hour later, when there was an enormous bang. The door blew off its hinges, we were covered in dust and the walls had split, letting in daylight. We emerged from the shelter in a state of shock and discovered that a bomb had hit a nearby five-storey block of flats, bringing down the whole wall. Beds and furniture on each floor were hanging out, ready to fall to the ground. Due to the damage, our shelter was unfit for use. My parents told my brother and I to go to our grandparents, who lived a short distance away. We stayed there for the night, with my grandmother complaining that she could get no gas to the cooker, totally unaware that along the road the gas main had been hit by a bomb and was blazing. We slept on the floor – not really sleeping, because of the noise and the floor shaking as bombs exploded. Next morning, we returned home, only to find that my friends' house had been hit by a bomb and demolished. My friends and their parents were killed. It was this which really brought home to me the reality of war.

We were living in Dagenham at the time of the Blitz, but all our family were living in the East End – my grandparents, my aunts, uncles and cousins, my great-aunts and uncles, and second cousins. So it was a harrowing time. I shall never forget that first time when the docks were alight and the bombing was so bad. It was a Saturday and the planes were coming over in their hundreds – all night – and it rained down incendiary bombs over Dagenham, and the men were out all the time putting out the fires. Came Sunday morning and an awful time was to come. On the buses from the East End – it was such a sad sight. They were full of people coming to their friends and relations. So many had been bombed out. They were there with what belongings they could carry, and, of course, their pets – dogs on leads, cats in boxes, birds in cages and fish in bowls. We were frantic to have news of our family and, by lunchtime, my mum decided to go to Poplar to find out what had happened, and, to this day, I don't know how she got there and back. Fortunately, our family were all right for the time being, but none of them would come back with her.

The experience of not having a home to return to was to affect all too many families during the Blitz.

The night we got bombed out started like any other. I lay in bed listening to the bombs dropping, heard the explosions and felt the house rock. My dad said, 'It's getting a bit close. I think you should all go in the shelter.' Nan got me out of bed, wrapped a blanket round my shoulders, while my sister got [her baby] from his cot and collected everyone's gas masks. Going from the back door to the shelter, I noticed the sky was alight – red everywhere – bomb blasts

. Blitz damage to Whitman House on the Cornwall Estate, Bethnal Green. Note the people still inside the probably dangerous building, and the municipal handcart on the left.

2. ARP Warden King, accompanied by Rip, begins his nightly duties along Southill Street during a London peasouper. Rip was adopted by Mr King's wardens' post, and was the first dog to help find people trapped by the bombing. He was awarded the Blue Cross Medal, known as 'the animals' VC'.

3. The railway arches, Arnold Road, Bow, showing the sandbagged entrance to the shelter belonging to J. O'Connor, the cooper and barrel merchants.

4. Bedtime stories in the shelter. The gas masks are stored on the ledge on the right, and Mum has little space to stretch out for the night.

5. East Enders experience nightly overcrowding and lack of privacy as they shelter – in this case in an uncompleted section of the London Underground.

6. Devastation in Poplar. ARP workers and wardens attached to Post B132 have the morbid task of digging out the victims of a parachute mine.

7. GIs lend Londoners a hand to clear up after a raid. On this occasion at least some of the furniture has been saved.

. Searching through the debris of a house in Cyprus Street, Old Ford, to see if there is nything left that might be rescued.

. This picture of September 1940 shows an ARP warden helping East End mothers and heir babies, made homeless by the bombing, move to a place of greater safety. It was assed by the censor as suitable for publication, presumably because it reassured the ublic that people could survive the terrible raids.

10–13. With the war lasting for six long years, ordinary domestic life, with its cooking and cleaning, still had to go on in our street, regardless of the extraordinary circumstances.

10.

11.

12.

13.

14. It wasn't only domestic work that needed doing; here the postman does his best to deliver the mail.

15. Sadly, this family have nowhere left to receive their letters. All that remains of their home is piled up on the handcart.

going off. I remember I wasn't frightened – like all kids, I saw no danger [and] anyway, my dad wouldn't let anything happen to me. 'You'll be OK in there,' Dad said. 'I'm going to stay here and watch for a while.'

The noise seemed to go on longer than ever before. The shelter door was left open for Dad to jump in quick if need be. We could see him clearly, standing on the back doorstep, looking up at the sky. My sister was crying and pleading with him to come in the shelter. 'George, come in here for five minutes to shut this girl up, will you!' Nan commanded. We saw him walk towards the shelter door, then [there was] one almighty bang and he was thrown inside, followed by dirt, bricks, everything. The doorway was blocked solid. So now we were all trapped inside, but Dad was safe and with us.

What a wonderful woman my nan was. She was not young and must have been terrified, but out came that commanding voice: 'Stop that noise and crying. We'll be all right, someone'll find us.' We'd listen for a quiet spell, then, 'One, two, three, altogether!' We'd shout, 'Help!' We waited for ages for that quiet spell – or so it seemed. We could hear people shouting, calling out in pain, crying. We had no idea what was happening outside. 'We're here together and alive,' said Nan. 'We'll be OK.'

Then the quiet spell came and we shouted, but nobody came. 'Quiet,' Nan said. 'Listen, someone's singing.' Sure enough, we could hear men's voices drunkenly singing 'Nellie Dean'.

'Right, now, all together. HELP!'

The voices we heard were two sailors – home on leave and out on the piss – we later found out. We never knew who they were, but they heard us and, with their bare hands, dug us out of that shelter. We emerged on to piles of rubble and bricks that were once our garden. The house was gone, flattened, and the spot where Dad had been standing watching the raid was a mountain of bricks. The bombs were still dropping all around us and the agonizing screams all around were deafening.

'Over the wall, Mother,' the sailor said to Nan. 'Cross the park and go to the church.' Waiting for my turn to be passed over the wall, I looked around me. There, on the ground, was [Dad's carving of] Hitler's effigy and next to it a human hand and part of an arm.

'Look, Nan, somebody's hand,' I said. My head was roughly screwed round in the opposite direction. 'Look where you're going, not all around you' – Nan's voice, taking charge again, trying to keep us calm. Over the wall into the park we all clambered in our nightclothes and there we saw where the screams were coming from. An underground shelter had been made there for people who had no garden. People had taken their bedding and gone down there on this night, the same as any other. But this night was not the same. In the very centre of the park, and spreading out all ways, was a massive hole. A land mine had landed there and so many people were there – dead, injured, trapped. In their drunkenness, the sailors had crossed the park and never noticed it, but they had, thank God, heard our shouts.

'Make your way to St John's,' an air-raid warden told us. 'That's where everyone's going.' Still the bombs were dropping, still the sky was one mass of red.

When we reached St John's and went into my Sunday School hall, it was like a family gathering.

'Hello, Lizzie, all right?'

'All right, George?'

'Give us the baby, Dora, while you get a cup of tea.'

No panic here, just people looking round for familiar faces.

'The park's got it.'

'Yeah, so's the Mason's.'

The chatter went on, and all these brave people, so glad to be alive, were exchanging news of the bombing, asking each other if they had seen or heard what happened to so and so and who'd 'got it', 'it' being bombed out. I looked around for familiar faces and there was [my friend] Joanie with her mum, sat on the floor, huddled together, as were so many other people – most in their nightclothes like me. The WVS [Women's Voluntary Service] and Salvation Army were there, dishing out tea to everyone, helping with the wounded and giving us kids an orange each. Where did they get these from, I thought. We hadn't seen any fruit for ages – 'There's a war on, you know' – and now these lovely people had found oranges, and tea, milk and sugar, from somewhere.

The exchange of talk continued.

'Didn't get you then, George?' someone shouted to Dad.

'No, didn't get me in the last lot, ain't going to get me in this' – the 'last lot' being the First World War.

'Got your Sunday best on, I see, Lizzie' – poor Nan's dress was torn and dusty.

'Well, it is Sunday, ain't it?' she replied.

For the first time since I'd been taken from my bed in my night-clothes, I realized it was Sunday morning. That night we got bombed out was the night 'they', as my friend Rosie had called them, set the docks alight.

After spending twenty-four hours in the church hall, everyone was getting edgy – 'What happens [now]? Where will we go?' As soon as it was daylight, Dad went back to number 12 [our home] to see if he could salvage anything for us. The only room left was the washhouse in the basement. He dug a hole in the rubble and slid down into the room that had the big brick-built copper [housing] and mangle in . . . When he came back later he had a suitcase [he must have found from somewhere] with a rescued pair of his old shoes, some papers, which I think were insurance policies, some baby clothes [of my nephew's] and there, on top, my doll that I had been playing with in the washroom while Nan did some washing the day before. The doll was missing a foot and half the other leg, but she survived the bombing in that basement. Clothes and other objects he was unable to reach, because they were all kept in the upper part of the house, which was now a flattened pile of rubbish. I wonder if he realized what danger he put himself in by getting that doll for me.

From somewhere the Salvation Army had got clothes given to them. They set up a stall and we all queued past them to be handed out what was most likely to fit us. Maybe there were no kids' clothes, or maybe they had all gone by the time our turn came, because there was nothing left to fit me. I was given an enormous pair of bloomers, a cardigan ten sizes too big, and the only shoes they had for me were a pair of red tap shoes. I loved those shoes and must have driven everyone mad with my tap-dancing up and down that hall. We were told that in the evening we were all going to be evacuated off the Island* to a place that never had any bombing, just the warning and the all clear. That place turned out to be West Hampstead.

If you were caught out by a raid when you weren't at home or at work, it didn't make sense to try to reach your regular shelter, and although there were plenty of stories about the bombing being a good cover for staying out all night with your sweetheart, these girls innocently caused their parents considerable concern when they failed to return home.

It was a Saturday evening and one of the first of the real raids. My sister met me outside the shop where I worked as we were going to a party at the house of a boy I knew. But then the siren went off and we both ran down Green Street and across the main road to an air-raid shelter, where we spent the night with strangers. Fire engines were about outside all night, putting out incendiary bombs. Next morning we managed to get a lift part of the way home. Our mum and dad were very worried. My eldest sister had also been out all night in Whitechapel, while Mum and Dad had spent the night in the Anderson shelter.

As the war dragged on, such eventualities became far more commonplace, and it sometimes seemed as if the bombing was never going to let up.

* The Isle of Dogs.

By the end of September we had been bombed every night . . . and then continuous bombing from October to the beginning of November, with the raids mostly from 6 p.m. to 6 a.m., and having to be at work at 8 a.m. Blimey, were we tired!

During the height of the Blitz, when we were going into the shelters night after night, I think we all ended up like zombies. It became an awful way of life.

Incendiary bombs landed outside our front door. One of my older brothers went and got Dad's window boxes and dumped them on them. There were a few loud bangs further away. That night we went to the shelters at the docks, to Free Trade Wharf. We went there every night for what seemed like months. We came home one morning to find a lot of damage to most of the houses in the street. So we were put on a lorry with Mum and the six of us, all under fourteen. We didn't know where Dad and my older brothers were.

It got to the point when we were happy when it rained or was very foggy – we were happy because the enemy did not come to bomb us when visibility was too poor! So we celebrated by having a drink in the Green Man and having a singsong.

A young nephew of my father's called on us on a twenty-four-hour pass, not knowing where he would be posted. After spending his leave with us, we all boarded a bus to go and see him off at the station. It was late evening and the place was full to the brim with servicemen. Any trains were jam-packed waiting to pull out. We hung around until it was very late and then the sirens went. Dad's nephew found a space on a train and squeezed into it. From the window of the train he said to Dad, 'If I was you, I'd get away from here. I think it's going to be a heavy night.'

We left the station and went out on to the road. I will never forget the sight that met our eyes. Red. Red. Red. And the sounds of bells clanging, fire engines and ambulances. Nobody was on the pavements, and no buses. Dad covered my head with his tin helmet and wrapped his greatcoat around me to shield me from falling debris. Mum was wearing high heels and I could hear her feet clip-clopping alongside of us. An ARP warden came out of a doorway and asked Dad where we were going, and suggested that he should 'Get the missus and the kiddie down the underground.' Dad, although then in the army, had actually been in the trenches in France during World War One – I still have his Mons Star medal – [and] would have none of it. We continued to walk and he called back to the ARP man, 'We'll walk till we get this lot behind us.'

I don't know how far we walked, but the City was well ablaze when suddenly, down a side street, a red double-decker bus slowly pulled up alongside us. It was blacked out, with blinds at all the windows, but we could see an outline of the driver's face. He called out to ask us where we were going.

Dad replied, 'Anywhere so long as I get them out of here.'

'Hop on, I'll get you home,' he said.

There were four or five other passengers on the bus. The driver carefully picked his way down one street after another, with burning buildings on either side, sometimes stopping and carefully reversing the big double-decker because of bomb craters in the road he had chosen to go through. Sometimes he looked back through his window and told us all to lie on the floor. It was quite an experience.

That driver managed slowly to get the bus and its passengers out of the City that night with all the devastation going on around him, not sticking to any route, just getting his passengers to safety . . . My dad went to the front of the bus and gave him some money, then turned to Mum and said, 'That man deserves a medal.' I often wonder who he was and whether he did get a medal.

It was estimated that Londoners were getting an average of just four hours' sleep a night during the bombing, so it was no wonder they were exhausted. Added to which, one in every six

Londoners had been made at least temporarily homeless during the Blitz, whether by raids, unexploded bombs, fires, fractured mains or the destruction of their homes. In a report on rehousing people made homeless by enemy action, written by the Bow Road branch of the Citizens' Advice Bureau, it was noted, rather poignantly, that the two most frequently mentioned problems were the loss of clocks and, even harder for those who already felt almost at the end of their tether, the loss of wirelesses. But, of course, there were far worse losses.

During the Blitz [I] was stationed near Gravesend. The greatest worry for us out there was for our loved ones back in London. Most nights there was a procession of German bombers passing high overhead towards the capital. When the anti-aircraft guns opened up it was bedlam, and we could climb on to the highest point of the roof to watch the terrible blood-red glow rising in the sky above east London. I'm sure I could have read a newspaper by the light from those fires. Our battalion was made up of London lads, some of whose wives, children or parents had not been evacuated. We anxiously waited to hear news on the wireless next morning and would selfishly feel relieved if the targets were away from our homes. My sister Phyllis was in our old home in Upton Park. I prayed that she was OK. I heard later that she was spending each night in the Anderson shelter in the back garden. During lulls in the bombing one night she thought she could hear a voice calling, 'Kitty, Kitty,' and eventually curiosity overcame caution and she poked her head out of the shelter. The old lady next door was searching the garden for her cat. What horrified Phyl was that the old dear was wandering around with a lantern in what was supposed to be the blackout. Phyl thought that was why our area seemed to get more than its fair share of bombs, although it was probably the railway that attracted the Luftwaffe. When the bombers were coming over night after night, Phyl used to get Mum into the Anderson before the sirens sounded, as Mum's crippled knee meant she took ages to get into the shelter. One night there were several explosions close by, followed by a heavy thud on the roof of their shelter. Phyl risked a glance outside the shelter and was horrified to see the silhouette of a large cylinder lying across the roof. It was outlined by the flames in the builder's yard at the bottom of our garden. Bombs were falling all around and shrapnel was whizzing about. Phyl decided it was too risky to try and get Mum away, so they stayed put – hoping that, as the bomb hadn't gone off when it came down, it really was a dud. It wasn't until the next morning that she realized it was just a length of drainpipe blown in from the builder's yard. Back in [Gravesend] two of the men were informed that their homes had been hit, but luckily their families had been in shelters and escaped with shock. The two squaddies were given compassionate leave immediately. While each German bomb didn't flatten too many houses, it would certainly damage hundreds of surrounding roofs that would need repair. Now in our company there were two Cockney lads who were tilers by trade and they were released from army service to help make the damaged houses fit for habitation. All the rest of us wished them well and regretted that we were not roofers as well so we could go back as civvies. Sadly, fate had its way and one of the tilers was killed in an air raid while mending a roof in Bermondsey.

Regardless of such tragedies, and demonstrations of courage in the face of terrible danger, it could sometimes take something merely horribly unpleasant, rather than actually life-threatening, to make you snap and drive you to tears.

Her mum was a lovely lady. She had snow-white hair, and on that day her daughter had set it all nice. Anyway, there's land mines, bombs dropping and all these incendiaries [they lived near the docks], so we all had to run out and get sandbags to put the incendiaries out. As she got her sandbag she put it on her head. And it was full of dog's muck. She cried her eyes out. She said, 'Ooh, just look at my hair!' It was all lovely and clean . . . snow white. It was different things like that that had you crying and laughing at the same time. It was all over her. I said, 'Right, you should be lucky after that.'

Some people really were lucky – with or without the 'help' of a dog – as they told me when they recalled stories of near misses. Others spoke of their failure to realize they were in any danger in the first place, or explained how they felt it was simply not their turn.

Our neighbour opened her sash-cord bedroom window to see if her son was going into the shelter in the garden. She called out to him, leaning out as she did so. Naturally, there was no light on in the house because of the blackout. As she leaned out of the window, a bit of the fuselage of an aircraft missed her head by just two feet, landing in the back yard.

My mother-in-law, who was at least sixteen stone, had to jump out of the second-floor window as all her staircase was alight.

I well remember standing at our street door and watching the fires all around and rushing to put out incendiary bombs with bags ready-filled with sand. This was stopped after a time when the bombs were also made explosive. Sometimes there were hundreds dropped and everybody seemed to be trying to put them out. There were quite a few casualties from the bomb and shell fragments or shrapnel. I had a narrow escape when standing in my doorway, watching what was, after all, for me a huge and very frightening firework display, and being saved by the steel helmet which we used to wear from a large piece of hot shrapnel which was deflected from my face when it hit the rim of the helmet. I finished up with the helmet over my face and the piece of metal at my feet. It is a pity that I never kept it as a souvenir, [but] we used to pick up hundreds of pieces so I suppose it was no novelty.

I was still at work and doing civil defence and fire-watching duties, but when I was at home I slept like a log, so I didn't bother to go down the shelter, I went up to bed. All sorts happened, so if I died in bed or in the shelter, so what? The next morning, when she called me for work, Mum said, 'Did you hear the bomb?' When I said no, she told me to look out of the window. Up on the telephone wires there was bedding and sheets hanging from them that had been thrown up there out of a house which had been bombed right to the ground.

Londoners talked about the quiet period after the Blitz, when the bombing at last abated and raids, though still deadly, were sporadic rather than unremitting. You could at least snatch some much needed rest and, with surprising composure, get on with life, even through the so-called 'Little Blitz' that rained down on London in 1944 from January through to April. And then there were the hope and relief that came in the June of that year, when newsreels, newspapers and wireless reports celebrated the successes of D-Day. However, rather than this being the end of the war, as so many had anticipated, the latter part of June was to present the people in our street with a new, deadly surprise.

Little did we know what Hitler had in store for us next. I'd stood many an evening on the doorstep with my dad, watching the planes fighting in the sky, seeing either Spitfires or German planes explode in balls of fire. Some just came crashing down. My nan would shout, 'Bring that girl in here, George, that's no place for her.' But I stayed. I saw no danger with my dad's arm round me, pointing out to me which plane was whose. But one evening we saw a plane come over with fire coming from its tail, the only sound coming from a droning noise. The tail fire went out, the noise stopped and – crash! – it came down to explode somewhere near the station, taking down several houses and causing many deaths. 'What the hell was that?' Dad said.

Very soon we found out that they were doodlebugs. A flying bomb, no pilot, just kept going until the engine stopped, then crash, straight down. Once more, Hitler's target was London. Night and day, day and night – they never seemed to stop. We didn't get a chance to have the warning sound before they were here. We would be sat in the kitchen, listening for the noise to stop, and then it would be, 'Quick, under the table!'

The Vergeltungswaffe – the V1s and 2s – were Hitler's 'reprisal weapons'. The V1, a flying bomb known as the doodlebug or buzz bomb, was actually a pilotless plane. Carrying a cargo of bombs and fuel, it flew towards its target with a characteristic sound that soon had it christened with its almost comic-book nickname, and then, when the fuel was used up, the engine cut out, the sound stopped and people sprinted for cover – that silence being the sign that the whole thing was about to come crashing down on whatever, and whoever, was below.

I remember lying in the gutter with my grandad – not his usual place of repose, I hasten to point out – as a V1 went over.

I remember the sound of the doodlebugs and how everyone seemed to hold their breath and wait to hear whether the engine cut out before it reached your house, overhead or beyond it. If it was overhead or beyond, then you were safe. It would glide down somewhere else and there would be a huge sigh of relief. I suppose it sounds awful really – if it didn't fall on us it fell on some other poor devil – but the relief was so intense that I don't think that was uppermost in anyone's mind, although someone would always say, 'Wonder who got that one?'

All would go quiet and we had to wait for the thud when it landed. We all felt a sense of relief when this happened as we knew we were safe, for the present at least.

*

Mum was walking along the street with the pram when she heard a doodlebug in the distance. She wasn't sure whether to run or stand still. She stood still and the engine stopped and fell, blowing up a house. Mum saw the whole thing.

On a quiet Sunday morning, after a warning had sounded, and after I had promised to leave my bed to follow my parents, who had left the house to [go to] the brick street shelter, a V1 crashed at the corner of the street about 200 feet away. [Our] home was completely demolished with me underneath, not killed because the bedroom door had somehow been blown in, [had] twisted and fallen over the bed, resting on the top and bottom frame, thus creating a space in which I was saved from being crushed. [That] door held the debris off me. I came to, choking through soot, dust and smoke, and terrified by the noises, shouts and screaming. [I] struggled and shouted until I saw a chink of light . . . above me, through which I eventually pushed my hand. [There was] a frantic effort to get to me by the rescue workers and I was pulled out naked and bleeding from numerous abrasions caused by flying glass and scratches from jagged wood. I had a coat or a blanket put around me and [was] carried carefully in the arms of one of the rescuers up and over the debris of my home . . . at that same time seeing both my mother and father, framed by what was left of the front door jamb, crying and in a state of shock and, at the same time, happy to see and hear me.

Still being carried after they had been assured that I was not seriously hurt, we were led over the smoking rubble, where so many people seemed to be tearing at the ruins of other houses where more people were buried still. Whether it was a reality or not, I remember seeing the head of an old lady who had lived next door lying on top of the ruins of her home and I believe it was detached from her body. Another horror came when, after a few yards, we stopped whilst a couple of the rescuers removed the boots from two legs that were protruding from the chaos of broken bricks, with the intention of putting them on me. I did not know [then] that the legs were artificial and belonged to a man who had still not been recovered – knowledge that would not have made the situation or nightmare any easier for me. We were led to the underground station, where there was some emergency help offered and word was sent to my sisters, who were living in Stoke Newington . . . We were collected soon after and [went to] the home of my sister Ada to recover. Over the next few weeks I used to return to dig in the ruins of my home, but there was little that was recoverable. Yet on one occasion, about three weeks later, upon raising the corner of our flattened kitchen table, I was horrified when a filthy, stinking lump of fur came into my hands crying and still alive – our old pet cat.

Another fact that came to light was that my brother had been rescued after some time in the sea when the landing craft in which he was sailing . . . was sunk. This was at the same time that the V1 had hit our home, and only came to light when, after a short stay in sick berth, he was allowed home on sick leave. Unfortunately, when he emerged from the underground, he was presented with the sight of demolished streets where his home had been. One shock on top of another so weakened his constitution that he never regained his old vigour . . .

Then, in September 1944, just a few days after the fifth anniversary of Britain's declaration of war on Germany, the first of a series of almighty explosions was heard across London. When these explosions continued throughout the autumn and into winter, the authorities could no longer try to keep matters calm by passing them off as exploding gas mains and the truth, that they were caused by V2 rockets, was finally made public.

It was two long months after the rockets first appeared that Churchill announced that London was once again under attack – two long months during which hundreds had been killed, thousands had been seriously injured, and untold homes and workplaces and other property had been damaged or destroyed.

Not until the end of 1944, when a rocket destroyed a branch of Woolworth's in New Cross that was full of lunchtime shoppers, was an attack eventually given wide media coverage. And even then the true extent of the tragedy was not made known. By this time, however, Londoners were only too aware of the terrifying power of these weapons, which were to be responsible for the deaths of almost 3,000 people and the serious injury of 6,000 others. At least the V1s, the doodlebugs, had had their distinctive 'buzz' sound, and so had given those in danger some chance to dive for cover. With the rockets no warning was given, and their height and speed made it impossible to shoot them down.

People were stunned. How could an enemy whom they had thought of as being as good as defeated be doing this to them? To add to the misery, the winter of 1944–5 saw the worst weather in living memory.

. . . we lived in the street just at the back of where the rocket had fallen. Our house was practically destroyed by the explosion. My dad and I had to rescue my sister. She had been trapped because the roof had fallen in on her while she was asleep in bed. She was saved because the bed was the old iron type and was strong enough to hold the roof off her. Once we knew she was safe, Dad and I went to see what else we could do to help other people. We were left with just the clothes we were wearing and some salvaged from the debris of the house. We had to go to the WVS in Romford Road to get 'handouts'. Because we had been helping out at the bomb site, there were a lot of people in front of us. Many of these people did not even live *near* us and were there to see what they could get. My mother had to point out that they were there under false pretences, but the WVS woman said that everyone was entitled to be there. My mother's answer to this was to lift her skirt above her head and say, 'Yes, but I bet they're not walking around with no drawers on!'

*

The week before I got married in 1944, we had a V2 rocket fall at the top of our road. The buses used to turn around and the drivers have their break there. One of the buses and all its passengers were lost, along with the buildings opposite. Our loss was negligible compared, just our windows blown in and all the doors off their hinges. We put a curtain up at the bedroom door for the wedding – no halls in those days, just a couple of crates from the corner pub and a good old knees-up.

[At first] the V2 weapons were not officially acknowledged by the government, [but] on the night of 21 February 1945, when one landed in our street, we were all only too painfully aware of what they were. I was asleep under the Morrison shelter when I woke to find it cold, with rain coming into the room. My mother made me get dressed whilst in the steel cage and told me to avoid the broken glass and rubble. I got up to find a hole in the ceiling and roof, broken glass everywhere and a terrible all-pervading sour smell rather like a very strong cheese. When I at last managed to get out into the street, I found that the smell was caused by huge mounds of clay that dotted the road like anthills. These had been thrown out of the bomb crater . . . and people were busy digging up these mounds and carting them away on lorries and horse-drawn wagons to allow rescue services better access. My mother and I got as close as we could to the still-smoking crater, in which the remainder of the [four] houses could be seen and where rescue workers were toiling away, and ambulances negotiated the debris to collect casualties that were still being found. [Back] home, my grandmother was comforting one of our neighbours, of whom I was very fond and called Auntie J–, her concern being for her close friend Mrs G– (I knew her as Auntie G–), not yet found in the wreckage of her home. Work continued throughout the day, with people coming and going and neighbours calling on each other with offers of help. Water and gas supplies had been cut, and people from adjoining streets not so affected supplied water, which was carried away in saucepans, kettles and even in tin baths. That evening, my mother, grandmother and I walked to the top of the street, where there was a timber company that had large workshops, which had been hastily converted into a temporary mortuary. A silent queue waited by the steel-shuttered door, waiting to be escorted into the building, where, by peering through people's legs, I could see stretchers on the floor, each covered with a black tarpaulin . . . A policeman or warden would lift a cover for someone to look, only for them to be tearfully led away. I then noticed my grandmother walking around on her own, stopping to lift each cover in turn and making a careful examination before proceeding on to the next. It was not long before she came out and went over to my mother, who was comforting a tearful Auntie J–, now more upset than before. We returned home in silence and, as I realized what I had seen, the excitement of the day seemed to be out of place and faded a little. My mother filled the kettle from one of several large saucepans of water and put it on a small picnic stove hissing quietly in the kitchen. My grandmother produced a small bottle and poured a little into each cup, including mine, before adding tea. In flickering candlelight, we sat round the Morrison shelter that was [also] our table, drinking tea and listening to the rain pattering down on the emergency tarpaulin cover over the roof. It was my first taste of whisky . . . [and] my first encounter with the concept of mortality. The effects of the whisky-laced tea, coupled with the sound of the hissing stove and the pattering rain, began to [make me drowsy]. Crawling under the shelter to my bed, I eventually fell asleep, my feelings hovering between a sense of loss and excitement, but none of fear and foreboding at what tomorrow might bring. Such is the resilience of childhood.

[3] *Childhood*

> I know it seems wrong to say it, but I was only a little girl and I enjoyed the war. It was exciting.

The first thing I remember about the war was seeing the barrage balloons floating in the sky like outsized silver elephants . . . [and] having to take our gas masks to school with us in cardboard boxes. If the siren sounded – an eerie, mournful sound – we had to file into a dimly lit brick building without windows with our reading books.

It is often claimed that people today are working so hard to provide their children with the material possessions they themselves never had that they have lost sight of the positive aspects of their own childhood.

But what was it that children *did* have back then? With schools offering somewhat erratic teaching at best and nothing at all at worst, fathers away in the services and mothers busy with war work, fire-watching and queuing for whatever they could get from the shops, children were left to their own devices more than ever before. There were certainly subsequent rises in recorded rates of juvenile delinquency and malicious damage, but there were also plenty of examples of children behaving with a maturity that seems at odds with their years. Yet despite having so much more freedom – if it can be called that – to rake the streets and get up to all sorts behind their parents' backs, children didn't have things easy. People recalled happy memories of course, but that is probably at least partly due to children's resilience – as previously mentioned – and sometimes sadness and fear were there as well alongside the laughter. I was also told stories of hunger, deprivation and straightforward cruelty too many times to ignore them as rare exceptions. But despite that, and the lack of awareness that things could – or rather should – have been better which characterizes many working people's attitudes in that period, there was surprisingly little dissatisfaction expressed. It was what people were accustomed to, the way things were, and most remembered their childhood wartime experiences – even some of the truly unpleasant ones – with impressive good grace.

Next door but one to the place where they moved us we found some East Enders who had been bombed out like us. They had been given a whole house and [the children] soon became good friends of mine. Once again I was back at the school where we'd been billeted after the bombing, but this time as a pupil. It was now forgotten by the other kids there that I was a 'dirty East Ender' and I soon made lots of other friends. One of our pastimes was to wait for the all clear after a raid, and then go round to look for plane or bomb wreckages to search for shrapnel. I collected many pieces – God knows what for – and used to study any markings on them. Usually they were numbers, which meant nothing to me, but Dad would look at them and make guesses as to what they were from.

In addition to normal lessons [we] received instructions on air-raid precautions and the use of gas masks. To this day I can remember the smell of my gas mask and the little cardboard box with a strap to carry it. We also had drills where we left the classroom and went to the basement room designated as a safe area. Boards on poles were placed in the playground . . . and we kids were told if the board changed colour – to yellow, I think – we were under gas attack and should put on our gas masks . . . Then came the Blitz. The anti-aircraft guns, the barrage balloons, the planes, the bombs, the sirens – all produced excitement and noise, and all the children I knew, not realizing the dangers, had a very good time. Lessons were interrupted, no regular bedtime, frequently not having to wash. People, family and other children around all of the time made a very happy life for many children, [but] adults did not find it so good and I often found my mother crying.

Adults, concerned for their families' safety and well-being, were very aware that their children were missing out on a normal life. But particularly for the younger ones, who neither knew nor remembered anything else, war was simply what was going on around them, the backdrop to their lives.

We had big maps stuck on our wallpaper from the *Daily Herald* of the British troop movements, and would look at them constantly.

Being a child in wartime was exciting and terrifying. The noise of guns and bombs was something I shall never forget. In bed we would shiver in fear, waiting for what was to come. Us children somehow thought that if we went to the shelter we would be perfectly safe, but Mum would not leave her bed until the bombs started to rain down. My father, who was with the ARP, would come over to our flats and get us to the shelter with tin hats on our heads to protect us from being hurt by shrapnel. If a raid occurred while we were at school, we would be ushered down in the cellar near the boilers. We would sit on mounds of coke and be told to sing as loud as we could – 'Old MacDonald Had a Farm'. Teacher said that if we sang it loud enough the Germans would be so scared of the horrible noise that they would go somewhere else and bomb.

My brother and friends found an unexploded bomb. They loaded it on to their home-made pushcart and took it to the local police station. The police immediately evacuated the station and called in the army bomb-disposal team.

I was a little girl, but the war didn't really frighten me. I found it exciting. The only part that did frighten me was the shrapnel – I thought it might come down and fall on my head. When we were in the big communal shelter for our flats in Bow, we listened in as all the adults were talking amongst themselves – they wouldn't have said this sort of thing in front of children in those days – and they were saying that London was alight, the whole place was on fire. We just wanted to get out and have a look at it. We didn't even mind being in the shelter. Mum's brother was very good on the banjo and we all sang songs. It was a happy time that I remember. We enjoyed ourselves, all in there together.

No matter how deprived their childhoods, adults, when looking back, will often be able to see that time positively, particularly if they were fortunate enough not to be touched personally by tragedy – probably because, as I was told when I wrote *My East End*, 'Of course they were the good old days, we were young!'

Our clothes had always come from local jumble sales at the Methodist Mission in Commercial Road. If you were lucky there were even toys to be had. My grandfather said once that I looked like a 'bookmaker's clerk' as I looked so smart in my 'new' clothes.

Looking back, I think that even though we did not have the types of toys, entertainment, clothes etc. we had a good life, which I enjoyed to the full. Of course, in those days social workers hadn't been invented and therefore could not tell us we were living in poverty and were hard done by.

We used to get these comics that had been sent over from America, and they'd have things in them like bananas and Coca-Cola, and we had no idea what these things were.

We had been used to having very little food. Days with nothing hadn't been unusual. In that way, things were better during the war, when Dad was bringing in regular money.

Those who did recognize that they 'went short' in their childhood are usually wise enough to concede that maybe they weren't really that badly off. Not only were there compensations, in the form of extended families, community and shared experience, in poor areas such as east London, but there was also probably someone in the street who was just that bit worse off than you anyway. Everything, even deprivation, is relative.

Compared with today, we had very little. No television, radios, computers, games, videos or bikes. No cinemas, McDonald's, theme parks, holidays, cars, telephones. The food was scarce and we had to survive on what we could scrounge or steal . . . I wonder who is better off: the kids of today, who seem to want for nothing, or those in my day, who wanted for just about everything.

Sweet-toothed youngsters, however, did feel hard done by when sweet rationing was introduced. It seemed doubly unfair that when, for once, your mum might have been in a position to treat you to a few extra coppers from the money she was earning working in the munitions factory or machining uniforms, the meagre supplies of confectionery in the corner shop let you down. Careful planning was required to work out which items would give the best value. Big, almost tasteless gob-stoppers were an often-cited favourite choice, as were the rock-hard sweet 'lollies' that looked like strangely bright red cupcakes with a little stick set in the base to hold them. Both of those would at least last a while, although probably not until it was time to go back to the shop to have your coupon clipped and for the whole agonizing process to begin again.

Apart from sweets, another item on most children's wish list, regardless of the reality of what was available and what could be afforded, was toys. There were some – at a price. But expensive shop-bought playthings had never really figured in the lives of the majority of youngsters who had been born into the harsh 1930s, and improvised toys and games were far more common. Skipping ropes were made from old bits of washing line and barge ropes; dolls were knitted, made from rags and remnants, or created by draping pegs in scraps of cloth, topped off with lengths of wool for hair; cricket bats were fashioned from pieces of wood stout enough to defend your lamppost 'wicket'; and carts and trolleys were cobbled together out of old pram wheels and orange boxes. But one woman recalled being a little girl who had owned some rather special toys – for a while.

I was born in Old Montague Street in the 1930s, when it was mainly a Jewish area. We played in a park over Vallance Road, across the street from Fat Annie's fish shop. Before the war I remember having a bike and a doll's pram, things I never would have once the war began, because my dad was injured and everything was sold off. We slept at night in Martinue's [*sic*] treacle factory, where we caught whooping cough. We caught a bigger cold early one morning when we came out of the treacle factory to find our house had been blitzed and the Troxy cinema bombed.

Although being a child in the war was frightening [particularly in the Blitz], it was also exciting as I wasn't aware of the real dangers. A heavy bomb dropped in our street – unexploded – and bomb disposal men were called. RAF personnel were there, and we all had to evacuate the street, and when we were allowed back, some of the RAF men had made a wooden V2 rocket painted green with red cloth attached like a flame! The holes in the road had been filled in the meantime and then a 'dip' was organized to see who would win the prized toy. I was the lucky one! Later, a piece of real V2 rocket came through our garret room at the top of the house and went right through the bed.

For most families toys were an undreamt-of luxury. What they lacked were more pressing items.

. . . we boys wore short trousers . . . That, combined with the holes in our shoes, and our socks that always had holes in them, made for uncomfortable living. The socks were made of wool and could be darned, but it was embarrassing to take our shoes off because of the holes, or darns in different colours. I bless the man who invented hard-wearing nylon socks.

If you were as confident and resourceful as the following young man, even the holes in your clothes could be a source of bravado, a badge of pride and courage.

Getting dressed for school was an art in itself. I first put on a coarse shirt with frayed cuffs, and short trousers with holes in the backside. To have street cred, as they say today, you measured yours against your mates on the way to school. You got these holes by sliding down the inside of a bomb crater. Being as I didn't have any underwear, I had to pull my shirt-tail down and between my legs and, using a safety pin, attach it to the front flaps to form the crotch – being careful not to damage my tackle that I would need later to produce my two strapping boys. The next thing to put on was your socks. My mum was no needlewoman, so when the sock sprang a hole you had to pull them down at the toe end and tuck that under. You'd carry on doing that until you got to the rib and then turn the sock so that the heel was on your instep, and start again. I had to put a piece of cardboard in my shoes to cover the holes that were in them. Of course, when it rained, you had a right soggy mess between your toes. My Uncle G–, who worked for Lebon's Coal Merchants, used to give me a lift on his coal cart to school. I think you can imagine the sight that captured the eyes of my teacher when I entered the classroom.

As far as the education of East End children was concerned, the government's intention had been that those schools in areas designated as danger zones – including parts of London and other strategic areas around the country – should be closed for the duration. The children were to be evacuated and the empty school premises turned over to various emergency-related purposes – vital first-aid and ARP stations, and reception and rest centres for those made homeless by bombing raids. But they hadn't reckoned on all those who either refused to leave the East End in the first place or who would very quickly return home.

With worrying numbers of children now left at a loose end, the authorities had to relent and schools that could reopen did so, but under strained and crowded conditions. Retired teachers were brought in to replace their younger, conscripted counterparts and in some cases a system of double shifts, with morning and afternoon sessions, was introduced to give pupils at least a modicum of education. For some, these changes worked surprisingly well, with older teachers rallying to their task and enthusing their young charges. Another change to school routine brought more widespread benefits. This was the increase in the provision of midday meals, to the point where it became practically a nationwide service. Intended as a necessary move to provide for those children whose mothers were now busily occupied elsewhere 'doing their bit', it was a particular boon for the ill-nourished children of poorer families.

On the whole, however, schooling was – as it now seems to be again – a case of either having to make the best of a bad job or being fortunate enough to strike it lucky, sadly with little in between to provide any choice.

Our school stayed open, but it got bombed, and so we had to walk all the way from Bow right down to a school in Chrisp Street. All that way and I was – what? – eight, nine years old, and my brother was a year and nine months younger. That's a long way for young ones.

[There] was a period of comparative calm during which schooling had been cut to half a day, because of the number of schools closed through bomb damage and the lack of teaching staff, schooling that was nevertheless serious and intensive where some of the older teachers remained.

At school, all the young teachers were away at war, so I was lucky enough to be taught by three retired ex-university men. I didn't appreciate it at the time though!

'Lucky' is hardly the word that would have been used by the youngsters below, who viewed the wartime education system as almost more of an enemy than the Luftwaffe.

I was absolutely terrified even thinking about that first day of school. Bombs falling and air raids, I could cope with all that – we used to go round in a gang of kids, we'd follow the older boys, and be happy to stand in the door of the communal shelter and watch the V1s going overhead – but school? That terrified me! And our school never closed either. Stayed open. I remember having to line up for injections. That place was a torture house. One terrible time, I'd run out into the road and been knocked over by a bike and hurt my leg, and my mum still insisted I went to school, and she had to push me there in an old pushchair – the shame of it!

My brother had started infants school and I had to take him. The teachers were nuns and were not very kind. My brother was left-handed and the sister teacher used to tie his left hand to his body to force him to use his right hand. She shook him and made him cry and he wet himself and had to sit in his wet clothes till school ended. When I collected him from school, I had to dry him with my scarf and I took my knickers off so he could wear them home, while I put his wet pants in my bag. You could say that Mum was annoyed, that was an understatement. She was all for going to that school and sorting the teacher out, but my nan stopped her. She went to the school instead! I don't know what she said, but things got better for [my brother] after that.

We kids were forever coming home from school with our hair full of fleas. They made our heads itch and we were always scratching our hair. Mum used a toothcomb to run through our hair to catch the little blighters. They were squashed between our thumbnails, making a squishy sound. The combs cut into our heads and we screamed and shouted all the way through the treatment, with Mum telling us off for being babies.

As a small boy, you were fair game for anybody to have a go at. Teachers would leap into the air in order to bring the cane down harder on your fingertips. Not content with one, they would do it five more times.

And it wasn't just the nuns and teachers you had to look out for. Even being at home with the family could present something of a minefield for an unwary schoolboy.

When we lived with [my grandmother] I seemed to spend my time there trying to avoid her around the house, as she would give me a smack round the head for any small misdemeanour, like getting in her way in the passageway.

The journey home wasn't much better, not with the 'real' enemy to contend with.

I was machine-gunned on the way home from school. Running along the street by a high fence, I heard the roar of engines and a thud! Thud! Thud! The fence shuddered. I looked up as I ran and saw holes being punched into the wood about four feet above my head.

But perhaps unsurprisingly, as these are childhood memories, it was the 'enemy' in the schoolroom rather than the one in the air who was most often recalled as being the biggest object of dislike, and tales of schemes to avoid school and of dreaded teachers were recounted with real feeling – all these years on.

I'd had very little schooling [and] at the age of seven I could not read. It was with glee that the teacher assigned to our form, who seemed only interested in painting her toenails bright red, caught me out and showed me to be the dunce of the class. This started bullying only matched by the Gestapo. Every time I got near the school gates they would set on me, sometimes seven or eight [of them]. Even when my sister and I took residence in the cupboard under the stairs during the raids [and] she taught me what reading meant – which I as a fairly bright kid latched on to quickly – the bullying did not stop. Added to the fact that Miss M–, she of the red toenails, had accused me of lying and trying to deceive her by making out I was illiterate, [which] made the situation far worse. It was a nightmare. The only respite occurred when, being a church school, we were not expected to attend school on Ash Wednesday, but, rather, were expected to attend an all-day church festival. I gladly took this to be a day's holiday – two years running – informing my mother that there was no school as Lent had begun. The School Board man persuaded her to the contrary, so she decided to [follow me] to the school just after I set off – just in time to see the bullies set about me. Hitler's rage had nothing on my mum that day, and I can assure you that the teaching staff were on hand always to nip any violence in the bud before I got hurt again . . . Nothing new, then, in victimization or bullying – even during wartime.

*

At school we had weekly shower baths in the playground. Everyone had a shower, as it was a way of getting out of lessons. The lorry came once a week and set up a canvas structure. It had changing rooms each end, with the shower in the middle section. When we children wouldn't come out when called, they used to turn the cold water on us and we all rushed out screaming.

I was enrolled at primary school on 17 April 1944 – admission number 407 – and our parents were asked to provide a photograph of their children for identity purposes should the school receive a direct hit and the worst occur. I remember the constant interruptions to lessons when we all had to troop down to the cellars under the school when air-raid warnings sounded, but these were welcome diversions.

There were others who had their schooling disrupted far more seriously, with some disappearing altogether from the notice of the authorities, their school days coming to a very premature end.

Most of the schools closed down, but if you were lucky a school would open for half a day. I was eleven when war broke out and was due to go to a secondary school, but one day a local shopkeeper asked me if I would like to help in her shop. Mum agreed, so off I went. That was the end of my school days. I worked there until I was fourteen.

I didn't attend school much . . . Incendiary bombs were setting fire to every street and all the buildings. Most of my friends were evacuated, but I stayed at home with my mum, because Dad was in the army.

As with the young girl who was mature enough to take a job in the local shop, not all children left to their own devices got up to mischief. Instead, plenty used their initiative to make themselves some money and, like these bright, sharp young operators, managed to turn a bad situation to their advantage.

We used to go 'coking' on a Saturday, down to the gasworks. We'd collect sacks of coke and earn a farthing or a ha'penny for every sack. People needed it, had to have it, to eke out their coal, which was very short. You'd have an old pram, a pushchair, but if you were lucky you'd have a barrow – like we had – so we could fetch more than one sack at a time.

To earn a penny or two I ran errands for my grandma. I would go to the Gas, Light and Coke Company with a pram and fetch her bags of coke. That same pram was used to take the washing to the public baths off the Highway, E1 [where the wash was done], for all the eight of us living in that same rented house – kids, aunts, uncles and grandparents.

. . . there was the wood collection from the bomb sites, where [we] collected wood and sold it at a profit to people desperately short of fuel for their open fires. What an earner that was – that is, until I was spotted by the ARP and shopped to my dad, who forbade any such activity in case we found something appalling on the bomb site.

As well as engaging in such entrepreneurial enterprises, children were expected to shoulder surprisingly heavy responsibilities during this time of crisis and just 'having to get on with things' and 'making the best of it'.

I was the eldest of the girls, although by no means the eldest of all us kids, but Mum had to work, so I became the mum. No, I wasn't very old, not even ten, but what could you do? We didn't dare answer back in them days – and what good would it have done anyway? How could I have left the little ones? My brothers wouldn't have had a clue. Or they'd have pretended not to have.

*

I was not quite six when war began, [but] as soon as my younger brother was old enough to be left in my care, Mum took a job at the local 'tin bashers' – a company that made tins and containers, and where her father was foreman. Looking after my brother was no real problem, because we were related to most of the neighbours – people did not move far from their roots in the East End of those days – whose doors were always open and who kept an eye.

Closely knit as neighbourhoods might have been, with extended families living on top of one another in often cramped conditions and with the war going on right on the doorstep, young people were still experiencing the turmoil of moving across the division between childhood and adolescence, and eventually into the mysteries of the adulthood world itself – although it might be a good while before they really came to understand what was going on in grown-ups' heads . . .

If I asked Granny Harris where anything could be, it was invariably, 'In the oven, behind the vice', and if you took food and left it, 'your eyes were bigger than your belly'. As I was considered too curious, I was a 'nose ointment'. When I pinched something to eat, Mum would call me a 'mumper' and if Dad went off to the pub he was 'going to see a man about a dog'. When I was headed for trouble, Granny Harris would say, 'You'll get your eye in a sling, you will.'

Rather more uncomfortable recollections – of not understanding quite what was going on with his feelings – are recounted by the man below.

My first feelings of a sexual nature occurred when my sister stood on a chair in her knickers and told me to paint black lines down her legs, which she had coated in gravy powder to simulate stockings. I had no idea what was happening to me. I was just flustered and all I wanted to do was go out and play on my bike. My sister didn't understand. She said, 'If those lines ain't straight, there'll be a clip round the ear for you.' It was some time later that I learned that a stick of chewing gum could buy you a look at a girl's 'forward anatomy'. The thing then was, at fourteen or so, you was still kids – not young adults, like they are today.

A slightly less disconcerting encounter with the 'adult' world was remembered in association with this visit to the barber – hair still had to be cut, and thus respectability maintained, even with bombs falling all around you.

My father took me to Harry the barber to get my ears lowered. I'd sit on a board across the armrests of the chair. According to my dad, Harry's dog got all the ears that got sliced off if you didn't sit still. I wondered if it would ever cotton on that lunging at you and growling would get it another tid-bit. After he had cut your hair he would give you a 'frizzer' that would make your brain hum, and then apply a generous amount of industrial-strength hair-setting lotion that would have tamed even Just William's unruly thatch. It would set your hair like a helmet, with a big quiff, but would crackle off in pieces the size of cornflakes that sounded underfoot on the kitchen lino like people trudging to the South Pole. One of the curtains of life was tweaked to one side when I twigged the meaning of Harry's question to the older young men and dads, 'A little something for the weekend, sir?', and the packet of three and the half-crown changed hands in a piece of slick sleight of hand that would have impressed Houdini. Then there were the Health and Efficiency magazines [there which] contained photos of white, pear-shaped Bibendums playing volleyball, riding see-saws, frying bacon, cycling, and all in the nude, naked, not a stitch on. Quartets of older ladies, each with her handbag beside her chair, each properly labelled – 'Mrs Doreen Clunch of Purley', 'Mrs Mabel Doorbell of Luton' – smiling at the camera to hide their china teeth, nipples discreetly tucked below the edge of the table on which was spread cucumber sandwiches and pots of tea. Each wore only her glasses and pearls. They could have been the semi-finalists of a strip-bridge tournament. All very heavy stuff for a young feller of impressionable years . . .

Then there were those who seemed to experience an even more confused mix of emotions, appearing sophisticated while dealing with the world on the one hand and yet still totally childlike and full of fear and wonder on the other. Perhaps nothing really changes, except the outward trappings of what we wear and superficially how we behave, when we present our diffidently maturing selves to the big, scary, outside world.

The shrapnel we collected! Tons of it. And each street had its own castles to be climbed and conquered, even if the day before they had been some little shop or a house until the bombs came. I was always told, 'Keep off the debris!' After a quick, 'Yes, Mum', I was out to see what new adventures Hitler had made for us. Until the day I fell through a roof and broke my arm. Off to the hospital, being fussed over by poor old Aunt Ciss, where the kind old nurse asked how I did it. 'Well, Miss, I slipped on a banana skin.' Mum was at work and I just knew she would kill me for climbing, but I don't think I had ever seen a banana in my life, just seen them in comics, and every skin somebody seemed to fall over. Both Aunt Ciss and the nurse fell about laughing, so at least I had a little hope that Mum would see the funny side. She did. In fact, it was 1944 and the docks were beginning to fill with troops . . . When some Yanks who had climbed over the dock walls for a night on the town – in essence they were confined to the docks for security reasons – gave me a banana, [that's] when I found out that it had to be peeled to be eaten. We kids had a great time in 1944. At the end of the street [on Millwall] there was a high wall – [the] dock wall – and night after night troops – Yanks, English, Canadians, Scots – would climb over to have a night out. We all put benches in our gardens and invited them in. Tears [as I remember this]. Two soldiers from Scotland left some letters with my mum to be posted if they didn't make it. We heard [somehow that] they were both killed and Mum sent off the letters. She put a little note with them and we got a reply in a week or so. The troops would bring with them all manner of loot. Corned beef by the large tin, beer, Scotch, chocolate, bubble gum and bread. Everything. All we did was to set up in our yards somewhere for them to sit and enjoy a break. It was a magic time. But, looking back, how sad. How many of those whose company we kept in those few weeks were to die? And some seemed no older than Joe next door. He was just sixteen.

. . . bomb sites and exposed cellars . . . became my playground. And, yes, I had my collection of shrapnel, often picked up whilst it was too hot to handle. I cannot walk past the junction of Goswell Road and Old Street without the peculiar smell of burning paper and wood soaked by water coming to my nostrils. During the Blitz a stationer's had been destroyed by enemy incendiary damage and my mates and I were rummaging around for what we could find. The smell of burnt paper and wood mixed with water pervaded the air. Can you imagine children having such freedom today?

Me and my mates worked out how to kill a German when – if – they landed. It took five boys and Maureen G–. She was blonde, self-assured and infinitely more mature than us. We were about eight or nine. The plan was that Maureen would flash her knickers, and the German would be dazzled by this display of beauty, and then, while this entranced him, one boy would grab a leg each, and one boy would each grab an arm – that's four boys. The fifth would stab him in the throat with a penknife. Sadly, the plan fell through as Maureen wanted to stab him as well.

Despite Maureen's enthusiasm for violence, it is often said, as if it is a simple fact, that children were safer 'back then'. In the words of just two of the people who consider this to be so:

There did not seem to be any fear of being accosted or abducted in those days.

You never had all these crimes and that against children that you do now. Never.

I suggest that the situation was more complex than that. The reality was that people were living in tight-knit communities – often in the same street that their families had lived in for generations – which meant that they knew the rest of the people in their community not only by sight but also by name and reputation. Children would be warned to stay away from any unsavoury characters who lived nearby and strangers hanging around would be challenged. There were local coppers patrolling the streets and, in the war, there were the air-raid wardens, who were familiar to everyone.

Even so, despite the view that there was nothing more frightening than bombs to worry about – and they were bad enough! – there were still memories that would have today's tabloid press up in arms and demanding that Social Services 'do something about it'.

We had prisoner of war camps in Carpenters Road near our school. The Germans kept theirs lovely. Very neat. The Italians didn't seem nearly so disciplined. We were curious and used to watch them – and the girls, whom I realize now were prostitutes, who used to turn up in cars.

[4] *Evacuation*

What a choice! Sending your babies away or keeping them here, at home with you, in danger.

Some London children had a very different, if sometimes only temporary, experience of living through the war years: they were evacuated away from our street and their East End homes.

If they chose to, the sufficiently well off, or those with family living away from any potentially unsafe areas, could make their own, private arrangements for their children, and maybe even themselves, to live elsewhere for the duration. For the rest of the population, it was the government-organized evacuation or nothing.

Bureaucrats divided the country into zones, with each sector falling into one of three designated types. There were the danger areas, which would be evacuated; the supposedly safe reception areas, which would take in the evacuees; and the remaining areas, which were deemed to be neutral. The populace was similarly sorted and labelled: children, pregnant women and those considered to be a priority, such as the visually handicapped, were to be shipped out of the danger zones. This was not only for their safety; it was important to clear the risky areas for strategic reasons. Buildings, from hospitals to schools, and staff, from medical personnel to communications workers, would be required for war work, not for looking after what might prove to be helpless, inconvenient or even troublesome civilians.

The complex plans required for mass evacuation were in place well before the outbreak of war, including the compiling of registers of everyone concerned, but things did not always go to plan. Originally, it had been thought by the government that up to 3.5 million individuals would be officially evacuated to places of safety, but this number was never reached, due to a combination of factors. Families showed a widespread reluctance to be separated, surprising the middle- and upper-class authorities, who were more accustomed to being separated from their children. There was also an increasing belief that things wouldn't be 'too bad after all' that set in during the Phoney War. And then there was homesickness, which on occasion was unfortunately exacerbated by the less than warm welcome given to those turning up in various reception areas around the country. Eventually, only 1.5 million took advantage of the evacuation scheme, but even in its abbreviated incarnation, this was an impressive accomplishment, especially as it was carried out in those comparatively car-free days, using mainly public transport.

On 1 September 1939, the gears were cranked and the massive plan was put into action. For the next few days, much of the country's train and bus network was given over to this unprecedented movement of people. Nine one-way routes were especially plotted by the police to allow vehicles to make their way out of London, while Walter Elliot, the Minister of Health, issued assurances that it was all only a precaution, and a shining example of what a free people could achieve when they put their backs and hearts into a job. With this vast scheme in place, the beginning of the blackout and the mobilizing of the ARP, it would have been hard to deny that war was really about to happen.

Some of the evacuees were to have very good experiences, being shown nothing but kindness and generosity by their hosts, and making lifelong friends with people who were, in some cases, to grow as close to them as family. Yet despite the minister's enthusiasm, evacuation was definitely not universally appreciated by those involved. Stories of hardship and neglect abound, showing that it wasn't only the enemy who could be cruel and

brutal. The ways in which some young East Enders were treated resemble episodes from one of Dickens's more harrowing novels more closely than the comforting visions painted by the local press of 'our kiddies' frolicking in flower-strewn meadows.

There were memories of being singled out for being Jewish; of a more general prejudice against 'dirty Cockneys'; and of experiencing such misery at their mistreatment that children ran away – one man even recalling the hospital care he and his sister required when they finally made their way back to their home in east London. As in other sections of this book, some people decided that they couldn't bear to have their stories told. Regrettably in this case, it was out of a misplaced sense of shame – which is perhaps hard for those of us who haven't experienced such cruelty to understand, as it seems so obvious that the adults responsible should be the ones who are ashamed.

There were plenty who, even before they left, had a good idea that leaving Mum and Dad behind and going off to live with strangers might not turn out to be the jolly adventure they had been promised.

The children who didn't want to be evacuated were tugging and crying, while their parents tried to hide their tears and their feelings, but were shattered by what was happening to them. There had always been togetherness, with families sticking together through thick and thin.

We were so little, with our gas masks and our little cardboard labels. Like little parcels waiting to be sent off, but to who knew where? It was so hard to understand what was going on. It wasn't as if one of our aunties or our nan was taking us somewhere. We were used to that. No, this was different. We were going off to be with these 'nice people' somewhere. But who were they?

Young Alan – speaking below – had a good idea, and he wasn't going to have any of it.

I remember a lady calling by to ask about me being evacuated. We had a tiny place – a dump really, no bathroom, no hot water – and my dad bawled up the stairs, 'Alan, do you want to be evacuated?' I called back down to him, 'No thanks, Dad.' I can hear to this day that woman's incredulous voice. 'Surely you're not going to let the little lad decide for himself?' 'Well,' said Dad, 'he's got to start someday, he might as well start now.' I was fully aware that I could be killed, but decided I'd rather go with my parents if we copped it.

If parents did agree to send their children – or to go with them, in the case of mothers with very young children and babies – the Londoners from our street didn't always settle in their new surroundings. And it wasn't only because of the welcome that some of them received. It was as much of a culture shock for those in the reception areas as it was for the East Enders, arriving as they did after the discomfort of their long journeys on trains and buses without lavatory or washing facilities, and with their city clothes and ways so unsuited to rural life.

We travelled by train and then coach, looking out on the pitch-dark countryside. The driver lost his way as all the signposts had been removed for security. When my mother found out that she was to be separated from my brother and me she said, 'I would rather sleep in a field than be taken away from my children' . . . Later we were found places with a family. From what she told me, I don't think all the local residents were too pleased to have us Londoners there . . . It must have caused disruption to their lives. Eventually we went to live in a rented stone-floored cottage . . . My mother found it quite lonely. [And when] there was a lull in the bombing we went home to London.

They weren't the only ones who fled, although some took a little longer to do so.

Mum took us somewhere out in the country. We got there on the Saturday and she went with us upstairs to unpack, then, when she went down, we packed all our stuff again. We didn't want to stay there. And so it went on – packing and unpacking. She stayed with us overnight and in the morning she couldn't bear to leave us. We went to the coach with her, and, even though she had no fare money for our tickets back to London, the coach driver was kind and let her bring us back.

When we were evacuated, Mum was pregnant with my brother, as were a lot of the other women, including one of my aunts. It must have looked like a human convoy of pregnant women and kids, all of us labelled and carrying bags and boxes and gas masks in cardboard-box cases. I was squashed into the corner on a big train, with my mum, aunt and all my cousins. We spent the night in a big hall, where we were given blankets, pillows, and packed food and tea were dispensed to us. Then on another train to where we were going to stay on the borders of Yorkshire and Lancashire. When Mum went into hospital up there to have my brother I was taken to see her. I can remember that hospital smell. She cried when she saw me. They'd cut off my hair because I'd caught fleas. And Dad had been given leave from the army to visit Mum and the baby, and I didn't know him. In the time between his last leave and him coming to see Mum and the baby, I'd forgotten him. Mum was so unhappy that she discharged herself from hospital and took us back to London to live with Nan and Grandad.

My nephew and I found ourselves most unhappily staying in a house with a woman whose husband was away in the army. She had only one son, slightly older than my nephew and me, and we hated him because he was a spoilt, over-indulged, fat brat who made our lives very uncomfortable. [We were not looked after and] soon learned what being hungry meant. We were half-starved, and it can be imagined how we felt when we were given half an egg weekly and the son had one or two each day, which he enjoyed eating in front of us at breakfast. This was in the countryside, where such items were not so scarce. We were sent out early mornings before school to search the fields for mushrooms in the surrounding fields – not particularly enjoyable, because the low morning mists [made] it hard to avoid the cow pats whilst fumbling for fungi. This led to a cold-water clean-up before [we were allowed] to enter the house on our return.

One day, during a rare visit from my sister Ada, her son told her how really unhappy we were and we were back to London in no time.

Various reasons were given by some of the Londoners who resisted returning home despite their unhappiness. These included having no home or family left to go back to, having gone through too much in the bombing to be able to face it again, and finding the strength to stay in the country because they believed it was the right thing to do for their children.

This family, for instance, was definitely not impressed with the countryside and its inhabitants, but the mother refused to return to London, deciding that it was best to stick it out for the kids.

Dad was in the army at that time . . . stationed about eight miles away. He used to walk the eight miles [to the big house where some of the children were evacuated with their mother], but Lady E– [the owner] was not too keen to allow Mum and Dad to be alone together in the house. Dad would have to climb through the windows without Lady E– seeing him. That is when my younger sister, S–, may well have been conceived . . . We eventually moved to a small empty cottage in the village. Mum had to squat there in order to have somewhere to live and to bring my three sisters from [where they had been evacuated to] and where they were not happy. Mum was a strong-willed woman and broke the law several times to protect her family. We were treated by some of the villagers as outcasts and were insulted frequently. We were told to go back to the slums of London and called cowards for leaving there. One day a bomb landed several miles from the village and most of them were at panic stations. We had the last laugh that day. The lady in the next cottage to us was always rowing with Mum and went too far one day. Mum either whacked her or threw a bucket of water over her to calm her down and had to go to court for it. When the magistrate heard the circumstances and the strife Mum was going through, he dismissed the charges. That did upset the neighbour, but she left us alone after that.

The villagers might have thought that the East End was a slum, but housing conditions in some of the reception areas weren't exactly plush.

The cottage was very small and contained the barest items of furniture . . . We had no running water inside and only an outside toilet. The only heating came from a large kitchen range [on which] all the cooking had to be done . . . In the winter, being the eldest son, but being only five or six years old, I had to go to the outside coal shed and defrost the only tap with lighted newspapers round the pipe until the water ran freely. I say a coal shed, because in one corner, next to the tap, was a heap of coal dust which I used to go through to try and get some small lumps to burn on the range. It never seemed to work because the coal was no more than dust and seemed to put the flames out. My sisters and I were always in the woods nearby, collecting logs.

[The] toilet was outside in a large shed away from the house. This consisted of a cubicle inside the shed that had a lift-up wooden seat with a hole in the centre in the shape of a toilet seat. Under that was a large round bucket for catching you-know-what. About once a fortnight I had the task of emptying the bucket . . . I would dig a large hole in the garden behind the shed under an apple tree and empty the contents of the bucket into the hole. I would cover it over with soil but because the contents were very smelly and very wet it took some time to disperse . . . The toilet paper consisted of any newspapers we could get hold of. This was torn into small pieces and tied together in bundles to hang on the wall of the shed. It was always a luxury whenever we could get hold of some old telephone directories or similar paper that was softer and didn't scratch the tender parts so much.

We'd tried going away, out to Norwich. But it was filthy. They kept their coal in the bath and they all had fleas. Mum tipped the coal out and we all had a good bath. Then all the kids from the family wanted a bath too. They were disgustingly dirty. At night, Mum would spread out a sheet of paper and comb her and all our hair out with a fine toothcomb, to check we hadn't caught anything off them. She couldn't stand it. She brought us all home. 'If we die, we'll all die together!' Back in London, the houses got damaged by bombs, but the mums did their best, they kept them nice, and, despite everything, dustbins were always emptied. My mum always had a paintbrush in her hand. She did her best to keep it nice, respectable.

After being appalled by examples of the lack of generosity and blatant unkindness shown by some in the reception areas, and the not always admirable behaviour of the evacuees, it was a relief to hear the much happier stories. Many people recalled with great warmth how they had kept in touch with their country 'families' for years after the war had finished.

I was one of the hundreds of mothers with babies evacuated from London. I took with me my little niece, who was too young to go with the school children. Together with a small bag of belongings, and with our gas masks over our shoulders, we tearfully assembled at the railway station at 7 a.m. The journey began some time later – delayed by a false alarm. The first stop was Colchester. Red Cross nurses were there on duty, waiting to top up our babies' bottles with water. The journey continued, with several more stops, until we reached Stowmarket in Suffolk. Scores of tired mothers and screaming babies were assembled in the great square in front of the station to await further transport. Again, volunteers were on hand to give us water and encouragement. I was eventually told to board a bus and finally arrived at a tiny village on the borders of Essex and Suffolk, close to Manningtree. Darkness fell as we entered the school to await our hosts, and a motley crowd they were – but no more than the crowd that had landed among them. It was now six o'clock in the evening and I was longing for someone to offer me hospitality, when one dear old lady came forward and invited me to stay. I answered rudely, 'I don't care where I go, so long as I can change my baby's napkin.' These words were repeated many times in jokes afterwards, and were the beginning of a wonderful friendship that would last to the end of her days.

When evacuees were sent to certain parts of the country, however, questions about their happiness weren't even raised. Admittedly, the smug privilege of hindsight again comes into play, and it is easy for us to see that some of the places chosen as safe havens for bombed-out East Enders were anything but, and actually put them right back in the line of fire.

We went from a school in Old Ford, where I lived. I was seven years old, my sister was only four and my brother was ten. [We went] to a village in Oxfordshire, where the women came out and took their pick of us. My brother took everything in his stride, my sister was too young to know about anything, but I was stressed out. I wanted my mum. I stayed with my sister and my brother stayed with someone else. We did not stay there long because it was near an airfield, but while we were there I had bad dreams and walked in my sleep.

However, the following young boy would probably have preferred to stay in the danger zone on the coast, where he was sent initially, than live on the farm where he and his brother eventually fetched up.

I went with my mother to St Leonards at Hastings. I mean, it's the most silly place they could send us. Everyone's talking about an invasion! When it did get naughty down there, I went with my brother to Wales. It was an experience that I can look back on with pride, because of the way the boys were picked out. My brother is much older than me and the farmers literally – and this is the Gospel truth – they went down the line feeling the muscles of the boys.

One of the farmers picked the boy's brother – who was twelve and well built – but because he was only seven and puny, they didn't want him. His brother, however, insisted they stay together, and they were both taken to the farm. It wasn't to prove a pleasant experience for either of them.

. . . we never saw a sweet, never had our sweet coupons, [and] they used to open every letter we sent home and open every letter my mum and dad sent to us. My brother sneaked a note in the post and that's how we got out. The thing I couldn't understand was what was so special about their toilet . . . The farm had a toilet outside, I'm not sure if it was a flush or chemical one to be honest, because – I couldn't understand why – we weren't allowed to use that toilet at all. We used to have to go in the field, summer or winter. I can remember looking at that toilet and trying to puzzle it out. We'd come from an LCC* flat and we had flush toilets, bathrooms and everything. I just couldn't understand that, why we weren't allowed the toilet. Just like I could never understand the London schoolteachers allowing those elder boys being lined up and the farmers feeling their muscles. I could never understand how they allowed that, because they were there, watching. We had to walk three miles to school and three miles back to [the farm, where] the farmer ruled the household like a rod of iron. His word was law. He had a son, and the only time I can remember me and my brother being treated was when we caught the son in a pub. His father was a strict Welsh Methodist and so the son bribed us by buying us a lemonade.

My brother worked really hard on that farm, but we weren't allowed to sleep in a bedroom. We slept on the landing. But they literally – and you can verify this with my brother – kept us so hungry, this is truly hungry, that in one of the bedrooms off the landing [we found] they used to store all their fruit. My brother, it's not a nice thing to say but it's the truth, he found that if he could put a knife behind the

* London County Council.

catch and pressed it, the lock would trip, and we used to eat fruit right, left and centre. We'd have to eat the apple core, the pips and everything. But it did rebound on us. We made ourselves ill with all the fruit and had to be put in hospital over Christmas. That was the best time we had in Wales.

There are other stories that, when we hear them as adults, make us wonder how anyone could treat children in such a way – no matter how differently they behaved from their host families, or what 'dirty Cockneys' they supposedly were. Even the following little tale of a child's real pleasure at being treated decently, and then feeling driven to eat foodstuffs intended for livestock, can make us gulp back the tears, as can the little girl's story after that, in which we hear about her panic and how she tried to protect the other children in her charge.

One of the local farmers took me to an American Air Force base nearby to collect the kitchen waste for his pigs. Whilst I was near the kitchens an American cook came out and asked if I wanted a sandwich. You can guess how I felt about some extra food and said, 'Yes.' He came back from the kitchen with two thick slices of bread containing a large cooked chicken leg. That was most enjoyable, and I shall never forget the taste of that huge meal. Another time I remember helping the farmer who was boiling up some potatoes in a large iron pot, bigger than a dustbin, in his yard. These were for his pigs and smelled quite nice. When cooked, the peel came off quite easily, so I took one and ate it. It tasted nice and I thought those pigs were eating better than me. I also went to nearby fields and dug up swedes and mangel wurzels that were meant for cattle feed.

We were evacuated with the first lot just before war was declared. We didn't want to go – it was just me and my little brother, I was seven – and we cried for a fortnight beforehand. We were sent to Wells in the West Country. It was a terrible billet, with a really terrible person.

She had six of us there. We all shared one bed, top to tail. Six in a bed! After breakfast she'd send us out, with me in charge – at seven, I was the eldest – and say, 'Don't come back till dinner time.' Then out you'd be sent again and be told not to be back till teatime. We all got fleas. And there was a centre where we had to report. They had a nit nurse – Nitty Nora – and, when they found we all had them, they said that the six of us had to come back the next day. We were so scared. Really terrified. Had no idea what to expect. None of our mums or dads were there, no one to talk to, to tell us what was happening. Why did they want us back there the next day? What were they going to do to us? So I didn't take them. Instead, I just took them all off to Wells Cathedral and hid them. All day. We were so scared of what was going to happen. At the billet we'd been hit, so what should we expect now? Our parents didn't even know where we were at this time.

If sending some children to stay with strangers far away seems like asking for trouble, and sending others to the coast seems foolish, then sending bombed-out East Enders only as far away as north-west London seems positively insane. Yet, close as it was to their homes, the reception they received there wasn't always a lot better.

We were all just loaded on to red double-decker buses to start our journey, when the warning went off. Someone decided to carry on with the evacuation, so off we went. All the way from the Island to West Hampstead, German planes swooped down, machine-gunning the buses. Us kids were made to lie on the bus floor all the way. I saw no danger, it was like an adventure, and when else would I have been allowed to lie on the floor of a bus? I remember looking up and seeing Sam, an old man who had also lived in our street. The bombing must have driven him mad, because he did that ride all the way with a tea cosy on his head, convinced that nothing could harm him while he had it on. I laughed and was given a good clout for doing so. One of the buses in front of us had been shot at and had turned over, but all the drivers had been told not to stop. Whatever happened – keep on going. So our bus did and we never heard what happened to its passengers. Once more we were dumped in a hall. [G– and her family had just spent twenty-four hours in a church hall, having lost everything when their home had been bombed.] This time a school hall . . . in Kilburn that was to be our home for a few days until we were billeted out. We trooped off the buses across the school playground in double file into the lower hall of the school. This time it was luxury we found waiting for us, in the form of used mattresses that were laid across the entire hall at two-foot intervals. We were told to keep in our family groups, find a mattress and try to get some sleep. Lots to see, other people to watch. Families were trying to keep together, four to a mattress; larger families scrambling to get two mattresses together. I wanted to see this place we had come to, this place where they got no air raids. I ran to look out of the window, only to find blackness – sandbags had been stacked up outside each of the windows. I must have fallen asleep with my only possession, my doll [her father had risked his safety by rescuing it for his daughter from their bombed-out home], with people all around me clutching paper bags and small bundles containing all they had left in the world except their families. [My sister], whose husband was away in the army, was worried that he wouldn't know where she was or how to find her. She had no nappies left for the baby and he, along with dozens of other babies, was crying and grizzly. We were assured that, 'Tomorrow everything will be fine.'

That first night we spent in Kilburn – 'The place that doesn't have any air raids' – the Germans bombed the hell out of the place. The building rocked, glass broke, and people were shouting and screaming. But not in our hall. We were all hardened to this. To us it was just another night like so many others. The minders, although trying not to show it, were much more frightened than us. Our Cockney humour came through – 'Blimey, if this is the place they don't get any bombs, someone's having a good fart,' said someone as another loud crash rocked the building.

There was only one inside toilet for us to use, so the men had to do a dash between the bombs to the outside toilets. There was no water to wash with. My long ringlets were caked down to my head with mud, dirt and dust from crawling out of our shelter [when the family were bombed out, now several days before] and I was beginning to itch! The following morning, in came the WVS with drinks, sandwiches and clothes, but this time accompanied by a barber. 'You've all got fleas,' we were told. 'As there's no water for hair washing or delousing, everyone gets a haircut. Kids first.' My dad loved my long curly hair, and I don't know who was more upset of the two of us when I came out of line with a straight cut – above the ears all round. My nan, who had long plaits wound round her ears like earphones, absolutely refused the haircut and took her long plaits with her to her grave. What a sight the rest of us must have looked with our new haircuts.

Between raids we were allowed out in the playground for exercise. The first time we went out there, a frightening sight and sound awaited us. The local Kilburn people were looking at us from the other side of the school railings. Word had got out about our fleas and unwashed state. 'Send the dirty East Enders back, we don't want them here!' Dirt, rubbish and anything they could find was being thrown at us through the railings. 'They've brought bombing here with them. We never had this before they came!'

In fact, they were right, the German planes did follow us up to Kilburn – machine-gunning us all the way and dropping their bombs for good measure before they returned to Germany.

Even if people didn't meet such unkindness or hostility, the so-called Phoney or Bore War did lull civilians into a false sense of security and, as a result, many chose to take their children back home to the familiar streets of east London. The not unsurprising attitude began to prevail that it all seemed safe enough and, if the worst came to the worst and people did 'cop it', then at least they'd 'all go together'. With minor variations in the actual words, this feeling was expressed to me many times over.

. . . the authorities thought gas would be a major weapon. My mother felt that, with a young family, she should take every precaution open to us, so we took off for Holland-on-Sea, where wet blankets were hung over each window to counteract the effects of poison gas. After a week of this futile operation, the curtains were removed, we returned to London and life returned to normal.

I had only been to St Luke's School in West Ferry Road, Millwall, once or twice when I was being labelled and put into a charabanc and taken to a train somewhere. My next recollection is being the last child chosen from those in the group. I never have and never will get over that experience. The family wanted me as little as I wanted to be there with them. After a few months of this, and little or no bombing, my mum and dad came down to take me back home.

I was nine when the war broke out. For the first few weeks nothing happened, then we were all evacuated with our schools. My school went off to Hopton-on-Sea, two of my brothers went to Haywards Heath with their school, and another one went to Brighton, leaving one small brother and sister with Mum at home and four working brothers and Dad – we were a big family, as you can see. Well . . . we all came back to the East End. I loved being back in Stepney with the family. Everything seemed normal. We played in the streets and went to the parks with our older brothers. But then, after a couple of months, the sirens went off.

When the war started, I was sent off to my dad's family in the north of England. But as we were not bombed or attacked, my mother took us home with the comment, 'Oh well, if it happens we will all go together.' As we now know, later all hell was let loose.

And it was that 'hell' – when the bombing began in earnest – that prompted another wave of evacuation. Not just children and mothers, but whole families were leaving London. And, not surprisingly, experiences were again mixed. The foster parents, as official leaflets and advertisements called the reception families, were again shocked by the inadequate clothes and footwear of the poorer children, and the sometimes impenetrable Cockney accents and the cursing of the 'rougher' youngsters were harsh on country ears.

As for the East Enders, some of them were similarly appalled, although it was the lack of cinemas, the infrequency of the buses and the fact that there wasn't even a local branch of Woolworth's to pop into that upset them. Going 'hopping down in Kent' for a couple of weeks a year was one thing, but being expected to actually live out in the sticks as a full-time proposition was quite another. Not only was there the culture clash between two groups with very different interests and expectations, but it was at a time when most East Enders didn't have a car they could jump into to get away from the place whenever they felt like it. They probably wouldn't have been able to get hold of the petrol even if they did have one.

The Blitz had begun and, because of the incessant bombardment, my mother thought it was time to seek refuge elsewhere. She chose Hertfordshire, where my maternal gran and aunt had taken a bolt-hole in two rooms in a house. We found two rooms in a nominated billet around the corner and, with our frugal belongings, arrived bedraggled and forlorn to a chilly reception by the house owner. The next morning revealed I had come out in spots – measles. Our hostess-with-the-mostest threw us out on the spot – sorry about the pun! – and there we were: Mum and two little girls, plus shabby belongings, on the grass verge for all to deride. I remember my sister putting me into an ancient pram someone had brought forward, declaring, 'This is no place for you, you're not at all well.' My mother and grandmother were so incensed by the attitude of the billeting officer of Hungarian origin, whom my grandma decided must be a German, that an angry altercation took place. This was only brought to a halt by a young woman called Muriel, who was seven months pregnant, with two other children. She ran on to the scene with pinny flying to offer her home to us three without question. For someone in a three-bedroom council house with 2.5 children, this was a true Samaritan act, and we lived happily together for some twelve months. During this time her baby was born, a little girl named after [us], the Cockney lodgers, and we'd found a firm friend at our darkest hour. It was also during this sojourn that we learned we had lost our home and the shop – at the drop of one bomb, our home and livelihood disappeared. This was the only time I saw my mum cry. She fought back, though, and the next day took us to the photographers, all decked out in dresses made out of some redundant curtains, to have our picture taken for Dad, with the message written boldly on the back, 'We're still here!'

Even the journey out of London was exhausting for those already battered by nightly bombardments.

An open-top lorry arrived the next day to take us and all our things to the place in the Essex countryside Dad had got us. We got on the back and sat on our chairs. As we drove through Ongar, my eldest sister, who was wearing a halo hat, had it taken off by a tree as we passed. We had been told beforehand that we had to help take things into the cottage directly we got there. When Father helped us off the lorry, we couldn't stand up we were so cold. The beds couldn't go up the cottage stairs, so we had to sleep on the floor until Dad cut the springs in half and then bolted them back together after getting them into the bedrooms.

At least that family managed to stay together. It is hard to imagine how torn parents must have felt between wanting their children to be somewhere safe and yet not wanting to be separated from them at such a terrible time. One little girl struggled to protect her small brother from the harsh treatment they received at the hands of the family with whom they were placed before being moved when her parents finally discovered the reality of their children's situation. Their new billet, in the second wave of evacuation, was with 'a lovely old couple' and the two youngsters were able to share the experience of those fortunate children who had found warm welcomes and kindness from the beginning of their time away from home.

The following memory carries a rather mixed message about what one child experienced.

At the age of ten I can recall my mother packing my things in a borrowed case and going with me to the school, where we were assembled, labelled and sent off to the railway station, [then] off to a small village near Cambridge. Really, I was lucky to be lodged at H–'s Farm, with a family made up of a middle-aged couple, the owners of the farm, and two very old grandmothers, one of which took more or less charge of myself and a boy called Smith . . . The farm was wonderful to someone like me, coming from a small place in the heart of London, familiar only with a very tiny back garden and one small pet dog . . . We were surrounded by orchards of every description, farmlands and stables, pigs and all kinds of other livestock, which made me wonder if I had come to a super zoo.

My two nephews, Harry and Siddy S–, were installed in a nearby farm, and my other nephew, Siddy N–, was in a small house with a farm labourer's family, also within a short distance . . . [We all had] the freedom of the place and assisted him in the feeding of the animals. Especially, we enjoyed the pigs, whether mucking them out or preparing the awful mixtures they ate; or catching the goats to be milked. We would turn their filled teats and, with a quick squeeze, catch one of our friends full in the face, or in an opened mouth, with a jet of warm creamy milk. There was the wonder of sitting astride one of the shire horses and feeding the goats, geese, hens and rabbits, and all the other farm activities that were so new to us.

Opposite the farm were the huge open pits of the cement works – a playground full of danger, about which we were many times warned – but we loved the place and never came to any real harm, apart from returning to a scolding when we were covered from head to foot in chalk and cement dust.

Whilst with the H–s we were well looked after, and I really loved the freedom to wander amongst the orchards and to climb trees overladen with fruit of the most delicious kinds. Often I would sit in a tree observing the activities of the nearby RAF air base, whilst eating my fill of fruit. One autumn, there was so much fruit that we staggered to school laden with sacks of pears, apples and plums to be given out in class to the other kids. Of course, this gave us a certain prestige that we enjoyed.

The old granny did so much for us, and sometimes used to fetch a huge tray of baked apples, or monster-sized fruit pies, from which we helped ourselves. But I cannot recall ever eating with the rest of the family.

That final line of the quote might startle the more cosseted individuals we are today – it certainly made me wonder if I had understood correctly – but what is impressive is the astonishingly good heart, or maybe sometimes the weary resignation, with which such tales were related. But there were some things that people still regarded as too painful to discuss, even all these years later. As an almost throwaway comment, for instance, I was told, 'When my cousin was evacuated, he had a label around his neck saying, "Bed Wetter".' When I investigated a bit further, I discovered that this was considered a major enough problem for official pleas to be made to foster families to accept this understandable shortcoming in their frightened little guests and not to punish them, otherwise it would make matters worse. But such was the alarm of the families – maybe partly defensible in those days before automatic washing machines and tumble driers – that the authorities eventually had to agree to set up special hostels for children with bed-wetting problems. Despite trying to find people who would be prepared to speak about their experiences of staying in such a place, I was unable to do so. Perhaps they have chosen to forget it, or just don't want to recall such unhappy memories.

Some unusual experiences, however, were recalled with pleasure. These are the recollections of an East Ender who was evacuated to far-distant Wiltshire. In addition to her surprise at the rural environment, she also speaks of encounters that, to an eleven-year-old kid, were entertainingly exotic.

We had two POW camps, one for Italian, the other for German prisoners. Both were within a short distance of each other, and my friend J– and I would often walk up to where the camps were to look at them. Of course, we couldn't get near to them. They were well guarded. The camps were surrounded by wire, a gap of about six feet and then another fence of barbed wire, but higher than the inner one. A grass bank to the side of the road allowed us a good view. We would wave to the prisoners, call out to them, and generally make a nuisance of ourselves to the British guarding them. All [the POWs] did was walk round and round the compound, some in groups, some alone. They looked bored and harmless – a 'what am I doing here?' look on their faces. Some waved back, some turned their backs on us. Some shouted at us in German, some in English. The only difference I could see in these men was that the Germans were in a dark grey, the Italians in brown. There was one other big difference – the Italians in their brown gear were allowed out during the day to work on the local farms.

The same former evacuee went on to remember how she met other foreigners who were also away from home and living in the English countryside, but for very different reasons.

We had another camp [nearby] but this one was quite different from the other two. This one was an American base, music, laughter and freedom being the only difference I could see. The men looked just as young, they looked just as bored – why shouldn't they? There was nothing for them to do. The Vista – two Nissen huts joined together – was soon erected and became the local cinema. Now, Nissen huts have tin roofs, so when it rained nobody could hear what was being said on the screen. But it changed programmes three times a week and was very busy. For the Yanks who had a day pass, there was no way they could make it back to camp by ten o'clock as the [timing of] the last of the two-a-day-only buses meant they couldn't spend the evening there. One Sunday, in chapel, an American bigwig got up after evensong and asked for the community's help. 'These boys are young and homesick, some of them never being away from their families before. They're in a strange land, waiting to go overseas, and they're afraid,' he said. 'Could the ladies of [the village] and their families do anything, come up with any suggestions, to make them more welcome, same as they would like their sons to be looked after in a strange country?' This struck home, the people were having their consciences played on, and a meeting was called of the Women's Guild after the service. One suggestion was to have a soldier to dinner on Sundays. Those that were willing put their names in a bag. The soldiers who wanted to go put their names in a hat. The idea was that one name was picked from each – that was the family he got, that was the soldier you got. Next week all names went back in for another selection. My aunt put her name in the bag, then proceeded to march us all – my uncle, my cousin Billy and myself – like her own private army, back home. All the way she was muttering, 'That's all very well, but where's the food coming from? I suppose they do know we're on rations. God knows what I'm going to give them to eat. I just hope they don't expect anything fancy, that's all.' But none of us reckoned with the Yanks. We had many soldiers to dinner. Every one of them brought something with them. I don't know how they got it – be it a bottle of something, to a side of ham; a packet of cigarettes, to tins of pressed meat; and, wonder of wonders – dried eggs – tins and tins of it. I'd already been treated to several sticks of gum and candy bars by them in the streets – 'Here, kid, have a candy bar' – but now dried egg! It was smashing.

Just as evacuees gave varying accounts of the warmth or otherwise of the reception offered to them by their new 'families', so their experiences of meeting foreigners could also vary.

I was with some friends on the bridge over the stream that ran through part of the village [where we were evacuated] when I first cast eyes upon some big American soldiers. We scrounged some chewing gum from them – 'Got any gum, chum?' One of them produced a nasty-looking knife and I asked him what it was for. He said, 'For cutting off little boys' heads'. I was very frightened and when they asked us if we had any sisters at home we took the opportunity to run off home. Thank goodness I did not know what they meant.

It wasn't only the foreigners who provided strange, new experiences for Cockney youngsters. Household arrangements could prove equally exotic and even baffling to the little townies.

I was evacuated in the first year of the war to a middle-class family in Swindon. The house had an indoor toilet and a bath! She also had a vacuum cleaner, a sewing machine, a dog and cat, and two children at college. They were very good to us – outings on Sundays, Women's Institute activities and Sunday School. She bought us coats with *real* fur collars.

Then came the sad postscript that the woman who had been so kind to this evacuee had committed suicide – presumably as the result of some war-related tragedy – and the children had to return home to London. But the reason that most young Cockneys were called home was the end of the Blitz.

Following that drift back to the familiar streets of the East End, there was yet another move to evacuate Londoners – when the dreaded V1, or 'doodlebug', raids began. As before, it was all down to chance where you wound up, and with whom.

I'd had my second baby, my mum had died and my mother-in-law had been killed when a bomb fell on her house, and the V1s had started dropping over London. When my husband was due to go back after his leave, he was afraid for us, so he found me and my cousin D– a place near Folkestone. It wasn't that far away, but we had a better life even though we did not have gas or electricity. We cooked by coal fire, which had an oven, and there was plenty to eat. The farmer used to leave us vegetables of all kinds on our step.

I went back to London to see how my dad and family were. Dad had my younger sister S– living with him then – she was expecting a baby. The bombing was so bad, with the V1s, that I made her go back to Kent with me and my cousin. And she had a little girl to think about. But I remember one lovely Christmas there when we were all together. My dad and sister Kit came with my brother Tom and his wife – another Dolly. All our husbands were on leave and Tom and Dolly brought a duck with them, which they sat and plucked. Then we all went to the pub – the only one down there for miles – and we got all the country folks going with a knees-up! My husband's sister won a rabbit, I had a chicken, and we ended up with a really good dinner, using the coal fire and all sorts of oil-fired gadgets. My sister had her baby there – we managed by boiling the hot water in saucepans for the midwife. Her baby was christened down there, as was mine at the same time. Our churches back in London had been blasted by bombs before I'd left, and I hadn't been able to have him christened until then, so we had the christenings in Swingfield in Kent, with RAF fellows for godfathers.

For children going away without their parents, having at least some family ties in an area – no matter how distant – could make an otherwise daunting wartime experience that bit more reassuring.

It was during this [time] that it was decided I should be evacuated. Welfare workers were asking mothers to go to the country with their children, or to let the children go on their own. My dad and nan were made to feel guilty and selfish for not wanting me to go. I didn't mind going. We had distant relations that lived in [the country]. I couldn't remember them, but it was decided if I had to go, I would be best off with family.

Off I went with my best friend, B–, who I had convinced to come with me. We left Paddington Station with our labels attached to our coats saying who we were and who we were to go with, our gas masks and one small parcel of clothes. There were lots of tears that day. Parents were not encouraged to come to the station, so goodbyes had to be said as we left the school playground to get on our allotted buses. Parents were changing their minds and pulling kids back at the last minute; others were pushing their screaming kids into the buses and running away home. By the time we got to Paddington, most of them had calmed down and were looking forward to their trip to the country . . . I was quite relaxed but B–, not knowing where she was going or with whom she was to live, was a bit nervous, but we had vowed not to be parted and went everywhere with our arms linked in defiance of anyone trying to separate us.

We arrived [in the country] with kids from all over London who had joined us at Paddington. A bus took us from the station to the school. Another hall! [She had already spent a lot of time in various halls used as rest centres after her family had been bombed out.] We stood in rows and were told, 'Smarten yourselves up.' How? The village people were then let in to look us over, to see who they fancied taking in. They walked up and down the rows of us sorry-looking sights and then back again until they made up their minds. This did not really bother me or B–, as we knew we were being called for by my aunt, but we had to stand in line just the same. I saw brothers and sisters being split up because people only had either sons or daughters that the evacuated children would have to share with. Two brothers were split because the five-year-old was sweet and quiet, while his brother was a proper Just William type and so the mother said no to the elder boy. Yet some were very kind. One woman, a farmer's wife, had come to take two boys and ended up taking a whole family of three boys and two girls whose ages were from five to thirteen. 'Oh well, what's a couple more,' she said. 'We'll manage somehow.' The hall was almost empty that Saturday afternoon, save for two or three kids who were sitting on their parcels looking lost and still hoping someone would take them, when my Aunt Bessie strode in, handbag on her arm, sensible shoes on her feet, and her clean cross-over apron wrapped around her. A small, bird-like woman with piercing eyes, she saw me, came over and gave me a hug, and said, 'Come on, young 'un.' I stood firm. 'This is my friend B– and she wants to come with me, she's my very best friend and we won't play you up, honest.' She looked at B–, back at me, linked one arm in mine and one arm in B–'s, then said, 'Well, we'd better get going then or the men will be in for their tea.'

Three abreast, we walked that long walk back to my aunt's, with her asking questions about the family, the train journey, everything – but no mention of the war or bombs. The men, being my uncle who worked on the railway, and my cousin Billy, eighteen and training to be a carpenter, were not in, so we were shown all over the big house, shown our bedroom, which overlooked the orchard, and were left to unpack our small parcels before coming down to tea. We spent the next half-hour opening cupboards and drawers, looking out to the orchard, where we could see a horse eating the windfall apples, and giggling on the big feather bed. It was smashing – we both agreed.

We went down to the large kitchen with its big table in the middle of the room. We were told to take the two back seats. 'They'll be your seats now,' we were told. She walked into a big cupboard we later discovered was the larder, and out came fresh-baked bread, pots of home-made jam and a big home-made chocolate cake. Aunt Bessie laid five plates in position. 'This will be your job from now on – to lay the table and in these places.' We were knocking knees under the table and ogling the chocolate cake. Billy and Uncle came in, having put their bikes in the shed.

'Hello, who you got here, then?' said Uncle. 'And who's this, then?'

'That's B–. She's –'s [my] friend. I've put them in the girls' room.'

The girls were my cousins, Gwen and Phyllis, who both lived away from home. Gwen was in service and Phyllis worked in a munitions factory in Salisbury and only got home occasionally.

The meal finished, Uncle took us to see the chickens, told us we would collect the eggs daily for him, and showed us where the gin traps were so we wouldn't step on them. 'They be only for rats, not little 'uns' feet,' he said.

'It's all very well telling us we can collect them eggs,' B– said later, 'but I'm not all that sure about going in there with them chickens. Say they fly out?'

I couldn't answer because I didn't know, so I just shrugged my shoulders. Within one week we were collecting eggs, feeding the fowls, mucking out pigsties and herding cows like we were born to it. We were given one week to get used to our new home and find our way around, and then it was back to school. A school bus brought children to the school from all the surrounding villages, [but] we had to walk as we didn't live far enough away. Our school playground was a large field. If the horse, Roofless, was not earning his keep, we were allowed to ride him to school and leave him in the field during lessons. Going to school on Roofless's back became a usual thing for the two of us.

After we'd been in the village for about three months, B–'s sister, Vera, who had met and married a Canadian airman during the war, came to visit and see if B– was OK. After she left, B– was not the same. I think her sister's visit had unsettled her. She got homesick, she cried a lot and, unbeknown to anyone, wrote to her mother to come and take her home. Once again the sister visited us, brought letters and a parcel from home for me and asked if I wanted to go back. 'No,' I said, 'I want to stay.' I loved the life there. The same day, B–'s things were packed and she and her sister caught the six o'clock train for London. It felt strange at first, but I can honestly say I didn't mind.

If, as for young B– above, it proved too much for children to have to live in a strange place and away from their families, returning to the East End could also be a problem, even a shock, after having had a taste of how other people lived.

We'd been put with a really terrible person first of all. Wicked. But then we'd been billeted with a really lovely couple, and their house was lovely and they had orchards and everything. We were really happy there. For the first time in our lives, my brother and I had a money box each. They used to give us thru'penny bits and their change and that. And we had more than one pair of shabby shoes. It was real luxury. The family had two grown-up daughters who were courting but who looked after us. We were spoilt rotten for the first time. I loved it. We were there for six, seven months. When the daughters married we had to come home, as there was no one [left there] to look after us. Really, we didn't want to go back home. And, believe it or not, back in the East End, we had the real mickey taken out of us because they said we'd come back talking posh!

It wasn't only a bit of teasing that the children returning would have to cope with. They were coming back to a place with no orchards full of apples and plums, no abundance of new-laid eggs to be collected every morning, no fresh air or pony rides. They were coming back to their families but also to a world of shortages, bomb sites and restrictions.

[5] *Rationing, Shortages, Making-do and Mending*

Poor working-class people had been rationed for years – by lack of money. But we weren't poor, we just didn't have any money!

Before the war, many East Enders might not have been very well off, but when the majority of people, including probably everyone down your street, lived in pretty much the same circumstances as you, and when you weren't being constantly bombarded with images of consumer goods that you *had* to have if you weren't to be considered a failure, it was less likely that you would feel discontented with your lot – no matter how basic that lot might actually have been.

But despite what we might now see as deprivation, there was still a reasonably affordable choice of essential goods that could be bought in the pre-war shops and markets, and from street hawkers. The following is a description of a not particularly unusual street a year or so before war was declared.

King David Lane was the street opposite our buildings.* Even though it was only 100 yards long, you could buy all your food there, from the Highway through to Cable Street . . . I can remember shopping there for Mum. There was a big pub called the Coach and Horses at the Highway end, and at the Cable Street end was the Crooked Billet. In latter years I used them both! There was the Salvation Army fifty yards further along from us – they used to practise quite often. H. White was the greengrocer; next to him was the fried fish shop.

* A familiar name often given to purpose-built tenement blocks.

When we went in there for a bag of chips we'd always ask for some cracklings.* Next to him was Smith's the cobbler's, and next to him was the baker's. They cooked their own bread on the premises. Hot cross bun day was a treat we looked forward to – a baker's dozen was thirteen back then. Next to him came the butcher's. Next to him was Maybury's the chemist's. Opposite was the corn chandler's, and not forgetting Con the tailor, who made a good suit at a fair price. So, you see, there wasn't even any need to go as far as Watney Street.†

With much of Britain's foodstuffs, raw materials and other goods being imported, the authorities were well aware that if war were to become a reality, the familiar scene described above would soon be a thing of the past. It had long been realized that this war wasn't only going to be won in the air, on the seas or on the battlefield; the home front, with its civilians as targets, was going to have to play a vital role if there was to be a successful outcome for Britain. Shortages would be inevitable and so measures had to be put in place to control the use and distribution of goods.

In these days of convenience foods and the bewildering choices in the supermarkets, it is hard to imagine how people coped with rationing, but of course they did – they had no choice, and that phrase was used again: 'We had to get on with it.' Surprisingly perhaps, the person who 'inflicted' rationing on the public, Lord Woolton – created Minister of Food in 1940 – was widely admired for his commitment to his post and the fairness with which he went about this vital war work. Using skilfully directed radio and cinema slots, and widespread poster and leaflet campaigns, Woolton's ministry ensured not only

* The crispy bits of cooked batter that fall from the fish while it's being fried and are then scooped from the hot fat to be enjoyed with salt and vinegar – preferably from the pickled onion jar.

† A market that was a short walk away.

that people didn't starve – even if they did sometimes experience hunger or cravings for unobtainable foods – but also that they were helped to make the best of what was available. The ministry introduced the British public to the cartoon characters Dr Carrot and Potato Pete, extolling the virtues and versatility of these easily grown vegetables as part of the 'Dig for Victory' campaign. There were regular items in newspapers; and helpful food tips and recipes were broadcast by Gert and Daisy, the popular comedy Cockney characters played by the variety artistes Elsie and Doris Waters. There was also the daily morning wireless programme *Kitchen Front*. The other vital popular medium in the ministry's campaigns, the cinema, soon had 'Food Flashes' showing alongside the newsreels and double bills of feature films.

According to the ministry, food was good if it was 'ship-saving, fuel-saving, and easy to prepare' – the final point being crucial for exhausted women, who were multitasking before the concept had even been invented. And it was essential for morale that people should be seen to be getting only their fair share. For this reason, in the autumn of 1939 everyone was required to register for his or her ration book, ready for when rationing itself was introduced.

This eventually happened on 8 January 1940. At first only butter, ham, sugar and bacon purchases were regulated, but then, in March, other meats were put on ration, although offal, sausages and fish were excluded. Not that these 'off-ration' foodstuffs were always readily available – or that appetizing in their wartime forms. But wet fish and fish and chip shops usually had an eager queue of women bravely waiting to see what sea monsters were being offered as the latest substitute for haddock and cod. Animal innards that had previously been considered fit only for the dog were reclassified as fit for human consumption, and as for sausages, what they contained was as much a mystery as it might be a lucky dip. By July even tea was being rationed and people had to become accustomed to putting in 'none for the pot'.

December 1941 saw a new measure introduced by the ministry. To ensure the even-handed distribution of any extra supplies of goods that might become available – for example, tinned items, such as fish – and which could help eke out the ration, adding a bit of variety to what was becoming a monotonously bland diet, the ministry introduced a points system. This was a monthly allowance given to ration-book holders to 'spend' – plus the price of the goods – in any shop that received a delivery of these non-rationed items. It has to be said, though, that shopkeepers tended to favour their regular customers and any such desirable items might well be kept for them 'under the counter'.

For all his ideas and his clever management of such a difficult, even potentially explosive, situation, Woolton will always be remembered by those who lived through the war years for two of the least popular of wartime culinary innovations: Woolton Pie and the National Loaf.

Woolton Pie was a brave attempt to make a tasty, nourishing dish out of not very tempting ingredients – or rather from a combination *lacking* the vital ingredients of increasingly scarce onion in the filling and fat in the 'pastry' lid. Convincing the public that cooking turnips, carrots, potatoes and parsnips, covering them in an insipid white sauce or oatmeal-based stock and then topping the lot off with a potato or breadcrumb crust wasn't easy. And as for the stolidly wholemeal National Loaf, it might have been healthier than the soggy white variety but it was off-puttingly grey and had about as many fans as the pie. But at least bread wasn't rationed – well, not until after the war was over.

Few of the people in our street with responsibility for combining limited ingredients with the abundance of information in order to prepare three square meals a day – predominantly women – had previously been offered much education in the nutritional values of foods, but they soon became well informed and skilled at stretching what was available in order to provide for their families. Despite all those well-intentioned efforts, however, it was eating to fuel their bodies rather than the pleasure of sampling appetizing dishes that seemed to figure in the memories of most people when remembering what they ate during those years.

We were hungry people on meagre rations, but we ate all sorts – sausages made from rabbit and God knows what else; whale meat cooked with onions – when you could get them – to try and disguise the taste; pease pudding – home-made with yellow split peas; faggots and sheep's heads cooked up and really delicious. American Spam – sliced up and fried in batter with some chips – made a good meal. If we were lucky, we'd get some beef fat off the butcher, which we rendered down in the oven and then had the dripping on bread for our tea. And remember, when it was cold, we had no central heating back then, so a stew – made with a little rationed beef, or tinned stewing steak, some carrots, other veg and an Oxo – would keep us warm. That and the piles of blankets and coats on the bed and a hot-water bottle for your feet. We survived!

Every bit of fat was saved and rendered down for a bit of dripping, but we survived.

We didn't get much food, but we survived. The people I admired most of all were the women. My mother was a widow with us three children to care for, and no pension. She did her very best to keep us alive. We had been children in the Depression in the 1930s and had little to eat, and at times had had to go on Relief to get food and clothing, so rationing did not come hard. Then, when we were old enough to go away to war, she was left on her own. To me they were real women. They had so little of their own.

*

I remember my mother cooking enormous bread puddings, cutting it up and taking it into the outside shelter in our street – incidentally, this was when she started smoking. Meals were corned-beef hash, shepherd's pie, stuffed hearts, and fish and chips from the shop. There were eggs from our chickens and our pet rabbits were baked! Any bacon went for sandwiches for Dad to take to work. There were stews, rice puddings and stewed apples – when you could get some free from the allotments. We were always hungry.

During the war the responsibility of food rationing fell to my mum and I was quite happy to eat what was put in front of me, but I know it was difficult for her as she had to make the rations go around. There was a lot of bargaining that went on. For instance, we didn't use very much sugar and one of the neighbours did, so my mum would exchange our sugar for her butter. That is the way a lot of people managed, and, like with everything else, we just mucked in. After I had my family, I was juggling the ration. A small joint of meat would be roast, then cold, then either cottage pie or stew. Mind you, I often do that now. Old habits die hard.

There were also references to how expectations of what you might find on your dinner plate were so different from those we have today, and how any kind of elaborate cuisine was definitely not part of most people's daily experience.

. . . it was difficult, and people were always on the lookout for something to stretch the rations, but remember that food was far more basic than it is today, and more nutritious – when there was money to buy it. I think, without sounding patronizing, we East Enders knew how to make a little go a long way. We did have that in our favour.

We hadn't been running the hostel [for elderly people bombed out of their homes] for very long when it was Harvest Festival time. [The vicar who set it up] must have told all the local churches about us, because on the Sunday evening and Monday morning the harvest food began to arrive. There were some tomatoes, apples, potatoes, and dozens of the biggest marrows I have ever seen. The big walk-in cupboard under the stairs was full of them! We had mashed marrow, stuffed marrow, marrow pie and I made marrow jam, and the cupboard was still full, so, in the end, we had a marrow party!

It wasn't difficult to cope with rationing. In the poverty-stricken East End it didn't make much difference; new clothes and excess food were luxuries few could afford. With Woolton's and radio recipes every day, it was relatively easy to produce a tasty meal from what you had.

At first, children didn't seem too aware of the problems presented by rationing.

On one occasion we had pork chops that had thick fat on the outside. I just could not stomach that and, when I left it on the plate, Mum told me off and ate it herself. She was so used to going without food and would not waste it.

I was about twelve and I used to go and collect our rations from the corner shop. You could fit the lot into about half of one of today's Tesco bags – I wonder now, whatever did we eat?

With the growing knowledge that shortages might – and eventually did – get worse, the concept of rationing became clear even to quite young children, and food items that had previously seemed rather ordinary could suddenly assume a new significance.

Mum had some prunes in the larder and I crept in there and ate one. [My sister] P– saw me and threatened to tell Mum that I had stolen one. I was terrified she would and begged her not to. She never did, but on many occasions she had me at her mercy to do anything for her, for fear of telling Mum about the prune. It would have been a lot easier to have told Mum about the prune, and taken the beating if there was going to be one, instead of living in fear for months.

While little ones carried on their usual rivalries and teasing of each other, older children and adults displayed a selflessness towards the youngsters that might serve as a lesson to us all.

I always likened our mealtimes to the parable of Jesus and the fishes . . . Mum was a great cook. Unfortunately, there was never any food left over . . . I have often thought, as I got older, how Mum managed to be so unselfish, to give us a quality of life that is hard to describe. It must have been sacrifice all the way. I never remember her buying herself clothes [or] cosmetics, and at most mealtimes, when serving us, there was no chair around the table for her.

I used to go to Hopwood's the butcher's, across Grove Road, and queue up for our weekly meat ration. Eggs were rationed, but I could have one for my breakfast every day – I think I had everyone else's ration in the house. We all lived together in the same house with my gran, grandad, uncle and aunt. Also my gran used to be forelady cleaner at the Bank of England and my grandad was a porter there. The other ladies would sometimes give my gran an egg for me from their own rations.

When I was in the Wrens, I had to go on to a submarine to do some work, and they had just come back from a tour of duty. They had bananas on board and gave me two hands to take to a primary school. The little ones had never seen a banana before and really didn't know what to make of them, but I'm sure they enjoyed them.

Of course, not everyone displayed such decent behaviour, and while the concept of rationing was generally agreed to be fair, with human nature being what it is, it didn't always mean that fair play would ensue.

[I] was the manager of one of a chain of grocery shops. R– and I became engaged during all the rumours of a war just over the horizon. Most people thought the threat of another war with Germany would blow over – I did myself – and just lived their lives as normal. I went to work as usual, and endeavoured to increase the trade and profit of the [branch] that I managed. There was no immediate rationing of foodstuffs, but many better-off customers started buying huge amounts of groceries, especially canned foods such as corned beef and other meats, peas and baked beans, pilchards, tea, sugar and tinned milk. You name it, they bought it. We were doing a terrific trade. Even my own boss had the van loaded with canned food and delivered to his home out in [Essex]. I clearly remember that van calling at each of our shops and each of us managers having to part with cases of tinned food.

For those without a chain of shops to plunder, or a group of managers to harass, there was the inevitable queuing.

I came home on leave in October 1940 to find the house empty. I went to Roman Road market and saw my mother waiting in the queue at the butcher's. As I spoke to her, the woman beckoned us forward to be served. At that moment I felt very proud and humble – the sirens had sounded and there were vapour trails in the sky, yet these indomitable women were more concerned with feeding their families.

The word would go around that there was a queue and people would appear from nowhere. Half the time they would not know what they were queuing for until they were near the front.

*

Somebody would mention there were rabbits on one of the market stalls and we would queue for hours. There would also be a long queue for horsemeat, but I'm afraid we bypassed that, although it was sold for human consumption, and people said it was lovely, but we took their word for it.

During this time there was little chocolate or oranges available and Mother, along with everyone else, would queue up as soon as word went around that the local shops had supplies, [and] an uncle in the Royal Navy sent us chocolate and some lemons in a small wooden box.

Not everyone had such good luck – either in the queuing stakes or in having such generous relatives.

As the middle-eldest child, my job was going to the shops, ration books in hand, and I'd be elbowed to the back of the queue many times before getting served. If I didn't get our full ration, I got a clip from my mum for dawdling.

Others had their own methods of coping with the queues and shortages.

[When] rationing got worse, if you saw a queue you automatically joined, having no idea what you were queuing for, [but] our neighbour always went to the butcher's for us to get our ration of meat. She would come back, plonk the meat on the table, rub out the butcher's mark, where he had marked the book, and then go back and get another lot. How she managed it we will never know, because there was a deep indentation from the mark that couldn't be rubbed out. He must have known. We also did a lot of swapping, exchanging marge for butter, and buying things that people didn't use or want, such as their tea or sugar rations. Our little dairy-cum-grocer's shop was very obliging and looked after us. We did quite well really and would queue for fish or the odd rabbit. In spite of everything we kept well – and slim.

Local shops, always an important focus for neighbours to meet up and gossip, as well as to buy their food, became an absolutely vital part of their community, as people had to register with their corner shop, their butcher's, grocer's and so on to get their official ration. Being a regular customer also helped to ensure that they would be 'looked after' first if there were any 'extras' to be had. This sometimes proved to be a problem for adult evacuees, who weren't always welcomed in the reception areas – either by residents or by shopkeepers – as people became increasingly proprietorial about 'their' shops and customers once the shortages worsened.

Our little corner shop was never bombed and so we continued to get our allowance, however bad the shortages got.

I'd always shopped there, and my mother before me, so course he was going to make sure he did all right by me. The war and the rationing were going to end one day and he might need my custom!

We had a very good butcher and good neighbours, so we didn't go short.

Mum would send me over to Evans the dairy. They had two cows in the barn at the side of the shop in Stepney, so milk was available and butter. In the corner shop – Meyers – we used to get broken biscuits, and dried apricots and apple rings. Our fish came via an uncle who worked on the market. But our treat was a penny block of lemon-flavoured ice wrapped in newspaper.

Despite the restrictions imposed by rationing and shortages, the war actually improved the lot of some of the poorer families – families, it should be remembered, who were living in our street, in the very back yard of the City, the richest square mile in the whole world.

I was a child when the war started. My father had been badly injured in the First World War and was unable to work very much, so we went without food at least two days a week. When the second war started, Dad became an air-raid warden. He could walk around, asking folk to draw their blinds for the blackout. He got paid, so it was paradise. We had food regularly for the first time ever. The few ounces of chocolate we were allowed a month was the first I had ever tasted. Apart from Hitler trying to kill us, it was glorious!

Mum always said that wartime was the first time that kids in the East End got enough food. The rationing, although things were scarce, at least meant we had a balanced diet.

Milk was a crucial part of that diet, with the government campaigning to actively boost its intake, particularly among children and pregnant women. Despite there being less milk available, as large areas of land previously used for dairy farming had been turned over to arable, this went ahead. Milk rounds also continued, even if the milkman delivering to your doorstep might now be a 'milklady', who would ladle it straight into your jug because of the shortage of glass bottles. The drive to increase consumption among the target groups was a success, as was the introduction of dried milk powder, which, along with dried egg, became an invaluable supplement to the increasingly sparse kitchen store cupboard.

Dad was a strict but loving father, but woe betide you if you didn't toe the line. As the breadwinner, his treat was smoked haddock on a Friday night, and I was given the treat of a slice of bread dipped in the water the haddock was cooked in.

*

It was hard for Mum to get food during the war years, and although we must have been fed properly, I can only remember eating bread and jam.

We had rationing, that's true, but I don't think the war made people poor. That had been caused by the lack of jobs in the 1930s. And it's true that there was a lot of comradeship during the war, but even so it was never a case of, 'Come round, any old time, and make yourself at home', because we never had anything to offer. We usually didn't have enough for ourselves . . . [But] through all the hardships, Mum and Dad were there for us, and a little hardship makes for good learning.

Ingenuity was sorely tested and began to be as thinly stretched as the sparse ingredients.

They were hard times, but you could still make good meals. I used to buy best end of neck of mutton and a few penn'orth of corned beef. I used to bake the chop end and roast vegetables with it. Then, with the neck, I used to braise it with onions, and fill the pot with whatever veg I could get. With the corned beef, you could stretch it by adding potato and making a little pie. My little daughter used to ask if she could have egg in a box! She meant a real egg, because we only had a few of those, but thank God for the American dried egg powder. We ate a lot of semolina, lived on the stuff. I baked it with powdered egg or boiled it with some cocoa to make it a bit different.

I never minded the powdered egg from America, it made a nice kind of omelette, or we had large tins of jam from Canada that tasted good on bread and in roly-poly.

We seemed to manage with the help of Marguerite Patten and Lord Woolton and his vegetable pie. There were all sorts of weird and wonderful ingredients that went into meals.

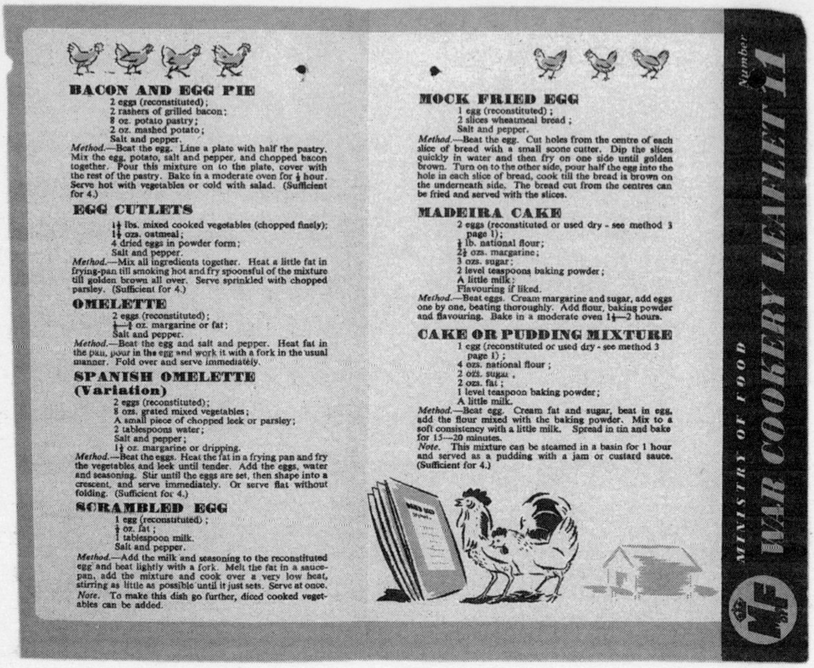

MINISTRY OF FOOD
WAR COOKERY LEAFLET Number 11

BACON AND EGG PIE

2 eggs (reconstituted);
2 rashers of grilled bacon;
8 oz. potato pastry;
2 oz. mashed potato;
Salt and pepper.

Method.—Beat the egg. Line a plate with half the pastry. Mix the egg, potato, salt and pepper, and chopped bacon together. Pour this mixture on to the plate, cover with the rest of the pastry. Bake in a moderate oven for ½ hour. Serve hot with vegetables or cold with salad. (Sufficient for 4.)

EGG CUTLETS

1½ lbs. mixed cooked vegetables (chopped finely);
1½ ozs. oatmeal;
4 dried eggs in powder form;
Salt and pepper.

Method.—Mix all ingredients together. Heat a little fat in frying-pan till smoking hot and fry spoonsful of the mixture till golden brown all over. Serve sprinkled with chopped parsley. (Sufficient for 4.)

OMELETTE

2 eggs (reconstituted);
½—¾ oz. margarine or fat;
Salt and pepper.

Method.—Beat the egg and salt and pepper. Heat fat in the pan, pour in the egg and work it with a fork in the usual manner. Fold over and serve immediately.

SPANISH OMELETTE (Variation)

2 eggs (reconstituted);
8 ozs. grated mixed vegetables;
A small piece of chopped leek or parsley;
2 tablespoons water;
Salt and pepper;
1½ oz. margarine or dripping.

Method.—Beat the eggs. Heat the fat in a frying pan and fry the vegetables and leek until tender. Add the eggs, water and seasoning. Stir until the eggs are set, then shape into a crescent, and serve immediately. Or serve flat without folding. (Sufficient for 4.)

SCRAMBLED EGG

1 egg (reconstituted);
½ oz. fat;
1 tablespoon milk.
Salt and pepper.

Method.—Add the milk and seasoning to the reconstituted egg and beat lightly with a fork. Melt the fat in a saucepan, add the mixture and cook over a very low heat, stirring as little as possible until it just sets. Serve at once.
Note. To make this dish go further, diced cooked vegetables can be added.

MOCK FRIED EGG

1 egg (reconstituted);
2 slices wheatmeal bread;
Salt and pepper.

Method.—Beat the egg. Cut holes from the centre of each slice of bread with a small scone cutter. Dip the slices quickly in water and then fry on one side until golden brown. Turn on to the other side, pour half the egg into the hole in each slice of bread, cook till the bread is brown on the underneath side. The bread cut from the centres can be fried and served with the slices.

MADEIRA CAKE

2 eggs (reconstituted or used dry - see method 3 page 1);
½ lb. national flour;
2½ ozs. margarine;
3 ozs. sugar;
2 level teaspoons baking powder;
A little milk;
Flavouring if liked.

Method.—Beat eggs. Cream margarine and sugar, add eggs one by one, beating thoroughly. Add flour, baking powder and flavouring. Bake in a moderate oven 1½—2 hours.

CAKE OR PUDDING MIXTURE

1 egg (reconstituted or used dry - see method 3 page 1);
4 ozs. national flour;
2 ozs. sugar;
2 ozs. fat;
1 level teaspoon baking powder;
A little milk.

Method.—Beat egg. Cream fat and sugar, beat in egg, add the flour mixed with the baking powder. Mix to a soft consistency with a little milk. Spread in tin and bake for 15—20 minutes.
Note. This mixture can be steamed in a basin for 1 hour and served as a pudding with a jam or custard sauce. (Sufficient for 4.)

Apart from following the information in broadcasts and leaflets, women used their own resourcefulness to produce all sorts of dishes. There were cheerily deprecating comments about some of the results, such as those of the 'We used to sing – "Whale Meat Again!"' variety, but there was also an insight into how people who lived down our street coped so admirably during the war.

One of my favourite tricks was to take a well-cooked parsnip, mash it with a little sugar, add a drop of vanilla essence and spread it on bread. The kids thought it was banana sandwiches.

I learned the art of cooking from my mother and elder sister and could – and still do – conjure up a meal from nothing or a few leftovers. I would get some bones from the butcher's with the minimum of meat on them, bung them in the oven with jacket potatoes, and then really enjoy the hot potatoes – slit open with marge – and the roasted bones: cheap, tasty food.

From the greengrocer's I'd get a pound of potherbs* and a few potatoes which would go to make the stew with dumplings. Sometimes we would have sprats fried in batter with mashed potato, or pease pudding and faggots. But the rest of the week would be bread and jam or syrup, but no butter on the bread.

You'd take the lid off the saucepan to see what Mum was brewing up for tea, and half a sheep's head would be staring up at you. Like with the sausages, probably best not to wonder what went in most of the things she came up with. I must admit I always drew the line at stuffed hearts. Perhaps if Mum had put some onion in to flavour the stuffing a bit . . . No, I don't suppose even then, really. Mind you, there were never any onions anyway. Don't know why.

Potatoes were our mainstay. They filled you up and you could fry, bake or boil them. If you could get the suet, you had puddings. Mum was a good manager and could make a meal out of whatever she had. We were sent out to try and get bacon pieces and onion, and she would make a bacon and onion roll.

If you could get some suet and half an onion, you were laughing. Suet makes a nice 'puddeny' pastry, you see, and onion gives the flavour. Roll out the pastry, wrap it round some bacon bits and onion – like a Swiss roll – cover it with a muslin cloth and simmer it in some water with plenty of veg till the pastry's done. That's really tasty, that is, especially with a touch of mustard! What I used to do was swap things I didn't want. Like I never was much of a one for sweet stuff, and everybody seemed to want sugar, and I was as happy with marge as I was with butter – so you could barter. If I could get

* Root vegetables.

hold of suet and a bit of dried fruit, I'd keep a bit of sugar back and make a lovely bread pudding. Tear up the stale bread and soak it in a basin overnight – cover it with a tea towel to keep it nice and clean. Next morning, squeeze out the water and mash it down with a fork, then you'd chop or grate the suet – it used to come in a lump, not like now – put in any dried fruit you'd got, add a bit of grated carrot if you were short, some sugar, salt, a good half a teaspoon of mixed spice, and enough milk to mix into a not too stiffish paste, spread it into a baking dish and stick it in the oven – medium sort of heat, for about an hour, till it's set. Lovely hot with a drop of custard, if you had some, or cold with a cup of tea. And sausage stew I used to make. You'd cut up each sausage into about three – you could get sausages – and put them in a saucepan half full of water, with as much chopped onion as you could manage, plenty of salt and pepper, and maybe a bit of carrot. Boil that up till the onions started getting a bit soft, and then put in some spuds that you'd cut up quite small, and carry on cooking until they were done. Made a lovely meal, that did. Good and tasty and filling.

There weren't many street pigeons left down our way, they all got trapped to stick in pies!

Fortunately for us, my grandmother had been in service during her early working life, graduating to being cook in a large house. As a result, even with limited ingredients, she was able to produce not only nourishing but very tasty food. Her accent on the 'nourishing' was largely due to her early life in Scotland in very hard times, and some of our meals had a distinctively Scottish flavour. In addition to fresh vegetables and fruit in season, our diet contained relatively – by today's standards – large amounts of fish, which seemed to be in plentiful supply. Our meagre meat ration was supplemented by the odd rabbit supplied by my uncle and, in addition to the inevitable Spam, exotic dishes such as pig's brawn and curried mutton were served up by my grandmother. Towards the end of the war I developed a taste for horsemeat and whale steak, the latter being subjected to a somewhat mystical treatment by my grandmother. This mainly consisted of marinating it in malt vinegar and peppercorns for twenty-four hours before washing it thoroughly, covering it in onion rings and grilling on both sides. Strange as it may seem, no 'fishy' flavour remained and it tasted delicious. Looking back now, it was a very healthy diet.

I know she did her best making grub for us lot, but you can't believe what a relief it was to have a plate of fish and taters. At least they tasted of something!

As well as fish and chips, there were other ready-cooked meals to be had, often from market stalls – the precursors of today's ubiquitous take-aways.

There were none of these pre-packaged meals that you see everywhere now, but you could buy ready-cooked stuff, things like faggots and pease pudding. I can remember my grandmother tucking into a brown paper parcel of trotters, spread out on her lap, smothered in strong vinegar, for her Saturday night 'nosh'. That would probably now be considered trendy cuisine.

The following quote might make those who nowadays prefer their meals pre-packaged by the supermarket chains feel rather squeamish.

Next [door] was a butcher's shop, which never seemed to have any meat. However, on occasions, the other kids and I would watch the butcher slaughter a pig. Several men would assist him and they would manhandle the animal on to a wooden stool, like a carpenter's stool. Its belly would be on the stool with the four legs hanging down either side. The men would hold it down by lying across its back while it screamed and struggled. The butcher would place a bucket under the pig's head and then pierce the neck with a pointed instrument to enter the jugular vein. He would then open the wound with a knife and catch the blood in the bucket. They made black sausage with that. The pig would scream for a while but soon die from loss of blood and then lie still . . . [It] was then laid on a small pile of straw, which was set alight. This would remove the coarse hair from the pig's hide and, at the same time, the trotters were pulled from its feet. The butcher would give those to us, which we would chew. They had a strong, singed, smoky flavour and were delicious. The pig would then be hung up inside the shed, where the butcher gutted it and cut it into joints. Imagine someone doing that nowadays. Just about every law on hygiene and cruelty was broken.

For those whose time was being stretched as thin as the contents of that wartime store cupboard – what with work, domestic responsibilities, sheltering and lack of sleep – a new system of communal, canteen-style eating was introduced by the government. This was the chain of British Restaurants. Economies of scale meant that these restaurants, often run and staffed by WVS members, could provide nutritious, good-value three-course meals for less than a shilling a head. Schools were called on to make similar provisions for their pupils, and whereas before the war the offering of midday meals had been the exception, by the end children having lunch at school was almost the norm.

As the war dragged on, getting enough food and coping with other shortages became a national preoccupation, and even when there was a lull in the bombing and things were momentarily easier, obtaining the everyday necessities overshadowed most people's lives. However, some shortages hardly affected poorer working families at all. For instance, in the East End, full indoor plumbing was still a rare exception. Bathrooms were, for many, unimaginable luxuries, and so the fuel shortage that had the government urging the public to patriotically confine itself to just five inches of hot water in its baths was not exactly relevant to families accustomed to taking turns in a few inches of rapidly cooling water in a tin bath in front of the fire.*

But it was the new meagreness of that fire which was to prove a shock. The availability of reasonably priced coal, and therefore reasonably priced gas, had been taken for granted by all but the poorest of households – not cheap maybe, but affordable. But then, after a period of almost wasteful use of fuel at the beginning of the war, the fall of France cut off an important source of supply. When shortages in domestic stocks began to make themselves felt, due to the numbers of miners being conscripted into the forces, and increased transport costs and restrictions on moving goods around the country started to bite – alongside the impact of some of the worst winter weather in living memory – initial murmurings were made by the government about introducing fuel rationing. The Conservatives objected strongly to this, as it was suspected of being a back-door means of nationalizing the coal industry, and it was eventually agreed that self-regulation would be the way forward. Again ingenuity came into play. Any coal supplies were pounced upon, but were regularly supplemented by coke fetched from the gasworks, tarry blocks 'collected' from damaged roadways and timbers 'salvaged' during the hours of blackout from bombed buildings – the fetching, collecting and salvaging often, though not exclusively, being done by entrepreneurial children.

Suddenly it was very quiet. For weeks now there were no raids, no bombs, just quiet. Songs were being sung about what we were going to do with Adolf when this was over. The few air-raid warnings we did get were not followed by bombs, not in London at least. Maybe someone else was 'getting it', but not London. It was just as well,

* It was the mid-1950s before I bathed in a 'proper' bath.

because my nan refused to go in a shelter again. 'Next time I go in a hole in the ground, it'll be in my box,' she'd say. We were all enjoying the quiet, and life went on as normal as possible, even though the ration coupons never allowed for enough food. Anyway, who had the money for more? And there was no coal man – he was away in the forces – so when we heard coal was in the railway yard, we got the old pram out, put the tin bath on top and walked to the sidings, where we all got our share, then pushed the pram full of coal back home even through the ice and snow.

In our profligate times, when rubbish bins are stuffed as full as fridges with discarded food, it is perhaps difficult to credit that those getting by on limited rations still had to follow regulations regarding waste. Failure to do so could result in considerable fines. Even throwing scraps to the birds was an offence. Whatever the leftovers – whether thriftily fine vegetable peelings, already scraped and boiled clean bones, breadcrumbs from the table or ragged and outgrown clothes – nothing was allowed to go to waste – that would have been falling prey to the Squanderbug!

Food was recycled in ways that would gladden the hearts of today's conservationists and environmentalists, and everyone was encouraged to 'Dig for Victory', with even the moat around the Tower of London being turned over to growing crops. But it was the campaigns encouraging salvaging that really seemed to capture the public's imagination. Whether it was rags and bones, paper bags, saucepans or kitchen waste, everything was collected and sorted by anyone who wanted to 'do their bit' to help the war effort. An often unpleasant task, it was undertaken by people ranging from schoolchildren to the ubiquitous WVS, who sorted through seemingly unlikely items: old boots beyond repair that could be made into fertilizer or even explosives, or bones that could be rendered down to make glue for fixing aircraft wing-coverings to their frames.

Then there was the collecting of metal. There is still disagreement about whether all the kettles and saucepans, railings and door knockers donated for Spitfire manufacture did anything more than lie rusting in discarded heaps, but people were so keen to help that it was a major propaganda coup which boosted morale, even if it wasn't either a practical or a necessary solution to shortages.

Some campaigns had more evident end results.

. . . we were issued with pig bins to put all our peelings in and the pig man used to come round regularly to empty them, and it would go to the farms to feed the pigs. We were encouraged to 'Dig for Victory' and flowerbeds were turned into veggie patches. Nearly everybody was at it, and there was quite a lot of competition.

If you didn't fancy saving your leftovers for someone else's animals, you could always start keeping a few yourself.

. . . we had the chance to rent a place with a bit of garden where we could grow vegetables and keep chickens that ran free during the day and were kept in a run to roost at night.

Livestock of all kinds had long been a feature of many East Enders' lives – a canary bought from Club Row* to brighten the day with its song; a cat to keep down the vermin; a dog for protection; a few hens for eggs; an occasional rabbit for the pot; even a donkey or pony to pull your cart; and, of course, pigeons to race and to show in breed and tumbling competitions (although the pigeon lofts in our street would remain empty for the duration of the war, except for those drafted in as official message-carrying birds, in case the pigeon fancier used his stock for treacherous purposes, such as sending messages to the

* East End street market selling animals.

enemy). But it was during the war years, with the scarcity of protein, that breeding animals for food came to the fore, albeit on a small scale and in the limited spaces available.

We were living in Bethnal Green, but when my father went off with the army, Mum and I went to stay with my grandparents and aunts in Leyton – all in one house! Grandfather kept chickens, rabbits and a goat in the garden, and my aunt kept chickens upstairs in the living room, behind a curtain!

Some Londoners, new to such matters, could prove a little soft when confronted with the harsh realities of animal husbandry.

Often we would take refuge in the cupboard under the stairs for safety with the dog, a wire-haired terrier called Nibs, and two cats – rescued from the bombing – one black and white called Benny, and one pure white called Bobby. This entourage, coupled with a selection of Rhode Island Red chickens, made up our family, the hens providing the eggs in their small back-yard residence under the leadership of Jenny, a redhead we loved dearly, and who would sound the all clear long before the official siren – always correct in her assumption that the last enemy aircraft had gone over. When it came to the crisis point of killing the chickens for sustenance, my dad could not do the dire deed and so they all died of natural causes. We kids had them buried under the sparse earth with crosses bearing their names.

In common with many households, we had turned our garden over to the production of vegetables and we also kept chickens. The day-old chicks, purchased from East Ham and Stratford markets, were lovingly reared by my mother and grandmother and kept us in eggs for the duration. We became so attached to them that they eventually died of old age! My uncle had a large allotment in the City of London Cemetery, supplementing our own vegetable crop, and neighbours would trade produce. On one memorable occasion of biblical proportions, we even had a supply of vegetables descend from the sky when a V1 landed on a nearby allotment and cleared the whole crop.

Making do and mending was to further test the resourcefulness of the already stretched homemaker. Turning collars and cuffs; patching shirts with material cut from their tails; mending sheets 'sides to middle'; unpicking the red side stripe from post office trousers to make them into a pair fit to be worn 'for best'; darning socks using a wooden mushroom to hold them in place as you stitched; unravelling old sweaters to reknit the wool into new ones; mending shoes with cardboard or, more 'professionally', with rubber from an old hot-water bottle or leather offcuts from the market; even fixing leaking saucepans with patches made from two circles of metal held together with a nut and bolt – leaving the pan a little wonky maybe but still functional, at a time when goods weren't treated as disposable.

It was such examples of ingenuity that could make the difference between getting by and going without. The shortage of crockery, for instance, which even after government directives on limiting ranges and decoration continued to be a problem, saw jam jars that were once only considered fit for swapping with the rag and bone man for a goldfish being washed out and used as everything from vases to basins, milk jugs to drinking cups.

Rug making became another home-based, do-it-yourself solution to shortages, utilizing anything from old rags to precious stockings that were finally, if reluctantly, declared 'past it'. And we think of recycling as a modern concept! Even an advertisement for Players cigarettes, responding to the shortage of paper and cardboard, urged smokers, 'In the National interest, empty your packet at time of purchase and leave it with your tobacconist.' Women's good nature was appealed to when they were urged to curb fashion and home-decorating tastes, and to realize that wood could be saved by making their high heels lower and their furniture simpler, and valuable supplies of material conserved by straightening and slightly shortening skirts.

But with the atmosphere of austerity hanging heavily over already bowed heads, morale needed a boost. People wanted something new to buy and might in fact even *need* something if they had been bombed out or were newlyweds just setting up home together. The government's answer was the introduction of the Utility range of standard items, guaranteeing a level of practical if basic design and quality – all at a fair price. Many families, including my own, were still using their Utility furniture long after the war had finished, and as recently as the 1970s I bought a man's white, collarless shirt bearing the Utility mark – two black circles with sections cut out, like slices of pie – in a charity shop which I wore as a 'trendy' maternity top. Items were made to last then – in every sense.

New clothes were rare, but my mother managed to make us things and to get us second-hand stuff. I always had dresses – usually out of gingham or something like that – socks and my one, single pair of shoes – plimsolls in summer, they were cheap – and cardboard in your shoes in the bad weather when they had holes in them. But, when they got too bad, Mum had a hobbing foot and used to mend the shoes herself.

Thinking back, I can't imagine what my mum must have been going through after we were bombed out. She was a marvel, getting second-hand clothes that she could unpick to make us clothes, and we soon had chickens for fresh eggs and meat again, and she was growing veg again. Nothing was wasted.

My aunt was a dressmaker and my mum did lots of knitting. I remember a dress my aunt made me out of parachute silk. I loved that dress. The first time I wore it I paraded up and down the garden like a queen.

My mother and grandmother were both very practical and good needlewomen, so clothes were patched and recycled, shawls and blankets were crocheted from unwanted woollen garments and shoes were preserved with Blakeys on the soles and liberal doses of polish. Everything was geared towards practicality, but a few pre-war items were lovingly preserved for best, even if they did reek of mothballs!

Two things stand out in my mind when I think about clothes during those years. The first is that we only had leather shoes or boots that wore out very quickly. No rubber shoes or trainers that lasted until they were too tight for the wearer. The soles of our shoes would wear out first and we always seemed to have holes in them that let in the rain and hurt when we stood on a stone or anything sharp.

We had to put cardboard or paper inside the shoes in an attempt to protect our feet. It never really worked, because I always seemed to have cold and wet feet. Another time, one Christmas, Mum managed to get me a new suit of clothes. A jacket and short trousers. She told me to be very careful and to look after the suit, as clothes were on ration and very hard to come by. The first day I wore the suit . . . I went over a barbed-wire fence and ripped the trousers. I was not very keen to go home that day and stayed out until the late hours, being very cold and hungry. When Mum found out, did I get a whacking. I feel very sorry for her now, because she must have been devastated after managing to get me a suit that was spoiled so quickly.

Sacrifices for the war effort took many forms.

I cut up my lovely wedding dress to make underwear for myself and my daughter.

*

Clothes rationing affected me more [than food rationing]. I have always, in the nicest way, envied young girls their fashions, and I think it was because we never had the opportunity to go through that phase, [but] again, we managed. We bought [clothing] coupons from people we knew, or cadged them from mums and nans – at least, I did. Stockings were a different matter. They were kept for best and our legs were covered with all sorts of colouring, including gravy browning, and in those days it was important to have a seam down the back. You would stand on a chair and somebody would draw a line down the back with an eyebrow pencil. If my uncle was there, he always did a really good job, but then there was the cry when I got in, 'Don't forget to wash your legs!' If you didn't, the sheets would be in an awful mess, and even soap powder was in short supply. When I went into the Wrens, we had our first uniform and clothing provided, but unlike the other women's services, we then had to buy our own. We could go to the slop shop,* where we could buy our naval gear, but not if you could help it; navy-blue bloomers were strictly for pay parade. Or we could get a chitty to let us buy outside. Mind you, there was a limit on the amount of gear you could request, [but] we used to take the chitty to a shop we knew would oblige, and black stockings would no longer be black, and navy knickers would be . . . Well, I leave that to your imagination. We got away with quite a lot. Lots of other items were in short supply and queues would appear outside chemists' if make-up or smellies were coming in.

Yet again, as the person speaking above put it so succinctly, 'We managed' mostly because of that extraordinary ingenuity that showed itself time and again.

Mum used to go to Chrisp Street market and buy material which had originally been used for the buses. It had been on a roller in the front of the bus to tell you its destination. She would bring it home and

* Navy jargon for the clothing store.

soak it in the bath till all the letters came off, then dye it for curtains and tablecloths, and blackout curtains.

Dad managed to get Mum quite a few flour sacks from somewhere and she made them into pillowcases and tablecloths. She even embroidered them, [and he] got hold of several bales of damaged material, which was a bit like lace curtaining. He sold it off to the neighbours and relatives and they all used it as net curtaining. Going around the streets, I remember I smiled when I saw it up at the windows – my dad had got that. Some had even dyed it different colours. People tried to keep up appearances even in those bad times.

As well as coping with the day-to-day practicalities of 'making do and mending' and always managing to 'rustle up' something to eat – all, it cannot be said often enough, after a full day's work, a stint doing civil defence and a disrupted night's sleep – women like the one described below also had the strength and optimism to look to the future.

Throughout the war [my mother] would religiously bank the small army allowances my three brothers made to her, not touching a penny. The savings were still there when they were demobbed.

[6] *Joining Up and Doing Your Bit*

There were lots of ordinary people who acted like heroes.

Exactly what you did for the war effort depended on the skills you had, your training and your commitments. And, as most fit young men would be conscripted into the armed forces, the Home Secretary, Samuel Hoare, appealed for a million volunteers, both male and female, to step forward to be trained for various ARP and other civil defence duties. There was plenty of choice as to what patriotic work you could become involved in.

There were air-raid wardens' duties to be carried out; fires that had to be fought; ambulances that needed driving; first aid to be administered; rescue, demolition and repair squads to be staffed; communications work to be done; and all the associated clerical and administrative duties to be undertaken. Then there was the WVS. Not designated 'Royal' until after the war, the Women's Voluntary Service for Air Raid Precautions seemed to be there to tackle just about everything not covered by anyone else.

Air-raid wardens worked from a post with up to five or six colleagues. In towns and cities with crowded residential streets, they had responsibility for maybe 500 people. Their role was vital to the neighbourhood. They were there to inform the appropriate rescue and medical services of any incidents, be they bombings or one of the anticipated gas attacks; to render first aid and to provide emergency rescue help before the services arrived; to investigate unexploded bombs and to put up appropriate signs and barriers. As well as ensuring that blackout regulations were being adhered to, they also provided sound local information, such as the whereabouts of shelters and reception centres, and made sure people knew how to apply for war damage compensation.

National figures show that up to one in six of the wardens were women. The following quotes relate to the experiences of both sexes, and to people at very different times in their lives.

My dad and uncle were older men. Uncle was in the ARP. One day, on his way to do his duty, there was a raid, and he saw arms and legs sticking out of a big pile of rubble. Of course, he stopped to dig them out. When he turned up at his post he was told off, reprimanded, for not reporting it in the proper way. He worked so hard and had saved those people. We were small children, but I can remember hearing those men cry at times. They must have come across some terrible sights, terrible things.

I was machining battledresses in a factory in Great Eastern Street during the day and was called up for the ARP when I reached twenty-one. I was on duty near home, which made it easier when I was off duty. As soon as the siren went I reported to the Fruit Exchange.* Hundreds slept there in bunks. After the all clear, we'd go home, wash and be ready for work. I never thought for one moment about being brave. We just got on with it.

I used to do nights up at [the factory] and we had to patrol [it] because we'd had a scare about parachutists. We went all around with rifles and gas masks, all the equipment, marching around in pairs, all around everywhere. Exciting days.

Another vital role for volunteers was fire-watching. The massive inferno that had spread so rapidly through the City of

* By Spitalfields market.

London in December 1940 made it apparent what a risk empty buildings presented. As a result, fire-watching duty was introduced. All designated areas were required to have rotas covering regular night duty. The volunteers' responsibilities included keeping a lookout for approaching planes, dealing with incendiary bombs and summoning help if a fire broke out that proved too much for their shift's stirrup pumps, buckets of water and sand.

The civil defence workers' views on the efficiency of their apparatus and safety equipment varied.

It meant being up on the roof – during an air raid – looking for incendiary bombs, which had to be put out straight away with a stirrup pump and a bucket of water. You were supplied with a tin helmet for protection!!!

All employees [did] fire-watching. It meant staying there during the night – usually one night a week. The duty was to try to extinguish firebombs – incendiaries – if they were dropped on the firm by planes. The appliance was a hand-held water stirrup pump. One person pumped the water from a bucket and the other directed the hosepipe on to the bomb. On three occasions, it was impossible to control the fire and the firms were burnt to the ground.

I was working, but I joined the civil defence as a messenger. I spent a lot of time helping wardens by covering for them when they needed a rest. For some reason I somehow felt safe with a helmet on my head, walking the streets, telling people to put out their lights. And on top of that we had to do fire-watching duties. That meant staying at work all night. We had a room with a bed and a dartboard for two of us. Even the boss had to take a turn. We only had one helmet, one axe and a hosepipe. That's all.

*

Our compulsory service was going on fire watch. But I also organized a first-aid service in the large air-raid shelters. I have a letter from Lady Mountbatten commending this effort.

During the early months of the Phoney War, members of the Auxiliary Fire Service (AFS) were treated as badly as the ARP wardens. But while the wardens were seen as little more than nuisances, apparently having no point in life other than to go round moaning about petty infringements of the blackout, the AFS volunteers were dubbed the 'Darts Brigade', 'duckers', 'parasites', 'idlers' and, referring to their allowance, '£3 a week army dodgers'.

But just as the public's opinion of the wardens would change, so too with the AFS, and many civilians owed their own and their families' lives to its members' bravery and commitment to a difficult and frightening job.

My husband's uncle was in the fire service – he got blown off a turntable ladder and killed at thirty-three years old. His name is on a memorial plaque at St Paul's. My own uncle was badly injured at Bank tube station in 1941, when a mine fell on him. He was blackened by the explosion and all his clothes had been blown off. My mum and cousin went to the morgue to see him. My cousin fainted when she saw his eyes move! They thought he was dead.

Women also worked in the fire service, in administrative, communication and driving roles, but all the fire fighters were male. The majority of ambulance drivers, however, were female – although some of their reasons for taking up that particular role might nowadays seem a little surprising.

I was on ambulances out in Romford. Mum, who was very Victorian, *made* me join the ARP rather than the forces, as she said [women in the forces] were no better than groundsheets for the soldiers!

I did it because it was a job that women could do.

There were also men working alongside female colleagues in the ambulance service, contributing their time and effort, and, like the women, doing so in addition to their other wartime responsibilities.

My husband was a brave man. He worked on secret government projects and several nights a week he also drove an ambulance. He saw some horrific sights that stayed with him always. One day, after a night on duty, he came home and was in the bath when a V2 dropped nearby. The ceiling came down and, mixed with the hot water, gave him a plaster coating. Imagine the sight I saw – he was standing there, stark naked, enquiring if I was all right. But, why, oh why, did he put his uniform hat on!?

From 1940 onwards, men who were unable to join the armed forces, because they were considered too old or too young for the regular services, or because they were in reserved occupations essential to keeping the country running smoothly, were given the opportunity to 'do their bit' in another way. It was a time of growing unease, with a sense that an invasion was a genuine possibility, and it was decided that a force of volunteers, based on home turf, would be the way to hold back any such onslaught until the army could be mustered to deal with it.

So it was that on 14 May Anthony Eden, the Secretary of State for War, broadcast an appeal for men to step up and offer their services to the Local Defence Volunteers (LDV). By August of that year, volunteers would become known as the Home Guard. The numbers of men keen to participate far exceeded those expected to do so by the government: rather than the anticipated 150,000 or so unpaid volunteers, over a million had been recruited by the end of June that year.

My father had been in the First World War. He had lost two of his three brothers in the trenches, and then his third brother in the 1920s, when he had been on the M1, a prototype submarine that went down just off Plymouth and never came up again. But he still did his bit and joined the Home Guard.

Father's job was classed as 'essential', which prevented him from enlisting in the forces, although he was in the Home Guard.

I commenced my first paid employment, receiving ten shillings a week, with John Meerloo near the Bethnal Green Road. When the Local Defence Volunteers – LDV on the armlet, and later called the Home Guard – was founded, I was the youngest member. I was instructed to clean a First World War Lee-Enfield rifle, which was to be shared among all the members. The barrel was packed with hard grease and I had to clear it. I solved the problem by using steam from the works boiler. The grease shot out of the barrel like a bullet. We all did fire-watching to deal with incendiary bombs. A nearby explosive bomb shattered the corrugated asbestos roof. The vertical boiler chimney stack, which went through the roof, was no longer upright. I climbed up and hit the chimney stack with a broom to straighten it up. It buckled and collapsed. Fortunately, no one saw me do it . . .

My dad was in the Home Guard and I got very excited when he brought his rifle home . . . Mum had been in hospital for an operation and my dad had to do all the cooking and we were glad when Mum came home. But on the day she came home a bomb fell just around the corner from us, blowing out the window in their bedroom and embedding the glass in the wall above Mum's head. Being in the Home Guard, Dad was called for. He had to go and help dig people out of the rubble. He came home a sad and bitter man. I can hear him now telling Mum how he only found arms and legs. He was so upset. The bomb had caused a lot of damage and when the WVS came in a van with hot soup, me and some of my mates pretended we had no homes or food so we could get a bowl!

The WVS willingly carried out an astonishing variety of tasks, far more than would be guessed at from the tea and sympathy image with which they came to be associated. Set up in 1938 as part of the call for volunteers, they were to play a crucial role on the home front. They were central to the evacuation process; organized nurseries; staffed hostels, social clubs and British Restaurants; transported and escorted hospital patients; did welfare work for the forces; organized food and clothing for refugees; made camouflage netting; knitted sweaters and socks; set up and ran rest centres to receive those made homeless by bombing; distributed ration books; collected nuts and bolts from factory floors and sorted them for reuse; set up Welcome Clubs for lonely GIs; comforted and assisted the bereaved; ran the famous mobile canteens for victims and rescue workers following air raids; distributed clothing and household items to families who had lost their possessions; and probably many other tasks and duties that weren't even talked about – which makes the following modest remark all the more poignant.

My mum didn't go to work because she had me to look after, but she did work for the WVS.

The WVS wasn't entirely made up of women – some driving, for instance, was done by male volunteers. But another extremely hard-working group was an exclusively female force: the Women's Land Army. Originally set up during the First World War, the Land Army was re-established with the same

16. Young Peter Hodgson sitting among the blitzed ruins of Single Street School, Stepney.

17. London families waiting for transport to evacuate the women and children from the bombing.

18. Little ones evacuated from Columbia Market Nursery to Alwalton Hall, near Peterborough, wave goodbye to their parents. Some children would not return home for years.

19. Older London lads, evacuated to Devon, being taught how to plough. The replacement of horses by motorized vehicles was, in many cases, halted by the war.

20. A long way from home – London evacuees and Italian prisoners of war. The POWs were being used as farm labourers in the West Country.

21. (*Above left*) Waste not want not – a young Londoner 'doing her bit' by adding scraps to the pig bin, which would be sent off to the local pig club or municipal piggery.

22. (*Above right*) A housewife 'doing her bit' by sorting tin and paper for salvage.

23. (*Left*) Queen Elizabeth pays a visit to the Sewardstone Road piggery in June 1943.

24. Models demonstrating the new Utility underwear. These standardized garments came in limited styles, but were well designed and affordable, and made from good-quality materials approved by the Board of Trade.

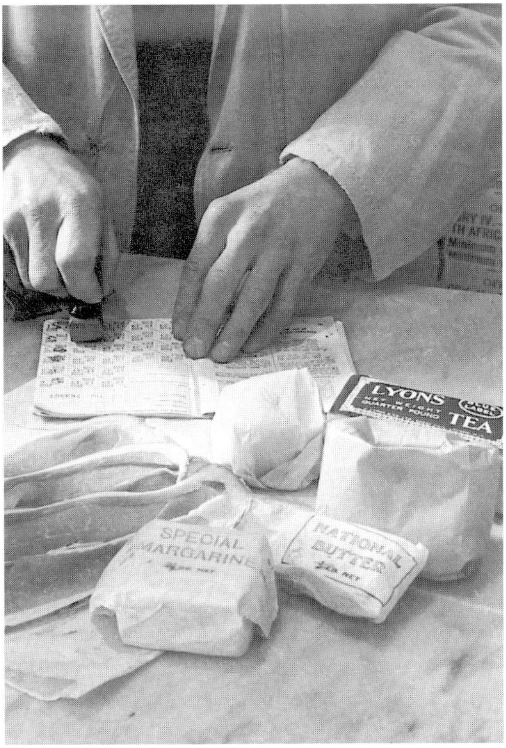

25. Cancelling the coupons for a customer's weekly ration, comprising tea, sugar, butter, cooking fat, bacon and the somewhat alarming-sounding 'special margarine'.

26. Even though goods such as tobacco, cigarettes and especially matches were not rationed, they were still hard to come by, although this shop-keeper could offer twenty Roys for half a crown.

27. Children in Russia Lane, Bethnal Green, clearing a bomb site to create allotments for growing vegetables.

28. Part of the astonishing 100 tons of scrap collected at Northumberland Wharf in Poplar after the mayor made an appeal for salvage in July 1940.

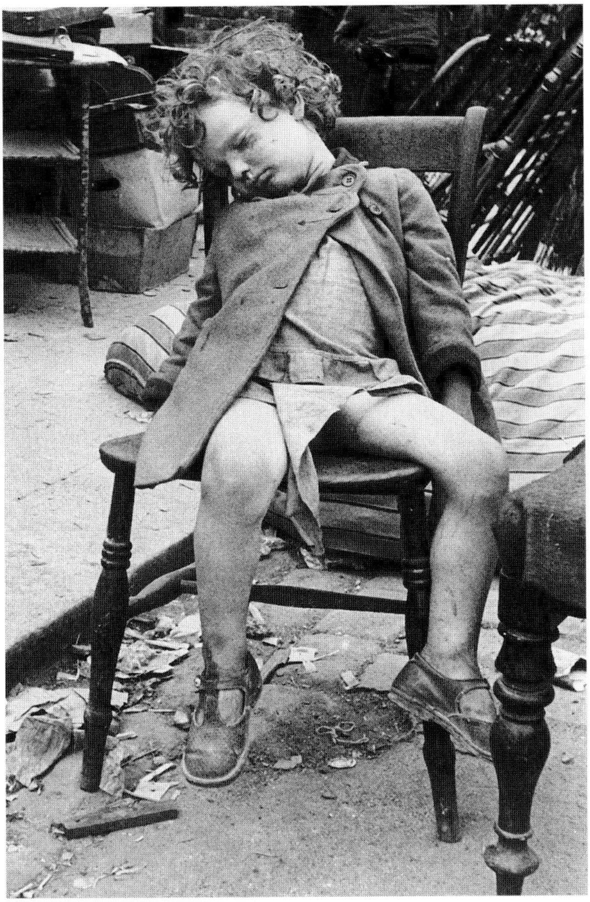

29. (*Left*) Exhausted and dirty but safe, a childhood victim of war is given what limited comfort is available.

30. (*Below*) An adult casualty being tended until medical help arrives.

31. The medical professionals themselves weren't immune. Here, nurses at St Peter's, Stepney – one of four London hospitals bombed in a single night in April 1941 – recover what they can from the debris.

purpose in mind – to ensure that essential agricultural jobs were done, and that the nation was fed – and even young Cockney girls, who had never before strayed very far, gladly joined its ranks and went off to stay in the countryside and learn about a very different way of life.

I joined the Women's Land Army at seventeen, and on my first leave I had my photograph taken at Griffiths' Portrait Studio in Armagh Road. How proud I was in my uniform.

I was glad to do my bit, but it wasn't like anything I'd ever done before, and the countryside took a lot of getting used to. And the work. I missed my family, but wanted to do it.

Travelling and working away from home wasn't strange to all East Enders. The proximity of the docks had meant that joining the Merchant Navy had been a widespread occupation for young men, who, like members of my own family, could sail to the furthest reaches of the earth by finding a job on one of the huge ships that were berthed little further away than the end of the street. But it had a far more important purpose than being a means of allowing young men to travel. The Merchant Marine played a vital role in feeding the country, bringing in essential raw materials and transporting its finished products all around the world. And during the war its role was central, as its ships struggled to bring in supplies, while under attack from the German navy and its U-boats, making its work every bit as dangerous as that of the armed forces.

It was 1940, and I was now turned conscription age, so, after Christmas and New Year at home, I went down to the West India Dock to see if any ship had a man short in the engineering department as a stoker, as I already had experience and a seaman's discharge book. As it happened, I got a job on an Ellerman's Wilson boat, leaving English shores as peaceful as any time I'd seen previous to war – although it was obviously still dangerous because German U-boats were playing havoc with English shipping. We went on a Mediterranean run on this 2,000-ton ship. But then Italy declared war and our job in the Mediterranean was very different. We were running up and down the Med in convoy with gunships protecting us from aircraft off of Rhodes, while we picked up steel-hardening chalk. But after six months I got malaria and was discharged to come home DBS [Distressed British Seaman] on a troopship. On returning home to England, we landed at Liverpool and I eventually caught a train from Liverpool to Liverpool Street Station in London. What a change! After having left a peaceful city seven months earlier, here I was, at night, with the blackout regulations really tightened, and anti-aircraft guns banging away. I managed to get a bus to Poplar. The streets were deserted – and it was only ten o'clock at night. It was eerie. And, when I got there, my home was deserted too. An air-raid warden told me that everybody'd gone to Spratt's dog biscuit factory, where my dad worked, and that people took blankets and anything necessary for sleeping down there for the night as it was a big strong building. And there I eventually found my people. Being a seaman, I was able to nick an extra bit of time ashore with my family before I got the letter telling me to get back to sea. Next, I took another, bigger ship – the *Inkosi* – over to the West Indies, and so it went on. And, thank God, despite all the U-boats and the bombers following us up and down the Med for days at a time as we went from Port Said to Greece, I've still managed to reach over eighty years of age.

A few people spoke with disarming honesty about their efforts to do anything rather than have to join up in either the armed forces or any other even slightly risky capacity, and there was certainly nothing like the fervour to join up that there had been in 1914. But because the war came so soon after the Depression of the 1930s, others saw it as an opportunity to escape from poverty. Having a regular income from the services

– regardless of how small the allowances were for the wives and children of the lower ranks – was a great relief after years of unemployment, and quiet pride could be taken in once more having paid work.

> To a [small boy] nothing much seemed to be happening with the war, [but] local men, including several relatives, were either being called up or voluntarily joining the armed forces. We were a poor family in a poor area and comment was made that life in the armed forces was paid work, and better than unemployment.

It wasn't only the diffident self-respect that was so touching when people recalled these experiences, it was how they spoke so matter-of-factly and with such humility about what were undeniably astonishing events. After he recalled his ordeal, this remarkably self-effacing man went on to apologize for being nostalgic.

> I enlisted in the army in 1941, when I was eighteen years old, and served four years. I landed on D-Day, fought through Normandy and finished up in Germany in a slave labour camp.

And the following quote is from a man who modestly describes his journey from being a clerk to taking part in the D-Day landings.

> I was sixteen when war started. I worked in the City and would go to work in the morning after a heavy night raid, with the firemen still trying to put the fires out. We had spent the previous night in the Anderson shelter with bombs falling and still got up and went to work and got on with our lives. Even though my two cousins, both girls, were killed a few roads away, we still got on with things. Then I joined the Home Guard, and when I got home from work I would put on my uniform and take my rifle to report for duty – watching

for parachutists and, to a man, to protect the reservoirs over in Walthamstow. Then I joined the army and took part in the D-Day landings as a tank driver and operator, surviving long enough to reach Germany. We had grown up in the Depression years in the 1930s with next to nothing and we had the grit to get up and face another day. I believe that was the spirit that was shown when our country needed us.

That final observation is reflected and supported in the following comments.

I saw many a young boy leave home and, after being in the forces for a few months, they would come home looking and thinking like men.

Conscription into the armed forces was at eighteen, [but] it was possible to volunteer to serve in the forces at the age of seventeen, [which I did. I went] into the army. The first six weeks was spent training at Bury St Edmunds, where we were taught how to march, use hand-grenades and various types of guns, and use a rifle fitted with a bayonet . . . running into a dummy representing a person. The whole object was to teach us how to kill . . . I passed the course and was transferred to the Royal Corp of Signals regiment, attached to the Royal Artillery.

Women also spoke of their memories of being in the services, although the part they played was defined as auxiliary.

My wife served in an ack-ack battery and, during the Battle of Britain, a Spitfire pilot from Hornchurch flew over so low he waved to her. I wonder if he survived. I hope so.

But their responsibilities should not be seen as inferior. Women who joined the Air Transport Auxiliary, for instance, were employed ferrying aircraft from factories and delivery ports to RAF bases, maintenance and test centres. They delivered nearly a third of a million planes, sometimes in basic airframe condition, flying without the assistance of radios or instruments. They would study master maps before take-off and memorize salient geographical features on the route and around their destination airfield. But the best memory in the world couldn't help them if they came up against either of the two main threats, apart from the enemy, to safe flying: the weather and barrage balloons. Probably one of the most famous members of the ATA was Amy Johnson, who died in January 1941 after having to bail out of the Oxford Mark 11 she was flying, plunging down into the icy waters of the Thames estuary. This work wasn't only brave, it was invaluable for the security of the nation, as it freed the increasingly pressed RAF pilots for action.

The navy also benefited from young women who came forward to do their bit for the 'Senior Service'.

My father played an important part in the Second Front; he was on a panel of people who planned the Mulberry Harbour. It was made and towed over to Arromanches in France, so that the ships could dock safely. My father was in charge of that, overseeing that the Channel was kept clear. [And] because I was working with the landing shipping, I was not allowed any contact . . . In fact, I was very nearly one of the first females to land in France. I was down below in one of the craft, checking the ammunition, when along came a matelot and kicked the hatch shut. After a lot of banging and shouting, I was heard and let out. I tell you, I was never more relieved . . .

When I was in the WRNS, I was in a Wrenery – a big house – which was opposite a static water tank that was always full of water for emergencies and had to have a red light outside it. I would like to have as many pounds as the times we came out in the morning only to find it on our doorstep, where some matelot had thought it was funny to put it there. Mostly we took it in good part.

Even children didn't miss out on the chance to 'do their bit', whether it was taking part in collecting for salvage drives like 'Saucepans to Spitfires' or maybe something a little more physical and 'hands on'.

The Italian prisoners of war were escorted by a British guard to work on the local farms [around where we were evacuated]. I came into contact with many of them, because us older children [I was about eleven at this time] were allocated out to different farms all over Wiltshire, to work with the Land Army girls doing potato picking, muck spreading, hedging and all the farm labourers' jobs that were not getting done because our boys were in the services. We loved it, because it meant a ride in the trucks with the Land Army girls, who were always so jolly – singing songs and talking about their love life – and it got us out of school and we earned pocket money. The Italians were so young, some of them not looking that much older than myself. Very few spoke English, unlike the Germans [in the other nearby POW camp], who nearly all spoke some, but somehow we conversed. I would share my lunch with them, as did the rest of my friends, but they were so afraid of getting in trouble and having their privileges taken away – of which farm work was one – that they always asked the guards' permission first. Permission was usually given, but they were closely watched. One Italian took my plastic tail comb from me one day. I thought he wanted to borrow it, and when he never returned it to me after work, I didn't say anything in case I got him in trouble. Two days later, the Italian truck with its prisoners arrived at the farm we were working at. At lunch time I saw him talking to his guard, saw the guard nod and he came over to me. 'For you, for you, photo, please, take, from me, Antonio.' I looked in his hand and there was a ring, made of the green tail of my comb, an oval piece in the middle, indented for a photograph to be stuck in it.

I stuck my photo in it and sent it to my dad. He wore it on his little finger for years, until it snapped and broke.

I joined the GTC [Girls' Training Corps] and took part in a radio programme called *Youth on Parade*, which, incidentally, I heard a snippet of some thirty-five years later. How embarrassing! Part of the training for the GTC was a first-aid course. We went to the St John Ambulance Brigade for our tuition.

So, if you weren't in the forces, you were expected to volunteer at least some of your spare time to 'do your bit'. And, as the majority of adults discovered as the war went on, the calls on them to make contributions to the war effort would only increase.

[7] *Work*

> My mother worked twelve-hour shifts in the boiler room as a clinkerman.

To paraphrase the wisdom of Studs Terkel, work is as much about our daily meaning as it is about our daily bread. This observation is probably never more pertinent than at times of national crisis, when people perceive that they and their country share a single purpose – in this case, defeating the enemy. And yet the tough, often demeaning conditions that people had experienced during the Depression of the 1930s were still making themselves felt, particularly among the unskilled working classes. Even with the call-up and the increased opportunities for paid civilian employment that were springing up throughout the manufacturing sector, the situation wasn't suddenly resolved overnight just because hostilities had begun. But at least there was hope that the country's economy would improve to such an extent that everyone would benefit, including the very worst off.

Then, ironically, another problem presented itself: labour shortages. It wasn't just that the now expanding economy was more than capable of supporting full employment; rather, the country's production and services needed to be ratcheted up to a level that could meet the demands of the war machine. Anyone of working age who was capable was called upon to get things going and to *keep* them going – flat out. Those who weren't called up for the armed services were required to either remain in their reserved occupation, if their job had been so designated, or do other essential paid work. They were also expected to carry out civil defence duties as directed and, at the same time, continue fulfilling whatever domestic responsibilities they might have. For some, this would prove to be a liberating, if exhausting, experience. In an odd way, it was maybe only because of the terrible conflict that this sort of liberation could have happened.

The next step in making up the employee shortfall was to call on people who had previously fallen outside the usual age range of the labour force.

My grandfather was past retirement age, but was employed by the Stepney Borough Council doing park-keeping duties. All the railings in the park where my grandfather worked had been removed to melt down to help the war effort, but the main gate was left standing. One day he came home, having finished his shift, when suddenly he said he had to go back because he'd forgotten to lock the gate!

Not all efforts to be more age-inclusive in the workplace were strictly legitimate, however.

I wasn't really old enough to leave school – by a good couple of years – but there was plenty of work about, and Mum could certainly do with the money I brought in. Believe me, it made a change for her not to have to worry about what was in her purse. Nobody took any notice of what was going on because there was so much commotion with the bombs and that, and the schools were shut, and I don't know if they realized how old I was.

It was women in particular who were being utilized as never before, often doing hard physical or technological jobs previously deemed well beyond their capabilities.

My grandmother [worked] at the local United Dairies milk-bottling plant.

My mother worked very hard on the railway. She and the other women were fantastic.

Me and my mate worked in a place in Ilford, and I reckon you could say we were doing jobs that the fellers normally did.

To keep small family businesses going, some women attempted to take over jobs from their menfolk, but this didn't always go according to plan. If the government decided you were needed for the war effort, you had little choice in the matter.

When the war started, Dad and his brother were working for my grandad as cats' meat men. They had butchers' bikes and would have the meat skewered on sticks. When they reached the flats around Brick Lane, they would toss the packets in through the windows for people to catch. When they were called up, my mum and aunt tried to carry on in their place, but that soon came to an end as they had to do factory work.

Single 'mobile' women – those without domestic responsibilities – were among the first to be coopted into 'male' roles, but it wasn't long before married women were also being actively encouraged to join the workforce, in some cases by the lifting of the marriage bar, which had previously been insisted on by trade unions to protect men's jobs.

To further free the female population for work – as well as for ostensible reasons of safety, of course – the evacuation of children was strongly promoted by the authorities. For those whose children remained at home, money was found to set up public day nurseries, and multiple shifts were introduced to get the most out of both the workforce, and manufacturing and processing plants.

Demands on female workers were high and schedules could be gruelling. In addition to the long, sometimes difficult hours they did in the workplace, women had to spend time queuing for rationed and scarce foodstuffs in their lunch hour or after work. They then had to go home, where they got on with their domestic responsibilities – caring, cooking and cleaning for their families – as well as meeting any civil defence obligations, including fire-watching, seeing to the nightly domestic blackout arrangements and, of course, ensuring the safe sheltering of the family in the event of a warning. These were the jobs and chores that made up their frantically busy days and nights. And, of course, bear in mind that their sleep might well be disrupted by air raids and frightened children, and that housework was a far more physical business in those days, before the wide availability of domestic appliances and hot water on tap, and with very little chance that any of them ever had any kind of paid household 'help'.

So the women from our street were proving their worth both to their country and to themselves. Those I met spoke about enjoying the financial and social benefits that came from taking an active part in society – a part they had previously been denied – and also the psychological benefits, as they knew they were doing something important at a time when they might otherwise have felt powerless. It was an incredible turnaround for them, but even the most willing among us can be pushed too far.

'We want to train some girls up to take the men's jobs,' [she was told at Tate and Lyle's]. It was actually refining the sugar . . . We were taught the running of the sugar, right from the beginning, where the raw sugar comes in and it goes through all the processing. Another woman and me had this job. [We used] a filter press, it was all big pumps and valves and things like that. So we learned the job . . . what type of valve we had to undo and which one we had to close and open. It was hot, so they said, right, we could work just by the tiny little lights so we could have a few windows opened, but the rest of the big lights had to be off. I stayed there practically all the war, but it was three shifts. I wasn't feeling good. I had my mother at home with me, and she had sugar diabetes. I was looking after her, doing the three shifts, and I had to do fire-watching in the street. In the end I just sort of ran out of strength.

Seeing the mess from the bombs in the morning was frightening, but we still went to work. I worked for a firm by Hackney Wick dog stadium, making ammunition boxes. We punched the nails in by machine and would often catch our fingers. Ouch! It was before B– [her husband] went into the air force, and he worked as a night watchman at the same place – running out to put out the many incendiaries. They were dangerous times. We used to meet at Temple Mills Lane, me going home after the finish of my day, and B– going on fire shift. B– worked with a fellow who followed dog racing, and he asked B– to take over his shift so he could go racing. When B– refused there was a punch-up. The fellow got the sack and B– followed a few days later – I presume when they got a replacement for him. I sometimes used to go back and B– would make me a lovely hot drink with milk he'd nicked from the canteen! I also worked at a factory, close to Burdett Road, making parts for Mosquito fighter planes, which were made out of veneered wood. A really pungent type of glue was used and the fumes used to hurt our eyes and make us fall asleep – which we did very often.

From the rest of her story, I suspect this woman was suffering from exhaustion as much as from the fumes, but it is a salutary lesson to hear how individuals rose to the occasion and kept in such remarkably good humour, despite the fatigue and the danger.

I was working [nights] at a factory that was right on the wharf. The water was lapping against the side and there was only the Home Guard taking care [of us]. It was such a cold night that one of the Home Guard, who also had a good job in the factory, thought he would take a drop of Scotch around to the men working on the wharf on guarding. And he gave this man the bottle to take a swig out of, and a bomb dropped and he let go of the bottle and it went right in the Thames! So he wasn't very popular. He got called a few names that night. That was the end of the Scotch, [but] we worked all during that air raid, worked during [all] the air raids, you know.

By 1943, approximately 90 per cent of able, single women and 80 per cent of able married ones were engaged in some sort of war work. But while, as noted above, some felt they benefited from the involvement, it did depend on the conditions in which you were expected to do your job. No concessions were made for the new recruits to the factory bench and the engine shop. Some environments, such as that in the sugar factory, could be really unpleasant. Surroundings were often dark, what with sandbags blocking the windows of offices and factories, and bulbs being dimmed because of fuel shortages. Production could even take place underground.

We had to endure working in the Ilford Plessey factory's basement all day, inspecting radio components for aircraft. The basement was the only place we could get any continuous work done. We had so many bombs land near us, it was as if the Germans knew exactly where our factories were. History has revealed that they had detailed aerial photographs, so luckily it was their aim that was bad! The basement was far better than the 'bomb shop', a section of the factory down in an unused part of the London underground line, full of grimy dust from the machining of high-carbon-content bomb casings. To be sent to the 'bomb shop' was the equivalent of the Russian front!

But enjoying your new-found freedom and status, regardless of how tired you felt, could soon be cut short if the realities of war impinged too dramatically.

Everyone was expected to do their bit, even us girls. I was one scared person, I must admit. I worked at a flourmill in Kingsland Road. It was dealing with food in the big warehouse where we had to fill the loading bays for the horses and carts and vans and so on. I started at seven thirty in the morning and worked until six at night. But us girls had fun there, and although the war was getting worse, we continued to carry on working while the bombs were dropping everywhere. One morning, young Tiny, as we called her – being a little bit on the plump side – was very depressed because she had had words with her dad. She told us all about the upset and said that she couldn't care less if a bomb dropped on her. We all gasped at what she'd said and tried to cheer her up. Every morning in work we had a roll call in case anyone was hurt or held up in the raids. Imagine what it was like when we heard that Tiny and all her family had had a direct hit and were all wiped out – that very same evening, as if she'd got her death wish. I shall never forget her, such a beautiful girl.

The story that follows is an example of how modest so many of the people I spoke to were when they told me about living and working in such extraordinary times. The woman here describes her transformation from a young girl whose mother worried about her journeying to work into a brave young woman serving her country – all in a matter of months.

I had been at work for a year when war broke out. I worked in the City and, like an awful lot of offices, the one I was working for closed down. It was only a small concern and I think they carried on at home. I had volunteered for the ARP just before the war and went to work in a first-aid centre full-time. I did really well with my exams, but then they found out my age, so I had to go. I then managed to get work in Old Street, making artificial flowers. I enjoyed doing that. I met and became good friends with two sisters, Franzi and Lisl – they were Austrian refugees. I worked there for a good while, but then we had the Blitz and it got more difficult and more dangerous to get there and back, so my mum made me give it up. I then worked making artificial flowers at home, sometimes in the shelter. Then I managed to get a job in the offices at Plessey, [but] as soon as I was old enough I volunteered for the WRNS. I enjoyed my time in the Wrens. It was hard, as I was outdoors on the ships. I was a quarters rating, which was a strange name for somebody who kept the guns in good repair. For most of the time I was stationed in Dartmouth, and the ships in were mostly minesweepers and destroyers. My 'oppo', Lucy, was from East Ham, so we became close friends, staying so until she died a few years ago.

But many workplaces in the City did remain open and some of them were engaging in important tasks, such as that described by the woman speaking here.

I worked in Ibex House as a clerk, copying out by hand soldiers' records that had been damaged by the enemy. Some of the soldiers were dead, others missing. To get to the premises, we had to contend with unexploded bombs and mines dropped from German planes. They had warning notices on them, as they were ready to go off at any minute. One day they were right by the entrance, but we braved those unexploded bombs for over a week, as we had to get the job done somehow – for all those missing and dead soldiers' relatives.

Danger in the workplace was such a constant that for many it became just something else to be dealt with while you got on with your job. But working in the docks had additional dangers, as the docks were a prime target for the enemy bombers.

. . . the night bombing [of the docks] was the worst and turns were taken to be in control of the air-raid-precaution staff – the night staff. I stood in the square just inside the dock and saw the flames. [It was] one of the more emotional times. I was in charge at night and the place had had thousands and thousands of incendiary bombs raining on it for two or three nights running, and our first-aid staff were essential. I told them not to go out of their dugouts unless they were called out, but somebody – ARP staff whose duty it was to try to put out these incendiaries – wasn't so keen on doing their job, and one of our more conscientious first-aid men was leading his group. He got to the top of his dugout stairs and saw so many incendiaries threatening a certain place that he thought he'd break the rules. It was some distance away, and the first I knew about it was that I was told an HE [high explosive] had fallen completely on their dugout. It would have wiped out the whole lot of them. He was one of the best foremen in my department and a chap I was very friendly with. So I went out, and lo and behold saw just the hole where the dugout was. And you know what I felt? I don't know what I felt. And then, behind me, a voice said, 'Lucky we weren't there!' He'd been right down the other end of the quay.

The following recollection of the hazards of working in the West India Dock is further impressive testimony of people's bravery and their determination to get their jobs done.

. . . it was the time of the flying bombs, and we got used to knowing what lanes they came over, and, of course, not to take too much notice of them while they were still buzzing. But directly they stopped, then your attention was grabbed. You could gauge to some extent the direction from which they were coming. On the day in question there was so much noise where I was superintending the lining up of vehicles for landing craft that I didn't hear a flying bomb coming. But a soldier who was on guard at the pumping house – quite near to me – suddenly said, 'Christ, look!' I looked up and there was this flying bomb coming down just where I was standing. Anyway, I ran to a place where I knew I'd be below the ground level, which was the superintendent's garden, and by our training I stood with my back to the wall, thumbs in my ears and fingers in my eyes, and just waited. There was a terrible crash. I went back up on to the level and there were several vehicles burning, and the soldier and the pump house had disappeared. I went into the first office and asked if everybody was all right, because all the windows were broken, and there were quite a lot of people shrieking and that sort of thing. I saw one of my foremen – I shan't forget this in a hurry – standing there with half a pane of glass sticking out of his rump. I said, 'Is he being attended to?'

The docks operated under really terrifying conditions at times, and on 7 September 1940 North Quay was very heavily bombed. We had tens of thousands of tons of sugar, which went up in flames, and a large number of the huge warehouses were damaged . . . One offshoot of the burning sugar, and the firemen's efforts with their hoses, was the formulating of a very nice thick layer of toffee over it. One thing we didn't realize was that it absolutely jammed up the drains – I mean to such an extent that they became useless. There were hardly any sweets in those days [and] the labourers used to come in and chip lumps of the toffee off the road and take it home. [They] told me, 'It's quite all right, we washed it when we got it home.' It took us a little time to reorganize after the terrific wave of so many days' consecutive bombing, but sooner or later we did get our department working for ship discharge purposes again, and we even got to the state when we would work after an air-raid warning until we could see, or hear, the aeroplanes coming up from Tilbury way.

Traditionally, those who worked in the docks also lived very close by, so even when they were at home they faced almost the same dangers as when they were on duty, the only difference being that some of the highly flammable cargoes were a little further away. This man recalls Black Saturday, 7 September 1940, the night mentioned above, when the docks caught fire.

When they came over that Saturday they dropped the bombs [and] flares and set so much alight. We had a little shelter there in Custom House, out in the yard. Me and my missus and three kids had to sleep there. During the night each bomb thudded – 'cos we were only 100 yards from the dock – into the ground, all around your shelters. *Bang! Bang!* And I really thought, 'Any minute now we're gonna have one ourselves,' or, in the morning I thought, 'When I go out there, there ain't gonna be a bloody thing standing.' This is how I really thought, because it was all night long. When we got up in the morning, they'd got it over there, and they'd got it over there . . . and the Island got it very bad. As I went into the dock – you'd go over to North Bridge and could see all the dock – there's ships all laying askew, where the bombs had dropped in the water and laid all the ships, you know, askew, right, and number 13 shed in the middle row, as they call it, that had a direct hit on the shed where they stored all the cargo . . . it was in a bit of a state. But work must go on, so we just carried on, [even though there] were only a few men available . . . So, right, I went there and you had these bombs dropping, and automatically you just carried on.

As he went on to explain, though, there were some for whom the threat of danger simply became too much.

I'll always remember, I won't mention no names, but there were still certain dockers who'd been discharged out of the army and they had this form of, er . . . when the sirens went they jumped out of the [ship's] hold and ran into the shelter. It's no disrespect, the poor sods, that's how it had got to them, and they ran into the shelter. Me, it was a way of life, it was going every day, so many days, and each night I was sleeping in the bloody shelter – straight home to sleep, and then back the next morning. And when you went out to work, you just didn't know – naturally. You can't grumble, it was a war, and you went on and you took that job and you had to see that job through, and if it could be done tonight, it was gonna get done tonight, and it was gonna sail and that's fair enough.

As well as discharged combatants, such as those described above, women, some of them just teenagers, were also drafted in to the docks to help reduce the labour shortage in what was such a fundamentally important workplace.

. . . they hadn't been used to having young ladies down where the men were. I was put in the export office and worked there for a while.

One of the things we were told was that we must not fraternize with the men. Then I went into the tobacco department and worked there for quite a while, doing jobs that men had done before they'd gone away to the war. On a Thursday I used to go with Mr S–, the pay clerk, and go down to the Albert Dock on the dock bus. We'd do the permanent labourers' pay and go out of the Albert Dock across the road and into the Victoria Dock with the money. Sometimes I used to get cheye-eyeked by the labourers . . . I was only about sixteen and a half, and when I think I used to walk around with this money in a sort of black tin box with a handle on it . . . It's amazing to think that you could actually do that. It made life interesting.

Not all workers were as content with their lot. There were instances of industrial action being taken during the war years, not only in the docks but also in the mining, transport and engineering sectors. The number of strikes actually rose from 940 in 1939 to 2,293 in 1945. With unemployment having fallen from a peak of almost 2.2 million in January 1939 to less than 80,000 by July 1944, employees had a degree of power not seen for years and those in key industries were determined to make themselves heard. It is perhaps an understandable response from those who, in the desperate times of the 1930s, had experienced the feelings of impotence that come from being breadwinners with no means of feeding their families, and who had no wish to return to such a situation when the war was over.

But for those who had no responsibilities or had not experienced bad times, it was possible to take it all far less seriously – as long as they and their loved ones didn't fall foul of the bombs. And even if they did have a brush with the enemy, the optimism of youth can be a wonderful thing. Despite having been bombed out of her home three times and missing most of her last few years of schooling, this woman remembered the somewhat strange work she did as a teenager with enormous enthusiasm.

I worked at Rainbow Corner, Piccadilly, next to the Red Cross. I was a photographer taking pictures of the Yanks as they queued up . . . and I became a cook – when I couldn't cook!

Factory workers in the East End also did unfamiliar work, as their firms turned production over to the war effort. Bryant and May, the matchmakers in Bow, made charges and safety fuses for use in demolition work. Albright and Wilson, the chemical company in Canning Town, became a major shell-filling plant. Wrighton's, the furniture manufacturers of Walthamstow, switched to making Mosquito aircraft – their carpenters being well suited to constructing the wooden-framed aeroplanes. Even what would nowadays be seen as quite mundane jobs were, in their own way, extraordinary, as people performed essential roles for which they had no previous training.

. . . my sister and I both got in the Port of London. My sister was in the Royal Albert Dock and I was in the Royal Victoria. We really enjoyed our work there. We were doing the men's [administrative] work, and about every ten days we used to have to do a night duty on ARP. There was a shelter for the girls and a shelter for the men, and, if the siren went, you had to get up quickly. We had one first-aid girl, my sister and I, and we'd have to go to the men's shelter. They had a big map there and you used to have to plot the aeroplanes coming in – you were in touch with Barking gun battery – and you had to give out a yellow alert warning and a red warning to the people concerned. You know, like the fire station in the Port of London and all that. So really you felt you were doing a good job . . . But you'd have to go to work again the next morning, even if you were up all night. My sister and I always used to volunteer over Christmas, because we felt that we lived right on the job and other people had to come a long way, so she and I always volunteered for Christmas duties. Even those evenings, when we were in the office, before we went down to the shelter for the night, we used to get a bit of food left for us to cook. It wasn't very much, and I always remember one night the superintendent, Mr G–, had gone out to do his rounds to make sure everything was OK, and we went into the kitchen and there was a piece of cheese there. It wasn't very big and my sister said, 'What on earth are we going to do with this? I know, let's make a cheese and potato pie.' So that's what we did, and we thought we were very clever . . . When Mr G– came back, we'd laid the table and set [the pie] on it, he looked at it and said, 'Where's my cheese?' And we looked at each other and said, 'We thought it wouldn't go around, so we've put it in a pie.' He wasn't very pleased!

Those girls were lucky to be able to fulfil their ARP obligations right there where they worked – even if it was one of the most dangerous places to be on duty. Getting in to work and back home again, and then over to where you were supposed to be for your local ARP and other civil defence duties, could be as exhausting and hazardous as the work itself.

Looking back, one wonders how we managed to go to work every day, and we did a long day at that.

And then there was all the other . . . you know, things we had to do. When you think of it now, I'm not sure how we did it. But then, it was what we did, and we were young, I suppose. Had the energy to do it. Somehow!

My fiancé worked at Plessey's prior to his army call-up, and would have to rush back to his lodgings at his sister's house to [get ready to] perform his nightly stint on the anti-aircraft rocket emplacement in the local park. One hectic night the rocket's exhaust incinerated his hastily discarded greatcoat.

Simply getting around London during the war years was complicated, and not only because of the blackout, the unexploded bombs, the fractured gas and water mains and the bomb craters in the road. Public transport itself was disrupted, overcrowded and understaffed. Just at a time when commercial, and even private, motor transport was being seen as the way forward, horses came back into their own for a while.

Private cars had been an unobtainable luxury for most East Enders – even before petrol rationing and shortages – and people were experienced in offering and accepting lifts in all kinds of vehicles supposedly on other business – as anyone who has memories of going 'down hopping' on the back of a moonlighting furniture lorry will testify. There were, however, only so many vehicles available, and as public transport was never going to cope with all those who needed to get around, people walked and cycled what sound like amazing distances to us twenty-first-century couch potatoes in order to get to work.

My apprenticeship completed, it was expected I would leave the company for experience elsewhere. However, the trade union, of which I was a member, circulated the membership, encouraging them to take up employment in factories engaged in war work. This I did, working at a factory in the Chiswick area, travelling by tube on the District Line, Bow Road to Stamford Brook. The work was the manufacture of giant gas masks to be installed in air-raid shelters. The work didn't materialize in the volume expected as the design was faulty. A group of us decided to seek other employment and started work for the Hawker Aircraft Company in East Acton. There were two factories, one for manufacturing aircraft petrol tanks and the other cowlings for aircraft. In the early years of the war they were Hurricane fighters and later the Tornado. Again I travelled by tube – Bow Road to Mile End, changing to the Central Line to East Acton. The journey brought me into contact with thousands of people using the underground stations as air-raid shelters, some still asleep on the platforms. The numbers fell during the Phoney War but went up again when the bombs began to drop. [I changed] my mode of travel, cycling from Ilford to East Acton and back each day. We worked a seven-day week. The journey was twenty miles each way. My route was down to Aldgate into the City and along Oxford Street, down to Shepherd's Bush and into East Acton. Much of the journey was in the early morning, during the blackout when the raids were still on. At the Hawker factory, many hours were spent in air-raid shelters with no production going on. Air-raid warnings went on for hours and hours. This had to stop – one to get the planes made and two to stop the wages being lost playing cards in the shelters. The government introduced a scheme of roof-top spotters who sounded a warning when the enemy planes were actually overhead and an all clear when they had moved over. Factories that adopted this scheme were issued with badges for the employees to wear. They were designed as the air force roundel, as seen on the wings of the planes. No one placed much importance on the badge itself, but it served me well on two occasions. During the raid that became known as the Great Fire of London, I was cycling to work and was held up by the fire at the main post office adjacent to St Paul's Churchyard. The police and the firemen refused to let me continue along the road, but when one of the firemen saw my roundel badge, he lent me a tin hat and allowed me to cycle through St Paul's Churchyard, leaving the helmet hanging on the railing at the other end. On another occasion, when approaching Oxford Circus, my cycle chain came off and locked into derailleur gear. It was still blackout and all I had for light was a cycle torch, which shone light out through a blackout slit. At that moment a policeman came out of the darkness, saw my predicament and directed me to a fire station in Glasshouse Street – quite a walk with a bike over your shoulder! On arrival, the firemen saw my problem and also saw my roundel badge. They took the bike from me, gave me a cup of tea and later returned the bike repaired. I had many experiences on that cycle ride, when unexploded bombs closed roads and lengthy detours had to be made. Once, when the Bayswater Road, near Marble Arch, was blocked, I was directed into Hyde Park. Finding all the exits closed, I cycled a complete circle round the park and finished up lifting my bike over the railings and riding by the unexploded bomb.

*

I went to work in Holborn, where I worked making spectacles for an optician. I left home at 7 a.m. to be there for 8 a.m. We had what were called workman's tickets, so if you didn't travel then you paid more fare. When it got bad and we were going to work, we only got so far on the train and then had to change and go by bus, using our train ticket. But we still only got so far and then we had to walk the rest – over streets full of hosepipes like cables stretched right across them. Life had to go on as normal as we could make it.

During the raids, as you can imagine, travel was difficult and dangerous. I know when I was travelling [to work] in the City, I did the best I could, maybe getting lifts or going different routes around the houses and maybe just walking part of the way.

There was always shanks's pony. We walked everywhere. We just got on with it.

Again the notion that you just had to get on with it – and you really did. If you were on one of the long lists of jobs made exempt from military service because of the essential nature of your employment, you had no legal choice. But, as requirements changed and more recruits were needed for the armed forces, workers in previously reserved occupations might find themselves called up after all, and in some areas exemption might be conferred only on what were considered to be the absolutely essential key workers within the occupation. Public opinion about the merit of such exemptions varied considerably, with some holding the view that people were 'getting away with it', while others felt they were bravely 'doing their bit'.

There was, of course, danger involved in any job in wartime, and in getting to and from the workplace after every shift, especially if you lived in a targeted zone such as the East End.

Dad worked as a fitter on the railway and, as this was a reserved occupation, he was exempt from joining the forces. Despite the fact that he wanted to join the RAF, he could not be released from the railway. So he joined the LDV, later to be called the Home Guard. During the Blitz, Dad went to work from 6 a.m. until 3.30 p.m. and sometimes later than that. After we had dinner, he changed into his uniform and went on guard duty with the Home Guard. He had to guard the railway line between Forest Gate and Manor Park stations, coming back home in time to go back to work at 6 a.m. In those days there was an undertaker's on the corner and one morning he was coming home, walking with a young lady who was also coming off fire-watching duty, when a bomb exploded nearby and they both ended up in the funeral parlour – not hurt but badly shocked.

Even in those pre-congestion-charge days, travellers were being asked, 'Is your journey really necessary?', not that they had much choice if they had to get to work. As we have already seen, all the restrictions and disruptions meant the success of a journey could prove something of a lottery, especially with priority being given to transporting anything or anyone with military or strategic importance. Public transport also had to work with the additional obstacle of place and station names having been erased, to confuse any members of invading enemy forces who might try to find their way to Stepney Green.

All this conspired to make journeys unpleasant at best and impossible at worst, and despite what has been called the 'Blitz spirit' and the often cited wartime camaraderie, tempers still frayed. When they did, the result could be comments which, to say the least, were rather robust . . .

A man was refused entry to our double-decker bus, which was full. 'Buses, I'd shit 'em!' he exclaimed. The conductor replied, 'Well, you'd better shit yourself one, then, mate, because you're not getting on here!'

[8] *Needing the Doctor*

You went to the doctor – if you had the five shillings.

Fearing gas attacks – which mercifully never materialized – initial estimates of civilian casualties were very high and London's hospitals were emptied. Many who would ordinarily have been kept on the wards for some months, including tuberculosis sufferers, were discharged. Those who were judged too sick to be sent home were ferried out to hospitals in the country – often to large houses requisitioned specifically for the purpose – being transported in any available, although not necessarily suitable, vehicle. Priority in London hospitals, as well as in other designated areas, was to be given to those injured in the war.

This enforced movement out of London also applied to pregnant women. From contemporary reports, it appears that civilian first-aiders were given somewhat cursory instructions in how to deliver babies in an emergency. But for those fortunate enough not to have to depend on such amateur assistance, and who could get away from the centre and the threat of raids, maternity homes – similar to the country hospitals – were set up. These were supposedly out of harm's way, some distance from London and other areas with potentially high concentrations of casualties, the idea being that women could experience their confinements in calm and safe surroundings, and introduce their babies into a peaceful world.

That was the plan.

I named her after one of the ladies in the nursing home, because her husband had died at Dunkirk. We had to register babies at birth because of all the bombing.

She was later sent away to Wisbech in Cambridgeshire, being a pregnant war-mum in danger, staying in an old workhouse specially converted into a nursing home for pregnant women. My mum always told me she thought it was an asylum. I must admit to being quite glad it turned out to be the former, as telling people you were born in a one-time workhouse is marginally better than being born in a lunatic asylum. That brought some very rude comments, as you can imagine. Mum didn't go for check-ups like we do now; she went once to her doctor and then no more until the time I was born. She was supposed to have an examination when she was evacuated, but there was an air raid and the nurses all rushed off to take cover, leaving her on her own. She said that when she arrived at the old workhouse she had to walk up a long, winding iron staircase to the ward where she would have me. Can you imagine having to do that when you're about to give birth? After I was born, Mum became very homesick and, contrary to popular belief, she felt she was no safer in Wisbech than in London. The Germans were bombing the Wash, which is quite close, and on one occasion, while walking down the street with some other 'large-sized' ladies, she had to run for cover as a plane rained bullets all along the street! I suppose I could say I was quite lucky – either not to be born in the street or to be born at all. Anyway, she came back to London with me and took her chances with the shelter in the garden.

I was quite pregnant during the early part of the Blitz and we had no shelter, but [a local firm] let us use theirs. The fire wardens were good to us, and one even brought me a deck chair from home so I could sit on it of a night instead of on a bench. One night my father-in-law came into the shelter and held my and my mother-in-law's hand, which was unusual. After a while he and the wardens relaxed. A barrage balloon had got loose and they had thought it was a land mine, which could have killed us all! [Then] I was evacuated to a nursing home in Somerset and went home fourteen days after having my baby. It was a nightmare getting back by myself on a train with a new baby and a large suitcase. But I managed with the help of some kind people. It was during the Blitz and I had rooms at the top of my aunt's house. One night we were fast asleep when my aunt was calling out, 'Get down here with that baby!' I looked out of the window and I saw a mattress all alight being thrown out of next-door's top window. It looked like the whole street was alight. A basket of incendiary bombs had been dropped. I hurried to get dressed, wrapped up the baby and ran downstairs. I decided to go to the [local firm's] shelter, but, you can imagine, the road was lit up like a Christmas tree. I thought, 'My God, there's petrol and oil in that firm.' So I ran back home again with my baby in one arm and my insurance papers and treasures wrapped in a bundle in the other. My sister saw me and pulled me into my mother's house. When she took the baby off me – horrors! – in the panic I had picked her up upside down. I'd been running with her upside down all that time.

Nowadays, many people are concerned about the medicalization of childbirth, which has resulted in what seems to be an almost exponential increase in the number of babies born by elective Caesarean section, but most of them would accept that intervention can be essential if lives are to be saved. Tragically, however, in wartime intervention is not always possible.

My mum gave birth to a baby girl, however she didn't live very long. As we were children, we were never told why, but we were allowed a little peek at her in the tiny coffin that was on the table in the front room.

Post-war parents, benefiting from cheap, reliable contraception and the existence of an – almost – free health service, might well be shocked by the following recollections, and will be further taken aback if they remind themselves that these incidents happened within living memory.

Pregnant again. The youngest wasn't much more than a baby. It was a disaster. How was I going to manage? Then after what happened . . . [she miscarried] God, I regretted those thoughts.

My aunt lived on the other side of the Island at Millwall. She was a widow, and had borne twenty-one sons but not one daughter. Only twelve of these sons lived over five years. Some died at birth, some died – one being a twin – of infant illnesses.

Members of that family who did survive their childhood were to fare little better, but their suffering came in adulthood.

She had seven of her sons serving in the war, and it broke her heart when her youngest son, Charlie, was killed overseas at eighteen years. Victor was killed in a Japanese POW camp. Ben and Ted survived POW camps in Germany.

The family just described was exceptionally large, but big families were the norm. With cramped and overcrowded housing conditions making complete privacy almost impossible, and with the terrors of war going on all around them, children had to grow up fast and find a maturity to deal with these monumental events. It might have been presumed, therefore, that they grew up quickly in other ways too – perhaps even more quickly than children do today – but from the stories I was told, this couldn't have been less true. Many people were surprisingly innocent of the more natural events of everyday life.

It was my friend who told me what my sister was expecting. When people said, 'I see Dora is expecting', I wanted to know, 'What?' So I asked Rosie. 'You don't know nothing, you,' she said. 'She's expecting a baby. And I bet you don't even know where they come from, do you?'

Rosie was right, I didn't know, so she proceeded to tell me. She wasn't quite sure how it got shoved in there, but she knew babies grew inside the mum's belly. As the baby grew, so the belly got bigger and the skin stretched. When the skin wouldn't stretch any more, it burst open and the baby came out of your bellybutton. I thought about this and imagined it like some Jack-in-the-box popping out.

As it was her first baby, Dora had the option of going off to a maternity home in the country for her confinement, but that wasn't always possible if you had other children to care for.

It was 1944 and I was going to have another baby. Mum was going to look after me with a midwife, but she was taken ill and died when I was only four months pregnant. In those days, you had to have someone at home to help – which Mum had done a lot of for people. But without her, I had difficulty finding somewhere to get in. St Andrew's Hospital accepted my booking in the end, but by then the doodlebugs had started. I was having my baby on the top floor of the hospital and there was a raid going on. They sent all the visitors out to find a shelter. In those days they used to keep the babies in a separate nursery, away from the mothers, just bringing them in to feed. But one night was so bad that they brought in all our babies and put them beside our beds. I suppose they thought we could grab our baby and dive under the bed.

I was told how expectant mothers who had no opportunity to book into a hospital – even one in the enemy's direct firing line – might rely on women who 'helped you out' or 'popped in'. And, if the forthcoming event wasn't a happy one, they could, in the words of one woman, 'see to young ladies if they needed help'.

And yet there was still the drive to procreate. Women spoke about feeling a real urge to become pregnant as a way of 'sealing' their marriage before their husbands were posted overseas. It was also suggested to me – although I have nothing but anecdotal evidence for this – that some babies were deliberately conceived as a means of avoiding the call-up for war work which could affect childless women without other dependants.

But while babies might be considered a blessing by most parents, having another 'mouth to feed' was never easy for the poorest families, even with the extra rations. In addition, the strains imposed by lack of sleep and air raids could result in perhaps understandable feelings of sibling rivalry.

My youngest sister, S–, was born sometime during the war. I do not remember much about her other than seeing her in a pram outside . . . She was an intruder, another mouth to feed, send her back from whence she came . . .

I wasn't keen on it. Not one bit. Bloody squawking baby in the shelter every night. *I'd* been the baby till then, if you don't mind! It was hard enough me understanding why I couldn't have stuff before it came along, so how comes there was stuff to be had for the baby when it arrived? I must have been a moaning, horrible little sod!

What happened if you needed to see a doctor because you were unwell? First of all, you had to have one who hadn't been called up, and then you needed to be able to afford the visit.

These comments are representative of what I was told – from the more fortunate to the resigned.

We were lucky in that our local doctor lived just opposite and was immediately on hand. Before the days of the National Health, people paid in to various societies or clubs to meet the bills . . . The one time I had need of medical treatment was for recurring tonsillitis. Following the removal of the offending objects and a subsequent post-operative infection, I spent ten days in Charing Cross hospital in 1944. Our family doctor must have had a fair amount of pull, as most of my contemporaries had their tonsils removed on the kitchen table or at the doctor's in what would today be described as 'Day Surgery'.

We had a panel doctor* so we were covered, but I know there were plenty where we lived who couldn't afford the little bit we had to pay in. So they'd have to pay at the time – if they could. It'd be a bigger, one-off amount, you see.

If you were ill, there *were* doctors' surgeries – some of the doctors were past calling up age – and if there was an accident there was always the hospital. But far and away the best cure for minor ills were home cures. We didn't go to the doctor's nearly as much then.

The doctors were probably very good, but on the whole, if you were ill you just had to get well again.

Being ill called for a case of 'grin and bear it' – as was normal before the NHS.

In those pre-National Health Service days – the NHS was eventually put in place in 1948 – and with most medical services being turned over to the war effort, the remaining facilities were often less than adequate, and, of course, many medicines that are taken for granted today simply weren't available. Despite our complaints about the present-day health service,

* An arrangement whereby a weekly amount was paid to a fund to cover the cost of any treatment.

we still have subsidized prescriptions, free emergency care, someone to look after our teeth, our eyes and so on. But these basics would have been luxuries for most East End families and a dose of 'jollop' – either home-made or bought from the chemist – would have been the most likely 'cure' for whatever it was that ailed you.

One way to maintain good health was thought to be to 'keep regular', and ensuring your bowels were in proper working order became almost a national obsession. This was in no short measure thanks to the 'Radio Doctor', Dr Charles Hill, MP, who broadcast during the daily five-minute *Kitchen Front* slot on the wireless. If you chose not to follow what is always described as his 'avuncular advice' – such as taking healthy exercise and making sure that you followed a sensible diet, preferably topped up with prunes – there was always my mother's favourite insurance against the dreaded constipation: 'liquorice wood'. This came in the form of bits of twig about six inches in length that could be bought from the chemist's. They were steeped in water during the week, until it was time to drink the pond-like liquor on Friday night. Like most children subjected to this home remedy, if we had to have the stuff, my brother and I much preferred chewing on the twigs, tearing at the bark with our teeth until the stringy white fibres showed through, rather than swallowing the vile liquid.

There were plenty of other equally nasty home remedies and patent medicines to choose from, and, in the days before advertising standards were imposed, all kinds of claims could be made for their products by the manufacturers. As just one contemporary newspaper advertisement put it, 'Just remember, nightly Bile Beans improve your health and figure' – presumably by stopping you ballooning up like a blimp as a result of your sluggish bowels. Syrup of Figs was another favourite for that particular organ, but other parts of the body and their associated ailments were not neglected.

People remembered small, niggling complaints that weren't serious enough to keep them from their daily routine but were bad enough to make them feel under the weather. These usually resulted from the close proximity of others, poor, damp housing and shelters, and, not unexpectedly, exhaustion. A simple cut or boil could soon become infected when your system wasn't in tip-top condition, but in knowledgeable households that was soon dealt with. My father, for instance, remembers the agonies of his mother applying steaming-hot bread poultices, and heating bottles until a vacuum was created and then slapping them on to his bare skin until the infection was 'drawn' – a procedure similar to the 'cupping' practised in Russia to this today.

High temperatures and flu-like symptoms would be kept well hidden from your mum unless you wanted to be dosed up with Fennings Fever Cure – a disgusting-tasting clear liquid in a square-shouldered bottle that seemed to cure just by the power of the patient seeing the cork being pulled from the neck. It was probably marginally better, however, than the boiled onion hung around your neck in an old sock recalled by some unfortunate individuals. If the cold 'went to your chest', then Friar's Balsam would be dropped into a basin of steaming-hot water and you would inhale the eye-stinging vapour under a towel tent draped over your head. Another well-remembered favourite to 'clear your tubes' was having Vick rubbed on your chest, although there were recollections of having the gooey balm rubbed on to the soles of the feet. Worst of all were the tales of having a good dip in the jar with your finger and then poking it down your throat. This sounds unbelievably horrible, if not downright dangerous, but I was assured by several people – including my own dad – that it 'did the trick'. Equally unlikely-sounding but probably not as risky – and also very economical – was the practice of saving the urine you collected in your po overnight and using it to soak your feet to cure chilblains – a then very common but no less unpleasant complaint. I think I would have preferred to daub my heels with the stick of patent ointment that was described to me as being like a fatter version of a modern-day lip salve – even if you did have to pay for it.

If all these wonders failed to work their magic and you still felt poorly – exhausted from lack of sleep and made jittery by the relentless bombing raids – there were various 'nerve tonics', such as Phosferine. This was claimed to be a 'proven remedy' for all sorts of physical ailments, and also for the nasty-sounding 'brain fag'. Then there were 'tonic wines' like Wincarnis, which were advertised as being good for most of what ailed you, and no doubt helped you to forget what did.

If you didn't want to be seen drinking wine – even of the tonic variety – there was another cure-all: a bottle of Dr Collis Browne's Chlorodine mixture. This was used for everything from upset stomachs to feelings of general malady; the fact that it seemed to work is no surprise, as its then not exactly secret ingredient was morphine. Less radically, there was always a nice cup of Ovaltine, Horlicks or Bournvita, but many people would still find themselves at the mercy of something their grandmother swore by.

If you were ill, you just went to bed and got over it with some junk your nan had cooked up. A sore throat was cured by rubbing winter green oil on your chest and having one of my dad's sweaty socks tied round your throat. A broken bone was dealt with by calling in the doctor, who had a pony and trap. He would get you to hospital to have it tended to and it seemed to me that in those days they were always boiling things. There was this grey sort of paste that they got red hot, spread it on some lint and smacked it on your leg to reduce the swelling. So you didn't break anything if you could help it.

Not that there was exactly a choice as to whether you avoided or gave in to health problems.

Perhaps it was the Blitz that destroyed our immune system, or, when we were evacuated, perhaps we just did not get on with the [country] air, but you name the illness and we got it. My sister endured chronic jaundice, and I nearly died with whooping cough after having had serious measles. My mum – a typical townie – thrust a pitchfork through her foot, and my dad, on one of his Sunday visits to us, nearly died in the bath due to a faulty gas geyser.

Some of the stories carried the weight of their sadness in the stark simplicity and stoicism of their telling.

During the quiet period [when the bombing had eased off for a while] my three-year-old half-sister died of measles and lack of medicine.

It was at this time [during the heavy raids] that my mother had an operation at the London Hospital to remove one of her breasts, and was sent to St Albans to convalesce. Our home in Bow was destroyed by a direct hit and we rented a place in Ilford where my mother went to after convalescence. My wife-to-be came too, to nurse her, and so we could see more of each other.

Close proximity to strangers, whether because of evacuation, being in a rest centre after being bombed out, taking refuge in a public shelter or, as in this woman's case, being in the forces, could result in some unpleasant problems – ones which could not be cured by something your nan had boiled up in a pot on the stove.

When I was in the Wrens, I came out in a rash all around my waist. I showed it to the rest of the girls in my cabin and they all came to the conclusion that I had shingles. The next morning, I reported to sickbay. When I saw the MO, he asked what job I was doing. When I told him, he laughed and said I had had a flea trapped round my middle. I was so indignant about it and told him that I did not normally have them. His reply was that he could see that, or else I wouldn't have made such a fuss.

Being among so many people in the shelter, anything contagious soon went round, and scabies* was *very* contagious, and hard to treat. You were sent to a clinic where they painted you with a strong disinfectant, which stung – a lot.

Irritation, however unpleasant, was one thing, but there were far worse problems, and not all of them caused by the enemy. If the very worst happened and your illness was fatal, funerals still had to be conducted. This was a particular problem in our street, as the East End has traditionally been a place where a 'good send-off' is seen as a matter of great pride, and where often elaborate wreaths are sent and memorials are erected to honour the interests and loves of the dearly departed. In the circumstances, families did their best.

My dad's parents died, and, being during the war, the funerals were basic. I remember seeing their coffins with only one wreath on top. My mum always made sure she had a bit of mourning to wear, and anyone could borrow that if they could fit into it. There were only a few mourners at their funerals, and a cup of tea and a sandwich when they came back from the cemetery. And that was it.

A couple of days after I came home from hospital with my new baby, my mother-in-law was killed by a bomb on her house in Stepney. The day of the funeral was calm [no bombs], but it was done in a hurry in case there was a raid.

* An extremely irritating skin infestation caused by tiny mites, which spreads rapidly in crowded conditions.

And in those austere, demanding days – even during the worst of the bombing – friends and neighbours did their bit to keep at least some of the traditions going.

Everyone who could turned out to watch, and men stood still and raised their caps.

The funeral cortège went really slowly past the pub on the corner where he used to drink, and everyone was standing outside, showing their respect.

Just as these sad, if everyday, rituals continued – a way of dealing with an inevitable part of life – so too did the war, causing disruption and further distress to already distraught mourners.

I was about ten at the time of Grandma's funeral – by then Dad had been called up for the army, so we had gone to stay with Grandma and Grandad at their home in [Shoreditch]. Grandma was lying in her coffin in the front room when we caught the blast from a doodlebug. It rocked the house and most of the ceiling came in on my bed, where I was sleeping with Dad, who'd come back to be with the family for the funeral. The ceiling came down in the kitchen too, all over the tarts and sandwiches set out for the funeral that was going to be that day. My uncle tried to salvage what he could by blowing off the debris – but without much luck. Auntie Ada was going upstairs when it happened and got the full force of the large iron doorknocker in her back. The front door had been wrenched right off its hinges. Everyone was so scared what they might find in the front room, but, fortunately, although the windows were caved in on top of the coffin, the coffin itself hadn't moved and everyone breathed a sigh of relief. The funeral went ahead, but the doodlebug had caused great devastation, scoring a direct hit on a nearby block of flats.

[9] *Courting and Weddings*

> I was married at Bow church and am happy to say we are still together, even though our little flat was flattened before we even lived in it.

Courting – not always the easiest of times for hesitant, or even bold, young couples – was made more complicated and challenging by the uncertainties of war. In more predictable and familiar circumstances, it wouldn't have been unusual for a young person to pair up with a boy or girl from the same street; or to become involved with the brother, sister or cousin of a school friend or workmate who lived just a few turnings away. But whoever your 'sweetheart' was, it was unlikely that he or she would be a complete stranger.

You might get to meet them in a variety of ways. You'd stop perhaps for a shy, shoulder-swinging chat as you wandered up and down the East India Dock Road with your gang of mates in the so-called Monkey Parade, pointing out who you 'fancied' – and making it clear by the way you looked at them. Or maybe you'd have a first, tentative dance together at a local hop, such as those run at the Tin Hut in Poplar, which might lead to an even more tentative first kiss. Others would size each other up in the queue outside the Troxy, while waiting for the next double feature to begin.

All these courtship rituals continued in their own truncated ways. But now there were other new, more adventurous possibilities to be embraced – or shied away from – as those same young people encountered potential partners they would ordinarily never have met.

They might literally bump into someone in the blackout; or

be thrown together in the less alarming but previously equally unlikely new woman-friendly workplaces; or even, and probably most glamorously, have met foreigners posted to Britain before being shipped off to the front. Young British men also went abroad with their units, of course, and would not only be experiencing new cultures, climates and landscapes, but also new possibilities for romance.

With the ugliness and horror of what was going on around them, and with so much uncertainty in the world, it is little wonder that solace was sought, and sometimes found, in the arms of another, regardless of whether those arms belonged to the one you loved or to someone you had just met.

There was plenty of evidence to back up tales of 'bad behaviour': an alarming increase in sexually transmitted diseases, which had the government issuing flurries of posters; a soaring divorce rate; and a marked rise in the birth of what were then referred to as 'illegitimate' – or worse – children. But there were also stories of charmingly 'old-fashioned', respectable young couples doing what was 'right', despite the topsy-turvy situation in which they were conducting their relationships.

I'd gone to meet my boyfriend and had told my dad – who was very strict – that we were going to the pictures, but in fact we went to the park! Two romantics walking hand-in-hand, with not a care in the world – but ourselves. But all of a sudden the ack-ack guns were blazing. We hid under a bridge until the raid finished. When we got home, there's Dad doing his nut. He was demented. The cinema where we had said we were going had been hit and he didn't know if we were dead or alive.

B– would hang around outside our house. He would perch on his bike waiting for my appearance – like a princess, he said – and I used to clean the outside of the sash windows, sitting on the outside windowledge with my legs inside the room. This was how we carried out our courtship chats, with Mum shouting, 'How long are you going to be cleaning those windows?' Other times, B– and his mates would sit over the road, fooling around to make me laugh. Lovely days!

When the war began I had just completed my sheet metal worker's apprenticeship at the Commercial Gas Company, Harford Street, Stepney, and was aged twenty-one years. My wife-to-be had come to London [from Norwich] to nurse at the Western Hospital, Fulham. Later, after we had met, she was transferred to the Joyce Green Hospital, Dartford, Kent, to nurse the soldiers returning from Dunkirk. When the first sirens sounded we were both walking in Hyde Park near Marble Arch. A– had to return immediately to the Western Hospital to deal with expected casualties and I returned home to Malmesbury Road in Bow. The alarm proved to be a non-event and we entered into the period of the Phoney War of alarms but no bombing. Our courtship continued. We usually met at Marble Arch and visited the cinema there. A– then caught the number 74 bus back to Fulham and I the number 8 back to Old Ford and Bow. Soon our courtship became more difficult, as A– was based at the Joyce Green Hospital at Dartford. Dartford was a restricted area and after crossing Woolwich Ferry or tunnel, permission to travel on to Dartford had to be obtained. On one occasion, when A– was travelling over to see me in Bow, a very heavy raid occurred. A–, crossing the Thames by the Woolwich Tunnel, was not allowed out and spent the night there, arriving at my home thoroughly fed up and in need of a meal just as I was leaving for work.

And, depending on your view, there was a comforting innocence or a stifling inevitability in working people's lives that seems so at odds with the earth-shattering events occurring all around them and that saw young adults still being treated as 'boys' and 'girls'.

I met my husband in a youth club in Poplar. It was run mostly to keep the young boys and girls off the streets during the blackout. We used to go there dancing to a radiogram. My [future] husband called in there with his friend for a cup of tea. He was on leave from the army. And that's how I met him – you know, talking about the tea and the dancing, and someone said, 'You know he's been in here several times to see if you were around, but you weren't here.' And gradually I got to know him, and from that time we went out for about two years, and I got engaged and then I was called up before the tribunal as regards war and going into the air force. I'd put down the air force, [but] my parents were rather reluctant at the thought of me going. So I had to face a tribunal, which was to decide whether I should do active service or carry on with the war work, which I was doing in [the factory]. I went before the tribunal and said I had an interest in the air force, but, unfortunately, my mother was unable to get about because she'd had her leg amputated and she was rather worried about me going abroad. So they gave me a three-month exemption and said that I'd have to consider whether I should go or whether I would get married. If I got married that would alter the circumstances. This was January 1943, and I got married April 1943, so I carried on with my work at [the factory] and also used to do fire-watching for the street.

I don't know if we were – how can I put it? – *slower* in them days, but I do know we never got up to much, well, not anything that would have got us, or should I say *me*, into trouble. I was too scared of Mum and Dad. If I'd have got in the family way – God help me! So I was a good girl instead.

Our courting days were so different to those today. Mostly it was done at the front gate, or sometimes in the living room, when everyone was out, and then you had to be more or less engaged. I remember at one time [I was a Wren] and I was going out with an air gunner I had been to school with. We stood close together, with our arms around each other, and it was quite a while before I realized the poor chap had gone to sleep. He was home on a forty-eight-hour pass and hadn't slept for a long time. Sadly, he was one of those who didn't make it. There were some sweet, precious times during the war. I married my second cousin. While he was out in the Middle East, we were just mates. Even as kids we were close. He was four years older than me, and I used to think he was the cat's whiskers. He went out there in 1940, and I did write to him while he was abroad, but I used to cheat. We used to write on what they called aerographs. The letters would be put on to a film reel and flown out and then processed that end. We used to number our letters in case they didn't make it, and, if I didn't write for a couple of weeks, I used to miss a few numbers. I did tell him about it later.

Living in such unsure times, and being separated from what you knew and felt comfortable with – all the while experiencing fears about what might happen to you and your loved ones – could intensify relationships in a way that makes some of today's more casual arrangements seem sadly lacking in passion.

But there could be a harsh price to pay for such powerful emotions. This woman remembers her cousin falling in love with a GI who was based near her aunt's village, to which she had been evacuated. He was one of their 'Sunday soldiers' – young, often lonely young Americans who were given hospitality in the homes of welcoming villagers.

'Guns' was . . . not his real name, but all his mates called him that as he was a tail gunner. My cousins, Gwen and Phyllis, were home the first Sunday he came, with a bag of goodies in one hand and his cap in the other. He was very shy, said hardly anything, and looked very uncomfortable. I was the ice-breaker because he said he had a little sister my age back in the States, so chatterbox me wanted to know what she was like – I got shown loads of photos – what did she wear etc. After tea, Phyllis started to play the piano. 'Do you know "American Patrol"?' he asked. Phyllis did her best and all the family joined in singing – as was usual when we were all together. He came to chapel with us, and on the walk home, he somehow fell in step with Gwen. I don't know how he managed it, but the next Sunday, and every Sunday after that, he was our Sunday soldier [where the GIs went for lunch was supposed to be decided by lot]. He started walking out with Gwen and you could see they were very much in love. The Sundays he didn't turn up he sent someone with a message that he was 'on duty', 'on a mission' or 'had no pass'. When he did get off, he would go round the house where Gwen was in service and wait for her to snatch a few minutes off. I was a regular go-between for them, running messages to and from the camp, asking whoever was on guard to give him the notes I carried if I couldn't see him. I became quite well known to the sentries, often getting treated to gum, and they gave me badges and studs off their coats.

One Sunday, Guns didn't turn up, so off I went with the usual message. I got no satisfactory answer from anyone I asked. I was told to 'come back tomorrow', maybe they would know something then. Nothing unusual in that. I often had to do that. Back I went Monday, still no satisfaction. Gwen made me go back again the same night. This time, a soldier whom I recognized was coming out.

'Seen Guns?' I asked. 'Gwen's going potty.'

'Go and tell Gwen to come down,' he said.

'She can't,' I told him, 'she's working.'

'Go and tell her it's important,' he insisted.

I was fed up with all this back and froing, so I took my time, stopping to lark about with my friend and not getting to Gwen until five o'clock. I went to the back of the big house where she worked. I knew she had seen me, but she was working and couldn't get away. I waited there for ages, when she finally came out, and I told her what was said. She disappeared into the house, this time only for a second, came running out, putting her coat on as she came.

'I'm going home for my tea now,' I said. 'I'll get told off as it is.'

'Please, come with me. I don't want to go on my own. I'll make it all right at home later,' she assured me.

So off we went at a running walk, ignoring passers-by. I looked up at Gwen. She was worried, really worried. Don't know why, I thought, this often happened – well, no, they never told me to fetch Gwen before. We got to the camp gate and the soldier was still waiting for us. He said something to Gwen, and I was ordered to stay where I was: 'Don't you dare move.'

A Jeep came out to the gate with Gwen sitting very upright in the back. 'Get in, kid. I'll take you both back home.' The ride was taken in complete silence. Something's wrong, I thought. Don't ask any questions, I thought.

Standing in the kitchen, Gwen told Aunt Bessie, 'He's dead. Guns is dead. He went on a mission and his plane got shot down. There's no mistake. His mates in another plane saw the plane blown up and fall to the ground.' She then shut herself in the bathroom and cried her heart out.

Some were fortunate enough to have happier endings to their relationships, or at least the opportunity to make them so. There was also more of a belief in, a desire for or sometimes an insistence on marriage. The number of UK marriages rose from around 409,000 in 1938 to around 429,000 in 1942. Many agreed that the urgency of the situation – the knowledge that your 'chap' was about to be sent overseas – heightened the romance and was the impetus behind much of the flood of hurried ceremonies.

My brother and his girl got married and he was sent to Gibraltar, where he spent six years with the air force. What a way to spend [the first years of] your marriage. But that happened to a lot of us.

I bought my wedding dress and bridesmaids' dresses before the clothing coupons came into being. I also ordered my wedding cake

– three tiers. There were rumours that we were going to be rationed and of course everybody started panic-buying. The baker's informed me in June that I would have to have my wedding cake soon as they were not being allowed to make any more. My goodness, what a cake! I imagine they must have used all the fruit they had left. What a beauty . . . My fiancé managed to get home the day before the wedding, so we waited with bated breath, praying for a peaceful day. The glorious day arrived and not one bomb was dropped, but, my word, didn't he make up for it that night. We had our wedding meal in the community hall, then made our way back to our flat. To say the walls were bursting at the seams would be an understatement. Nevertheless, we all crammed in and sang our hearts out. 'Knees up, Mother Brown' had never had such a rendering. If we had to go, at least we would go happy. The wardens were constantly knocking at the door to report a light showing, which rather puzzled us, until we realized that every time they knocked they got a drink, so they were taking it in turns. My husband and I had seven days together, then he had to return to his unit and I didn't see him for five years, but, thank God, he survived.

Not all marriages that began with so much hope and desire would have anything like such joyful endings.

I was married in early 1940. My husband had joined the army and I got pregnant right away – silly me – but I loved her lots and still do. [He] was a different story . . .

It seemed so right at the time. The thing to do, the *only* thing to do. But it was a big mistake for both of us. We got carried away. Caught up in it all. And I'm sure we weren't the only ones who made a mistake. It felt like everyone was getting married. What's that saying? Marry in haste, repent at leisure. That was us, all right. Shame.

At the beginning of the war, it was still possible to find all the trimmings for the big traditional 'do' so loved by people in our street, but as rationing and restrictions took hold, ceremonies and celebrations had to be adapted accordingly.

With a little help from family and friends, however, there was usually something that could be pulled out of the hat to make the day special. There were stories of cardboard edifices taking the place of wedding cakes; with ingredients being short and sugar icing not permitted, these covers might hide a plain cake or even have a little drawer containing a small piece of fruit cake. In one case, the 'real' thing was donated to the bride by someone who had saved a layer of her pre-war wedding cake, having intended to ice it for the christening party of her first child. Others told of borrowed wedding dresses. In the case of people who spoke to me, these came from family or friends, but there was a scheme for women in the services, run by the author Barbara Cartland, which allowed them to borrow white wedding gowns so that they didn't have to marry in uniform. Some women opted for a stylish but 'sensible' two-piece costume, which could be worn again. Food rationing and alcohol shortages were seen as a challenge rather than a disappointment, and travel restrictions and a loved one's leave being cut short were practically expected. Yet despite all that, the happy couple could still be spliced in good heart and their guests entertained, even though the newlyweds realized they might not see each other for months or maybe years.

The reception was held in the home, so food rations were saved up and food scrounged by all the family. I know one of my aunts turned up with a catering-size tin of fruit cocktail. We never did ask where it came from . . . The family all saved and helped towards the ingredients, and we had a very helpful baker who called every day with his horse and cart. He took the ingredients away and, like the fairy godmother, came back with a lovely cake. So many had just a plain effort or a fruit cake under a cardboard cutout of a wedding cake.

[My boyfriend was] away for a long time then. When he came home, he came to the house on the Saturday. He'd been away for nineteen months. It was lovely to see him. I went back with him to his mother's to stay and we got engaged in the December . . . But then he sailed in the January [and didn't return until] March on a week's leave. He said, 'Shall we get married?' So I asked my parents if it was all right. They said yes, but my mother said, 'Not Thursday, leave it till Saturday.'

Quite honestly, to this day, I don't know where all the food came from. The customs officers [at work] let us use their dining room, and my friends came, and even a square wedding cake with icing came from somewhere. I don't know to this day where it came from. I had a lovely white wedding. My father gave me his coupons, and I had a white dress because my mother wanted me to get married in white. My boss at work was a really very nice gentleman and when I told him I wanted a fortnight off to get married, he said, 'Fools rush in where angels fear to tread', but he was wrong that time, because we've been married a long time now and it's been very happy.

Jack and I married on 11 February 1942 by special licence – a Wednesday, a borrowed dress and veil – my dear dad went with me, to get [the licence] at Westminster, forty-eight hours beforehand, because I was under twenty-one – in fact, under nineteen. [On the day] an auntie kept looking up the road to see if there was a soldier in sight, as we didn't know if he would get home – he had already had embarcation leave three weeks earlier, when we became engaged. Yes, the wedding took place. We had a lovely party – like they used to be. Everyone contributed and we were still dancing the night away at eight the next morning! But Jack left six hours later. I didn't see him again for three and a half years, and then it was for just twenty-eight days' leave. Then Jack had to return overseas. He was a corporal in the famous 8th Army and I am so proud of him. We wrote to each other almost every day. It certainly was love.

Not everyone's timing was as propitious or as welcome, and it is important to remind ourselves again that these events took place within living memory and yet describe experiences very different from what we would expect, or accept, today. There are stories of adults being treated by their parents in a manner that suggests they are still infants, but parents back then expected to have considerable influence over their grown-up offspring, to the extent that a couple might be coerced into going through what was little more than an enforced marriage.

I came home from work one night and Mother was so angry. My elder sister and her young man had told her that my sister was pregnant. What a disgrace. Mother had a special licence organized in no time. The sad thing was that neither of them wanted to get married. Mum's family all rallied round and provided them with different items, [but] it was not a happy marriage.

When I got married, my new husband was billeted in a place where you were allowed to visit – some places you couldn't travel to without a permit – but my mother was quite against it. So I didn't visit him.

I managed to get leave for my wedding [by saying] I had to get married! On arrival at my fiancée J–'s house, my father-in-law-to-be had a quiet word with me. He said that J– should stay at home to continue to help her mother and that nothing would change other than her name. He then, to my utter amazement, gave me a book by Dr Marie Stopes [about 'married life'] to read. After the ceremony we went back to the house for the wedding breakfast, then Father-in-law proudly announces a visit to 'his' local pub for a few drinks. Father-in-law, in full uniform, led the way and headed the entrance. What followed then was complete mayhem! As we went in, we heard the landlady tell her beer-pullers, 'Drinks only for the regulars and for service boys and girls.' J–'s dad stuck his head under the shelves above him and said to the landlady, pointing to his stripes, 'What the bloody hell are these, then?' Or words to that effect! And shook the shelves in anger. Glasses were strewn all over the place and, not to put too fine a point on it, we were 'ushered out', all twenty or so of the wedding party. On the pavement outside, the landlady followed with much screaming. She pointed at my poor mum and shouted, 'You started all this,' and slapped her face! Mother-in-law intervened and got shoved roughly to one side. After a while, all was calm and we trooped back to the house. Me? I was going on honeymoon to Devon [he had family evacuated there] the following day and didn't want to arrive with a black eye, split lip or cauliflower ear, so I kept my distance but close enough to look after my family. All was calm when we arrived back at the house, but Father-in-law would not give up and took us to another pub. By this time I was much concerned with how the night would finish, as there was the sound of buzz bombs coming to their noisy pitch. In the meanwhile, someone had quietly spoken to Dad and told him that a Black Maria was outside his house. Luckily, all things – including the buzz bombs – calmed down and I slept with my new bride for the first time, who cuddled me like I was a baby and told me not to worry! To this day, my dear wife has never shown panic, bless her. Amazing woman!

Once the restrictions and regulations of war really took hold and the bombing raids became almost inevitable, an increasing measure of resourcefulness was called for if a bride was to have an occasion even slightly resembling the wedding she had dreamed of.

We had to rush about to make arrangements to be married in a different church, because the one we'd thought we were going to get married in was bombed to the ground the week before the wedding!

*

Two weeks before my wedding, Mr Hitler kindly blasted the entire roof tiles from my aunt's house, where our reception was to be held. It was only due to my uncle, a resourceful petty officer, and a press gang of naval ratings plus a large tarpaulin that the reception went ahead. The wedding [itself] was punctuated by explosions still destroying the neighbourhood. At the reception, as we proudly stood up as man and wife to make a thank-you speech, my new husband clumsily knocked a vase of daffodils from the windowsill behind us. I ended up having my photo taken in the garden with a very wet rear.

At the rear of the vicarage [where they rented rooms] a bomb-disposal unit was stationed. The vicar regularly buried those who had given their lives in this dangerous form of military service. He worked with another vicar from a nearby church, sharing responsibilities. He did one week of weddings and one week of funerals! He maintained that it always rained when his turn came round for funerals. When couples came to the vicarage to rehearse the marriage ceremony, I was often asked to stand in as best man, usually in my dishevelled working clothes after my twenty-mile cycle ride home from work in the aircraft factory! My wife and I were married by the same vicar – at no charge as our wedding present – in November 1940. He loaned us a gold and silver cutlery set for the wedding party. Aunts, uncles and friends who could make it attended the wedding party in the vicarage. Mother was a dab hand at creating something to eat out of the rations.

The woman speaking below served as a Wren during the war. Here she recalls the novel role that circumstances thrust upon her on her dear friend and fellow Cockney's special day.

I was 'best man' at her wedding. She was married at St Stephen's Church, East Ham. Her brother-in-law was supposed to be best man but his ship was held up, so I stepped into the breach. My mother said that it looked as if we were on parade, as all the wedding party were in uniform – including Lucy's bridesmaid!

Such a charming and relaxed attitude to what might have been considered the 'proper' way of doing things can't help but be impressive. However, on other occasions the resourcefulness wasn't always of an entirely legal nature.

I had a white wedding with three bridesmaids and a black-market reception – it was very good!

If we hadn't have had all that gear from under the counter, we'd have had bugger all to give the guests! It was a smashing do.

The standard of the 'do' wasn't the only thing that mattered. The simplest of gestures could help make the day special, as could what at any other time might have been thought of as very ordinary, everyday gifts – second-hand, maybe, but treasured items to help establish the couple in their new home.

There were a few wedding presents – one or two being possessions treasured by the givers.

Honestly, you wouldn't believe how grateful we were. Grateful for anything anyone wanted to give us. Not like kids today, who expect to move into a fully furnished place with all the best of everything. I remember the first time I saw one of their wedding lists – bloody hell! It was more a case of what wasn't on it than what was! Thing is, daft as it sounds, we weren't doing too badly for once. My new husband was in the forces and I was doing uniforms – piecework, good money if you were fast like me – but there was nothing to buy. Nothing.

*

My wedding was austere and limited due to rationing and we set up home with the minimum.

Furnishing our home was, of course, a matter of having the coupons. We only bought the basic furniture, which was made to wartime 'Utility' standards, and the stairs had no carpet on them for years.

Plenty of people expressed views on what they thought was important in a marriage, and quite a few commented on how the focus today appears to be on the wedding day and all the very expensive, yet ephemeral trimmings rather than on the union that is being solemnized.

Like many couples, we had one room with family. With us it was my family home. We did get some coupons to get some Utility furniture, and the rest we begged or borrowed, but things were so different then. Expectations were not as high as they are now. It was a different world. It is hard to explain unless you have experienced it. We lived in that one room until we had enough points for a council house, and that wasn't until there were five of us – the two of us, a three-year-old and three-month-old twins. We used to sleep on a bed settee, my eldest on a bed chair, and the twins in cradles. It used to be quite cosy during the day, but at night it was a different matter.

We made up our minds to get married. My father wasn't too keen but he didn't object. He was worried about the war and told me what was in front of me, but we prayed that nothing would happen and had a beautiful wedding in spite of food rationing and coupons, no wedding cake, a honeymoon in an air-raid shelter and in a church that had been bombed in the Blitz.

It was him I wanted to marry, not a fancy frock or a big party. I'm not saying I'd have said no to all that fairy-tale stuff, if I could have had it, but it would have been extra, on top of everything else. Like a bonus, if you see what I'm getting at. It was my Jack I wanted. To be with him for the rest of my life.

The tragedy was that in such uncertain times even good marriages might end in premature heartbreak.

We got married, childhood sweethearts. Then he went away. He never came back.

A family four doors from us went to a wedding in [Bethnal Green] when the siren went. They took shelter in a big building that had a very good shelter in the basement. But a bomb went right through the ventilation shaft and many of those sheltering were killed. There was S–, who had lovely ginger hair, he was on leave from his unit for the wedding and was killed. So were two of his brothers. The whole family was either injured, badly shocked or killed. It took years for them to accept what had happened.

In spite of the danger, the often improvised celebrations and the lack of home comforts, plenty of wartime marriages proved to be great successes, some lasting for what might seem to today's newlyweds an astonishingly long time.

The tutor at the St John Ambulance Brigade, where we trained, was a man called Ernest. I married him in June 1944 and was married for almost fifty-seven years. Our wedding was wonderful. Family and friends rallied round with clothing coupons and so on, and we had a traditional white wedding at Bow church. We went off for a few days to Olney, and the day before our return a V1 doodlebug dropped on our home. My father and his workmates had made rooms in my mother-in-law's house into a self-contained flat for us. Had we been there, no doubt we would not have survived. We gathered what little we could salvage and went back to live with my father.

*

My mum and dad were married in November 1939, before he went [into the Royal Marines]. It was arranged in a rush by my gran, who put the banns up for them. I think they wanted to wait, but it was taken out of their hands. Apparently it poured with rain all day and the photographer was drunk and didn't take any photos. My mum had to dress up in her wedding gown a couple of weeks later and stand in the garden just so she had a record of her wedding day. I was born in the following September, so I suppose that makes me a Christmas baby!

The fact that some marriages lasted longer than the majority do now, however, doesn't necessarily mean that they were better or happier, or that relationships 'in the good old days' were all bastions of mutual understanding and sweet harmony.

Nanny F– would not let Grandad smoke his smelly old pipe in her presence and, because she could not read, didn't allow Grandad to do the same. To get round this the family waited until she had gone to sleep and then gave Grandad his pipe and papers to enjoy without her knowing. A chair would be put up against the bedroom door to stop her coming out and surprising him.

Do you know, I can't remember my parents ever talking to each other. They talked about what was for tea and that, but never about anything – properly. And they went through all that together and all – the war and the bombs and the Blitz and that. I reckon it was more like a habit than a love match. It wouldn't have done for me. It would have depressed the hell out of me, I reckon. But we have more choices, I suppose. It's sad, though, when you think of it. I never said anything to Mum about it, never mentioned it, but they might have had a chance to be happy with someone else.

More serious than disputes over tobacco were the problems experienced by married individuals away from home caused by the unfamiliar proximity of members of the opposite sex. A combination of loneliness, brought on by separation from family, and an undermining of society's usual expectations and views on acceptable behaviour drove some people to 'enjoy' themselves regardless of the cost or the consequences. Unfaithfulness flourished in this world of confusing and rapidly changing mores, and the increase in 'Dear John' letters, divorces, illegal abortions and sexually transmitted diseases reflects this change.

It was hard to cope with being separated. Very hard. And there were lots of tears. But you had to keep full of hope, and that's what we did, we stayed at home and hoped, although there were plenty who had affairs while their husbands were away.

I saw a fight between a soldier and a spiv. By the shouting, I could gather that it was over the soldier's wife. It seems spivs had the knack of not being called up and always seemed to prey on married women while their husbands were away.

You'd spot her of an evening, going 'up West', done up to the nines. A real soldiers' friend she was – and sailors' and airmen's. Pity she wasn't more of a friend to her old man when he was away in Africa. Took him for a proper mug.

I am afraid to say that there was a certain amount of playing away. I myself was going around with a naval officer for a couple of weeks, until one of his shipmates told me that he was engaged and that was the end of a beautiful friendship. Loneliness was hard and some people found it too hard, especially when they were away from home, or did not have any family to turn to. There were so many 'Dear John' letters in those days, but then there were some who were just looking for a bit of company for the day or evening . . . Then again, there were some who just thought that 'while the cat's away, the mice will play'. Life was tough.

Accusations and disapproval were, of course, not always warranted.

My mum was forever accusing my dad of having affairs with the nurses that he had to work with in his job. He didn't deserve it, though, because he was a big old softy and he adored us.

However, if suspicions were in any way well founded, rough justice would prevail – usually within the confines of the family unit – leaving the straying individual with little choice in the matter.

One of my aunts ran off with a man from the next street, but my uncles and their friends formed a posse and she was hunted, captured and soon brought back into line. That was how it was.

Perhaps more sadly, it might be the innocent parties who had the choices about their relationships taken away from them – not that they were necessarily rendered helpless or didn't get their own back in some way.

Life wasn't too good for me. I couldn't stand sheltering with my daughter in the underground any more, so I got her into a place in [Kent]. I missed her terribly and was working really hard. My husband was away in the forces. He had risen to being an officer at this stage and, being an 'officer and a gentleman', was supposed to pay me my allowance by cheque, which I never got. I came home one day from work and there he was with a German woman, standing bold as brass on his mother's doorstep! He had been carrying on with her, the widow of a U-boat commander! I decided there and then to go to the police. When I told them, they were astounded and said, 'Don't worry, mate. She'll be gone by tomorrow!' And she was. May I say she did me a favour, as I wouldn't have had the wonderful life I have today with my second husband. But at the time he broke my heart. He was my first sweetheart.

I was on leave one day, in a pub in Bognor Regis with my wife and her dad, when who walked in but the wife of one of the chaps I'd worked with back in London, and whom I knew very well. But her escort was a Canadian soldier. You can imagine the look on her face when she saw me. They say it's a small world!

My nan told me, 'Your mother won't be coming home, 'cause she's buggered off with a bloke.' She would come round and take me out sometimes. My dad never stopped her. Just me and her, until one afternoon she brought me home late, left me on the doorstep and left. My dad was worried and cross. He asked me where we had been. I told him Chrisp Street, and to the church. My dad asked, 'What did you go to the church for?' And I told him: 'Mum and a man was playing jigger-jiggs on the railings.' I didn't know any different, but my dad soon worked out what had happened, although, as a child, I thought it was playing. I never went out with her alone after that. Another time, a man knocked on the door and my nan answered it. He asked if he could see R– [her mother]. Nan said, 'She isn't here, but I'm her mother.' At which point the man almost fainted on the doorstep. Nan called my dad, who gave him some water. He then told my dad that he had given R– the money to buy a new black coat for her mother's funeral. No wonder he nearly fainted.

[10] *Family Separation and Loss*

> The thing that stands out in my memory is of a long train carrying troops – my husband amongst them – and me standing at St Pancras station waiting for him. Lovely when he was coming home on leave, but so sad when he was going back.

It wasn't just being called up for the services or for civilian war work in another part of the country that could separate you from your loved ones. This woman remembers a wartime childhood in which she not only lost her home when it was reduced to rubble by a bombing raid, but was then taken away from her neighbourhood and herded from one reception centre to another. The authorities and hard-working volunteers tried to do their best for her and her family, but they were still obliged to stay – camp out, almost – in what were essentially bleak, inhospitable halls requisitioned from schools and churches. And, when her family were eventually found somewhere more permanent, she then suffered the additional loss of being separated from her mother and sister.

The next day there were more tears. We – our family – were being split up. My mother, now remarried, with her two-year-old baby daughter and my sister with her baby son were told that a clippie* in Netherwood Street would let them have her back bedroom and share the kitchen while her husband was away in the army. The parting came with many tears and hopes that we – Nan, Dad and me – would

* A female bus conductor.

not be billeted far from them, and vows of seeing them as soon as we could. We got billeted at West Hampstead with a Mrs I–. She had a ground-floor flat there and was willing to let us have her back room. Her husband was away in the air force, and she lived there with her baby son. We were taken there by car and it seemed miles away from where my sister was, in Kilburn – which caused more tears.

'We've just got to make the best of it,' Dad said, as we looked around our large but unfriendly room. It had one big double bed, a table and some chairs, a chest of drawers – that we had nothing to put in [as everything had been lost in the bombing] – and a big built-in-the-wall cupboard. This cupboard was to be our shelter, Mrs I– explained. She slept with her son in a cupboard under the stairs during the air raids, as she had no shelter, and that cupboard of ours, she assured us, was as safe as houses. *Safe as houses?!* [Her family home had just been flattened by a bomb.] From our window the garden ran straight down to the railway lines, and as railway lines seemed to be the next hitting point for the German bombers, we spent many more nights with bombs dropping all around us. Dad took the mattress off the bed and put it on the cupboard floor, and there we slept night after night. I was OK, being only small I was inside, but Dad and Nan were only in it up to their waists. 'Well, if they drop a bomb on us now, Mother, we'll be legless!' Dad joked.

We found where my sister and mum were and did the long walk from West Hampstead to Kilburn most days, sometimes while a raid was going on. I saw enemy planes fighting with our planes and bombs actually leaving the bomb carriage of German planes many times on that walk to Kilburn. 'If it's not got our number on that bomb, we'll be all right,' Dad used to say, and still we kept walking. Come to think of it, what else could we have done? There was nowhere to take cover anyway. And how could you tell what number was on them? They fell so fast. And I didn't know what our number was anyway. Unless, I thought, it was my identity number.

My sister and mum were quite comfortable with Blanche, the clippie. She was friendly to them, and us, when we called around – unlike Mrs

I–, who insisted we kept ourselves to ourselves, and only mixed and talked with us when absolutely necessary. Dad pestered the WVS to find us a place of our own, nearer the rest of the family. 'We're a family and we don't want old Adolf to part us now,' Dad told them.

Families from our street weren't exactly spoiled for choice when it came to what they could do and where they could go following the loss of their homes in the bombing. The issue was usually settled pragmatically and, to put it bluntly, they had very little say in the matter. But most people realized that if they were to keep their head during those difficult times, they would have to do what they could and make the best of things.

One woman spoke of having to take shelter in Aldgate when an early-evening raid damaged the workshop where she was employed as a machinist. She reached home many hours later, in the thick of the blackout, to find her family home had also been bombed – in fact, razed to the ground. Frantic for news of her family, she ran up and down the street in the dark until she came across someone picking through the remains of their equally devastated home, searching for anything that might not be damaged. The neighbour was able to tell her that her mother and sisters had put what was left of their belongings into a borrowed pram and had gone looking for lodgings a few turnings away, where someone had said that a woman had a couple of rooms available. It was the first time her family had left the street in which every one of them had been born, the first time they had not lived in the same street as her aunts, uncles, cousins and grandparents. It is hard to imagine, with the geographical mobility available to us today, the shock and wrench of such a separation.

Some less fortunate individuals didn't even have the benefit of those limited choices – about where they lived and from whom they were separated.

My father went into the army, my mother had to do war work in a factory, and it was decided I was to be evacuated. I did not go with the school but went privately for ten shillings per week. Our rent for the house was a pound and money was very short for Mum. Before I was evacuated, to help out with the housekeeping, Mum took in a lodger, W–, a sixteen-year-old German Jewish boy who had managed to get away from Germany just before his family were sent to the concentration camps. He settled down well and to me he was a big brother. But he was interned and ended up being sent to Australia.

Sadly, even for previously very close families, separation could sometimes become permanent, as close-knit bonds unravelled due to enforced relocation following enemy action and the demands of war.

What with the bombing, evacuation and the need to change jobs, families and neighbours in the East End were split. Many never renewed contacts or went back to live in the close family units that prevailed before the war. My uncle, who lived opposite us in Bow, had to leave after the bomb hit our houses. He ended up in north London. During my childhood and up until the bombing, he had called in to see my mother practically every day. After he moved he was seldom seen.

You have to realize that we didn't have phones and the computers like you do now, or the cars to get around as you felt like it. A few miles was like the other side of the world. Anything more than a few turnings away was as good as being abroad.

It is easy enough to be fearful at any time when you have been forcibly separated from loved ones, wondering if they are well and safe and happy, but during wartime those fears are elevated to new levels, as you are all too aware of the dangers they might be facing.

. . . there were couples who were separated for years. Some husbands, fathers and sons were taken prisoners of war right at the beginning and had to spend the whole war in prison camps. I can't imagine what that must have been like. It was bad enough Ron being in the Middle East for three and a half years.

*

Separation was one of the hardest things in the war. Our family were all in different places: my mum was at home; my dad, a dredging engineer with the Merchant Navy who was seconded to the Royal Navy; my brother evacuated to Wales; and myself in the WRNS. Just before D-Day my mother was frantic, because neither my father nor I could be in touch with her. My mum used to ring me every week from the telephone box on the corner of our road, so when she rang and did not get through she didn't know what to think.

It was because most homes didn't have telephones that letters were still the routine means of keeping in touch. And while the sight of the telegram boy was feared because of the bad news he was sure to be bringing to your doorstep, a visit from the postman was always welcome, as he just might be bringing you news of your loved one. Whether it was from your husband, boyfriend, brother, son or maybe even your daughter, and even if it was telling you all leave was cancelled, at least you knew they were all right. Well, up until the time they had written that last letter . . .

You tried to cope with the separation by living for letters, writing them all the time. Sometimes you had to wait weeks to get one.

I worked at Blackfriars for a good few of the war years and when there were delayed-action bombs dropped we used to have to work on invoices etc. in the back of the company's lorries. The company manufactured paint that was used on ships, planes, tanks and so on. We backed on to the River Thames, and there was a flat roof where we could go up and eat our sandwiches at lunchtime, and I could sit and write my love letters. They would begin, 'Darling, I am on the roof looking out on the Thames and writing to send my love all to you, tucked in this envelope.'

The shock, followed by denial and then the pain of realization, and then the months and probably years of mourning, experienced by those people who would never get another letter was always there as a possibility, hanging in the background whenever your loved ones were away. But it still seemed so unfair, so wrong, when it happened. Having gone through so much already – what with the bombing, the fear and the uncertainty – they were now having to pay the 'ultimate price' of permanent separation.

A single bed was put in my room alongside the double bed. My aunt said I was to sleep in the single bed as my cousin Phyllis was coming home. Poor Phyllis, her boyfriend had been killed in action, and she had been given a few days off [from the munitions factory]. She cried herself to sleep for three nights. I crept out of the single bed in beside her in the double and we cuddled up until she cried herself to sleep.

R– was to become a pilot in the RAF and, sadly, lose his life.

There was the awful dread of seeing the telegram boy. You knew it was bad news for some poor soul.

[My brother] was, in my eyes, a great guy with an outstanding personality. He would date all the girls, but made a lot of fuss of our beloved mother and would be seen accompanying Mum and Dad into their local for their once-a-week drink. When the call-up came, she took it deeply to heart that her boys were to go to war. [My brother] never failed to write great letters, full of humour to boost her morale when times were low. I believe his letters, above all else, were the tonic she so needed. Sadly, he was the son not to come back. I still feel the grief as I write this. It was to change her life for ever. She deserved so much more. Her life, her very existence, was for us, her family. [My brother] to die at twenty-two years of age was to be our biggest family tragedy.

*

V– was to go to France with the British Expeditionary Force and disaster was to strike the family. He went missing. Most of the soldiers were back via Dunkirk but alas no news of V–. There was a death knell over our house, but he was to arrive home unannounced. Apparently his platoon was cut off at Dunkirk but he managed to drive along to Brest, which at the time was surrounded by Germans, where he boarded a merchant ship and managed to get home with all his equipment. There was joy at home and celebrating into the early hours – the favourite son was home – but sadly the joy was to be short-lived. V– was to go abroad again with the 8th Army to Africa. His letters would continue to flow and provide real morale boosters to all of us. The letters contained no complaints. As I get older I find there is little time to spare, it simply flies by, but in those days, with three brothers abroad in the army, we at home seemed to live in limbo land and time stood still. Tragedy was to strike finally. V– was taken prisoner in Tobruk whilst serving in the 8th Army. We received no word until, to our relief, one post saying he was a prisoner of war with the Italians in Benghazi. There was total relief in the family, but, again, silence. V–'s closest friend, S–, was to turn up in the Ship – the public house opposite our home. He would not come to the house to give the tragic news. He had been on board the prison ship with V–. There were 500 troops battened down below. There was no Red Cross flag. S– was taken for his stint of air on deck. A British submarine fired over the bows of the ship, signalling to heave to. The ship started to run the gauntlet [and] the submarine sank the ship. There were only seventeen survivors, including eleven crew. S– survived because he just happened to be on deck. The tragedy was called 'The Missing Five Hundred'. We got the tragic news that night from S– and it appeared in the *Evening News* with V–'s picture. S– had obviously given the story. This sad event was to alter our whole concept of family life as we knew it. It would have been far better if Mum had had a nervous breakdown, but no, she was to carry on for the sake of us all. [It was] as if half of her had died along with him.

*

One of my father's brothers, L–, was killed in the jungle wars with the Japanese in Burma. He was just twenty years of age at the time and is buried in one of the vast cemeteries near Rangoon. No one in the family had known where and how he died, [but] I found out that L– was a member of the famous Chindits and was killed along with thousands of others in the most horrific circumstances. I don't suppose for one minute that he, or other youngsters like him, realized the dangers.

Such tragic stories cannot help but touch us – not least because of the youth of those involved. And as this was a war that put civilians in the firing line, there are equally tragic stories from there too, right on the home front, in the middle of our street.

. . . how we survived seemed a miracle, when every morning on your way to work you saw the terrible devastation, and men digging under the rubble hoping to find some survivors. Thank God some of us survived, but thousands didn't, and our hearts went out to the families that lost their loved ones. I lost some of my friends. One, on his way home from work, was literally blown to pieces by a land mine, only because that night he had to take the shop's takings round to his manager's house, which was in the opposite direction to his normal route back home. The land mine dropped and blew him to smithereens. His wife was left with a little boy of three years old. She never married again. Then, less than a month later, the police came to her door and told her a bomb had gone off in the underground. They had found a body with her address in his pocket. She ended up identifying her husband's brother, who was dead, his wife, who had been critically injured, his mother, who was just about alive but who had had her leg blown off, and his little five-year-old daughter, who was also dead. Soon the whole family was gone. Another friend, whose husband was on leave, came out of the shelter during a lull and went indoors, probably to make a cup of tea, and the house got a direct hit. They were both killed. She was expecting their first baby.

A young member of my family – he was twenty-six – was in an exempt job. He was helping the wardens when a land mine fell nearby and he was crushed by the wall of a shop falling on him. When he was taken to the mortuary, his age was stated as being about sixty years, so he must have died a terrifying death. Six weeks after he died, a letter arrived telling him he was no longer in a reserved occupation and would be called up. Who knows, perhaps if he had gone into the services earlier on he may have lived.

Living and working close to the Thames was one of the most dangerous places of all for civilians.

Her three brothers and her father worked as lightermen in the docks, two on one shift and two on the other. One day they were on the barge, changing shifts, when the barge had a direct hit with a bomb. They were all killed. It was so sad.

It was Saturday and Sunday night under the Morrison for us. [The bombing] was so bad on the Sunday night that my father said I was not to go to school, but he had to go to work. I went up to lie on the bed. I was quite bad-tempered, because I'm awful if I haven't slept. My mother went to lie on the couch in the sitting room and [her father] rode off to work on his bike. People told us afterwards that every morning he would always get off and look at the boats. We didn't know that. After a bit there was this great wooooooofff! The ceilings came down, the windows came in, the door evidently just missed my mother and she came and screamed at me, 'Are you all right?' I walked to her over the rubble and she said, 'Get dressed and I'll go and ring your father.' There was only the pub that had a phone, and she went down and phoned [his firm] and said, 'Will you tell my husband that we're all right?' And they said, 'He's not here yet.' And she said, 'Oh, that's funny, he should be. Anyway, he'll be there in a minute.' So she came back, and I can remember that she said [her father's name] all of a sudden and ran out down to the river. She knew what had happened and I ran after her. My mother found him. He was lying there on that piece of the shore . . . As I got there, an ARP man was just coming up to Mum [and he] put his arms round her, saying, 'There's nothing you can do for him.' My dad had been killed by the blast, and, you know, he looked perfectly all right, but my mother said afterwards that his neck must have been broken, because it was at an angle. And I remember that my friend A–, who lived in the flats behind – evidently this thing, so people told us, had been coming towards our houses, and it had caught these flats and they'd gone to powder. A–'s brother, who was on his paper round, had seen this happen, and had seen where his parents had gone. They were dug out because he was able to direct them in, so his father and mother were in hospital. A– was all right, [but] they'd lost their home. Old Mr L– and Mrs L– were killed, and young N– and his father and mother and the new baby were killed, and young K– downstairs and her father were killed. She was eighteen, a pretty girl. I can't remember who else – people on the riverfront. That really was the end of a whole chapter. Our lives changed completely.

Despite so much sadness, there was also good news for some, with the long years of separation at an end – for the time being, at least.

I was on a little break from work in London, staying with my aunt and uncle at their home near Oxford, and my young brother, who was seventeen, made the train journey from London – Gran paid his fare – to bring me a card from the army. It said in bold print, 'I AM COMING HOME. Do not write any more until you hear from me.' And it was filled in by my Jack! Remember, we hadn't seen each other for three and a half years. I packed my bag and caught the next train home, pinching myself – was it true?

[11] *Community Spirit*

> In spite of hardship and heartaches, the people I knew showed an indomitable spirit of support, sympathy, sharing and caring.

As with the stories about people 'getting on with it' and 'doing their bit', much has been made of the selflessness displayed as a result of the so-called 'Blitz spirit' that permeated the home front, which saw people facing all kinds of dangers as they put the needs and safety of others above their own. But some have questioned whether that spirit actually existed, wondering if it wasn't rather a response to the massive propaganda campaign that the authorities quite rightly saw as essential for bringing the war to a successful conclusion. Newspapers, newsreels, wireless broadcasts, posters and leaflets urged people on and congratulated their good humour and exemplary behaviour in dealing with the exhaustion, the horrors and the austerity.

The Blitz in particular was a good leveller of most people. We most of us had nothing, or very little, but that very little was shared.

It was the horrors of the bombing, particularly the Blitz, that made people more aware of their neighbours and family and drew them all together. It made people closer to their neighbours.

Whatever the reasons for such feelings, they certainly had a lasting impact on the people who lived during that period. I was told many stories of great heroism and of pride at the way people managed to carry on for the sake of others during such demanding times. And there were memories of outstanding generosity that might shame many of us today, when we have so much more – in material terms at least.

One day, when I was about twelve, Dad took me with him to deliver a load. We were making our way to Rotherhithe Tunnel when my dad saw an old drunk sprawled out on the pavement. It was cold. Dad, although he was teetotal all his life, got out of his lorry and took a ten-bob note from his wallet, put the note into his jacket pocket, then took off his jacket and somehow managed to put it on to the drunk. He sat him up and we drove off. Dad said, 'Don't tell your mum, boy.' I'm sitting here with tears in my eyes as I write this. At my age! Ten shillings was a lot of money. When we got home I heard Dad say [to my mum], 'I left my bloody coat at the delivery today. Sod it.' Years after, I was talking to Mum and I asked if she remembered this and she said that she did. She also guessed that Dad had probably given his jacket away. She told me that he even tried to tell her he had lost a pair of boots while he was bathing his feet one day. My dad and his dad were the salt of the earth – I think I knew it at the time. Just wish I could tell them both.

On several occasions, my father brought a strange soldier or sailor into our home. He would sleep on the floor in front of the fire with a greatcoat over him. He had usually met them in the local pub, looking for relatives whose homes had been destroyed. Mum would share what food we had with them and send them off with dripping toast for breakfast, so they could go and look for their families.

Two streets were flattened by a mine. I lost friends and relations, and my grandmother was trapped for eight hours under the debris. A Salvation Army boy crawled through a hole with a feeding cup and stayed with Gran, singing. Gran had a good voice, even though she was eighty. Everyone outside sang with them. That's Londoners.

With the fragmentation of communities and the subsequent opportunities for a media-fuelled fear of crime, we have become suspicious of strangers in a way that would have been totally alien for most of the people who told me their stories about living through the war.

The good thing I remember is the friendliness of the people. Complete strangers would practically drag you into their house if you were caught outside in a raid, and as a child it seemed everyone was an 'aunt' or 'uncle'. The Home Guard managed to throw a party for local children who had their fathers away from home on military service or who had lost relatives in the bombing raids.

I was running along – scared, if you really want to know. I wasn't much more than a kid, but I'd got myself lost and didn't know where I was, and this lady, she opened her door and she took me in. She took me out to the back yard and let me stay in her shelter with her. I suppose she could have made a ricket,* and I could have nicked her handbag, but she saw I needed help and so she helped me. She might have had young sons my own age. But whatever reason, how genuine is that?

Of course, not everyone's stories showed people displaying anything like such kindness to others, or even having the slightest trace of community spirit – a balance to the sort of memories of childhood in which the sun was always shining.†

Talk about selfish. We always tried to help our neighbours – sharing what we had, and even putting on as good a party as we could if it was a child's birthday in the street – but this woman . . . We were sitting by her in the shelter, and nobody could get any fruit – well,

* A mistake.

† See *Pull No More Bines*, my history of hop picking. The final part of the book deals with the use of personal testimony.

maybe one orange if you queued up for an hour. But this lady took out a large bag of oranges, grapes, bananas, apples and so on, and sat and ate them all with great relish. Our mouths were watering as we sat there watching her. I think she enjoyed our pitiful hunger. She didn't offer us even one little bit of her precious fruit. Where she got all that fruit from, nobody knew, but it was a scene I'll never forget. That woman had no conscience!

She was always all right for everything, that one. I'm not saying, or suggesting, that there was anything out of the way, but she could have shared it out. Given the kids a treat now and again. But no, that didn't enter her mind.

Boils down to what you're like as a person. You're either generous or you're a nasty bastard. I know what I'd rather be. You can't take it with you, can you? And in the war you never knew if you were the next poor bugger who was gonna cop it. So what was the point in being greedy?

Even if you were an established member of a community and regularly treated the local kids, being foreign could absolve your neighbours from any sense of gratitude or loyalty during those frightening and sensitive days.

[There was] the café round the corner in Green Street, Jack's Café was its name, and Jack was an Italian who would always give the kids a free penn'orth of ice cream if they took their own cups along. It was a shame about Jack the Italian man, because when Mussolini brought the Eyties into the war on Hitler's side, our local grown-ups smashed Jack's shop windows and did a lot of wreckage there. The police took care of the situation by getting him through the crowds outside and accompanying him to the local nick. From there he was posted to an internment camp for enemy aliens until the end of the war.

There was also antagonism to other kinds of people who were noticeably different – not, in this case, because they were foreign, and so potentially in league with the enemy, but because they were 'posh', that being another way of saying 'idle rich'.

There was plenty of criticism of those who continued to dine in expensive restaurants as a way of getting round the rationing regulations. There were supposed to be restrictions on what was available in commercial dining rooms, but there were ways of 'avoiding' such inconveniences. Those same people were also sheltering safely and in some comfort in the basements and cellars of the grand hotels and restaurants where they dined. It is no wonder that resentment was felt by East Enders who, nightly, piled down below the streets on to the overcrowded, squalid underground platforms, sharing a bucket latrine with hundreds of others.

It did surprise me, however, that so many comments were made along the lines of the following two quotes, when the generally accepted view of Cockneys' feelings has always been different.

We're always hearing now how popular the Queen Mother has always been – with everyone, no exceptions at all. 'We all feel a warm glow round our hearts when we think of this wonderful woman' blah, blah, blah . . . Well, not in my experience, no, certainly not among East End adults in the 1940s. Then, in the East End, in my experience she was deeply unpopular, especially among women. They rather liked the King . . . But her? No. 'Fanlight-bloody-Fanny. Always got just one too many furs or feathers on. And that silly bloody flapping paw of hers! Gets right up my nose, that!' I heard this over and over again whenever she was mentioned. While her famous remark after Buckingham Palace had a window broken, 'Now I can look the East End in the face' – well, that didn't sit very well at all. Nowadays, it's always quoted as if it was a wise, lovable utterance. Then, quite rightly, it was regarded as being a crass, incredibly stupid one. People who had lost homes, everything they'd once owned, didn't agree that having the brickwork scorched on one of one's twelve mansions was quite enough to qualify as an equal sufferer.

Before the war I'd been a follower of the royal family. I felt sorry for them about the abdication and that – you know how it is with families, one of them causing aggravation for the rest – but I felt, when they started showing up round here, it was like Lord and Lady Muck. Strange, but it had never occurred to me before to think of them like that. We're standing there in rubble – the remains of *our homes* – and they're doing all the sympathetic bit: 'Aw dear, what a shame!' But if their place got bombed they had plenty of others to go to. They didn't have to go and sleep in no poxy church hall. I used to read all about what they did in the papers and the newsreels and that before then. I still do, a bit. But they stopped having me over then. I saw through them and what they were all about.

But save a few comments similar to these – although not as strongly worded – the majority of people who spoke to me believed and remembered that the royals were welcomed on their visits to the East End. They were not treated like the celebrities of today – gawped at and clamoured around – but were regarded with a degree of reverence probably unfamiliar to younger generations, who have experienced the very public unravelling of a royal family previously shielded from such intimate scrutiny.

But regardless of people's views on the King and Queen and their entourage, it would always be the closeness to loved ones and community, rather than a visit from the royals, that they really craved.

[Despite their house having had a direct hit] my parents moved back into a house in the same road in Bow, so strong was the attraction of the area and the people they knew.

*

We lived close to all our relations – my mother's mum, my dad's mum, and all my aunts and uncles – all within short walking distance.

. . . we moved into Stepney after having been bombed out of [our home] at the Abbey Arms area of West Ham. Here we lived in a three-storeyed house with my mother's family – aunts, uncles, Grandad, Grandma and Father. Being a big dock working family, cousins and anyone who was not taken on for work in the docks that day would sit around having tea and toast, telling stories. My old gran, being the matriarch of the family, would serve them and fuss and worry over us all like an old hen.

As the war went on and the bombing got worse, houses got more and more overcrowded. But you didn't complain, you bunked in where you could. Good job we got on with the rest of the family or there'd have been murders!

The man speaking above, a young lad during the war, makes a good point. Intimacy was fine if you got on with those you were being forced to live with in such close proximity. But what if you needed privacy or had a secret you didn't want to share? Then the closeness could become claustrophobic, resulting in a fear of gossip that could be the consequence of too many people 'knowing your business'.

A young girl in our street got pregnant before she was married. The disgrace made the family feel that they had to move away. Sadly, her parents insisted the child be put up for adoption and she wasn't allowed to bond with her baby. It broke her heart, because she was engaged to marry the father the following year.

There were rumours about her being a bit too friendly with one or two chaps while her husband was away fighting. One of the old girls next door said so to her face one day and that was it, she did a moonlight [flit] and we never saw her again. Or her husband. Suppose she wrote to him with some old fanny about what had happened. Some pack of lies. She was one of them who'd flap her eyelids and get her own way.

But the majority of stories were both positive and moving in the way they told of people doing whatever they could to help one another, even when they themselves had so little or had suffered personally from the bombing or the loss of someone close. They spoke of emerging from the shelter in the morning to the sights and smells of their street after it had been hit in a bombing raid – a raid that hadn't just damaged the fabric of their homes but had cut off electricity supplies and the gas and water mains – and how someone still managed to fetch water from somewhere and boil a kettle on a Primus stove, so they could share a cup of tea with their neighbours before getting down to what might otherwise have been the completely demoralizing task of going through yet another clean-up.

Or, as in the following woman's case, there were stories about just trying to make life that little bit more pleasant, despite being tired out after a full day's work.

I'd been in a tap-dancing troupe since I was six [and] I left school at thirteen and three-quarters, when war broke out. I didn't want to be evacuated so took a job. My first was with a company in Chadwell Heath as a messenger girl, taking a suitcase full of papers to Aldgate, twice a day on the Green Line coach. Then, when I was fifteen, I went to work with a friend in Aldwych. We used to go straight from work to meet up with the rest of the troupe to entertain in works canteens, such as Tate and Lyle, Gillette's, Yardley's and so on, and forces clubs. We did lots of variety shows and pantomimes in theatres – Collins's Music Hall, the Theatre Royal in Stratford, the Brixton Empress, the Trocadero, Golders Green Hippodrome, to name a few. We also put on entertainment in the London parks, as the government was encouraging 'Holidays at Home'. We appeared with some well-known names of the day, including Donald Peers, Adelaide Hall, Kitty Masters and Wilson, Kepple and Betty. We often went down into the shelters around east London. We'd rig up a stage at the end of the platform where, later, the people would be sleeping. The trains were going by, the war was on, but we took it all in our stride!

So the government's continual stream of well-placed newspaper stories, radio and cinema broadcasts, posters and public information leaflets appears, on the whole, to have had the desired effect of keeping community spirit in good shape. But behind all the enthusiasm and jollity, other information was also being distributed that displayed a full awareness of conditions on the home front. The authorities knew that people not only faced danger and even death from the bombers, but also might be required to do something rather more challenging than making a cuppa for members of their community.

For instance, there were leaflets with phonetically spelled German orders for if you came into direct contact with invaders. Use of this linguistic skill would, apparently, facilitate their immediate surrender and allow you to march them to the appropriate authority. Rather more alarming was the pamphlet that detailed another possibility: if you were, for some reason, in possession of 'some kind of a bomb or hand-grenade' when you spotted the enemy in a vehicle on British soil, you must 'let them have it', regardless of whether it was being driven by someone you knew well who had been forced to do so at gunpoint.

But it has to be remembered that this was a time when public appeals of all kinds saw people responding in a patriotic and admirably selfless manner for the good of the community as a whole. To give an example, when a request was broadcast for the women of Britain to donate everything they had that was made of aluminum, so that it could be melted down and transformed into 'Spitfires, Hurricanes, Blenheims and Wellingtons', an overwhelmingly generous rush of donations soon filled the WVS-run collection points. Questions were asked after the initial eagerness subsided a little. Why, for instance, were the scrap merchants not cleared of their aluminium? And why hadn't the stock of new aluminium goods been impounded from shops and warehouses, leaving housewives with their cooking pots? Cynics suggested that those sources would have required payment rather than personal sacrifice on the part of the civilian population, but the whole event was such a great propaganda success that few complained. Soon railings from private and communal gardens and parks alike were to become part of the same salvage drive, such was the desire to do what you could for your community and the country as a whole, to be part of one of the many battles it would take to win the war.

[12] *Breaking the Rules*

Someone walked into our house during a raid and nicked the clock right off the mantelpiece.

Statistics show a rise of over 50 per cent in crime during the six-year period of the war, with civilian murders reaching a peak in 1942. One notorious individual, the mass-murderer John Christie, was to kill his first known victims in 1943 and 1944; and Gordon Cummins, the so-called 'Blackout Ripper', pursued his infamous career under the cover of wartime lighting restrictions, his six-day spree of murder and mutilation in 1942 still able to appal a public already assaulted by the atrocities of war.

There was also, as there is now, a fear of crime as well as crime itself, and there were many rumours and unsubstantiated scare stories about perverts and robbers preying on women as they made their way home from work in the blackout. Other stories can be authenticated. One well-known London career criminal has freely admitted in both print and television interviews that he was only too pleased to take advantage of the abnormal circumstances of those extraordinary times. He has recently been quoted as saying that rationing and shortages were, for him, a 'thieves' charter' that made the war years the best of his life – 'paradise', to use his word. He further went on to claim that he would never forgive Hitler for losing the war and thus curtailing his business opportunities.

The authorities were obviously aware of these problems and worried that the rise in crime would undermine the morale of those living in the bomb-ravaged capital. It was even feared at one point that law and order would break down altogether and the military would have to be brought in to restore calm.

But these scares apart, it was the more commonplace crimes that affected the general public, for – just as in peacetime – most people were not touched by the horrendous crimes of the likes of Christie and Cummins. For the person on the street, their experience of criminals and their doings would be limited to the activities of black marketeers, spivs, looters and, indirectly, profiteers.

There were always those who were fed up going without and weren't averse to buying the odd pair of 'dodgy' nylons or a half-dozen fresh eggs and a few rashers of bacon from someone who had the 'contacts'. It isn't often that money can't buy privilege, whatever form it takes: larger portions in a fancy restaurant, 'under the counter' extras from the butcher or a new winter coat to keep you warm despite your lack of coupons to buy one.

There was a lot of dealing done on the black market. We could get shoes without coupons for £5 a pair and could pay through the nose for food. I don't remember going hungry.

My pal C– had this little old motor, a truck, and he'd always got plenty of fuel for it. We used to go out to Essex, to the farms, in the early hours and fetch back a load of gear to sell. We had regular customers and could knock out any extras we had in the pub. Food? Yeah, course it was food. It weren't horse shit we was selling!

Dad would come home on leave quite often and I remember him placing the rifle that he had to carry in the corner of the kitchen. He and his brothers were, for a time, stationed at an army supplies depot. I have heard many stories about his two brothers, who were always stealing small items from the store to sell for beer money. Dad was a gentleman at heart and was too frightened to steal, or so it seemed. On one occasion, Dad took me for a walk up to the main road. Suddenly a large army truck went past, slowed down but didn't stop.

The canvas cover at the rear opened and a large case containing tins of sardines was thrown out on to the road near us. I had to pick them up while Dad kept watch, and I also had to carry them home. They went down a treat over the next few days. I got the feeling later in life that I had to carry the stolen goods in case the police stopped us. Dad would have been sent to prison for sure for stealing food during the war. I wonder what they would have done to me . . . [When] sugar was on ration and hard to get hold of, Dad took me out one day to a pub in the Mile End Road called the Three Crowns. He came out with a carrier bag containing several bags of sugar, which I had to take home whilst he stayed in the pub drinking. It was obvious that the police would not stop me – at least, I'm glad they didn't.

Pubs have always been places where 'deals' of all kinds could be done.

There was this feller who came in the pub. Not a local man, but he could get you anything you could afford to buy. It was all 'ask no questions, get told no lies'. We'd have stuff off him now and again. Good stuff. Not that much, though – we couldn't afford it!

Of course, some of the deals didn't turn out quite as expected.

In the pub, somebody said to my mum that he could get her a bit of black-market pork if she fancied it. She was well chuffed – our rations were so tiny. Anyway, there was a knock on the door and a man staggered in with half of a huge pig. It was as tall as him, with the head still on it. I can see those ears now! Mum went crazy: 'Get it out of my house. I don't want it!' I couldn't stop laughing.

Another focus for those interested in obtaining supplies from what is now called the 'informal economy' was the docks. The criminally minded have seen the ships and warehouses on the Thames as profitable sources of luxury and hard-to-get goods for hundred of years. Offences ranging from pilfering, through large-scale theft, to outright piracy were such a problem by the end of the eighteenth century that the River Police, the first professionally organized force in the whole country, was set up to cope with the embarrassingly huge losses. But the image of the docks as one huge Aladdin's cave, regularly topped up for the sole benefit of thieves, continued despite their existence, and the war would prove no hindrance either. If anything, the shortages became a spur.

Of course, being near the docks, we saw a good supply of stolen food – sugar, tea, currants, meat. I remember these all being on offer from time to time.

You'd have to be on fair terms with the dock coppers, then you could come out with more or less what you fancied. To an extent. You wouldn't take the piss or anything.

The stories they'd tell you about how they brought the stuff out – stuffed down their trousers, strapped to their bellies, carrying stuff out in a bucket or a barrow right out in the open, like you was entitled. Some reckoned that that was a good way to nick buckets or barrows – pretending you was fetching something out in it, when really it was the barrow or bucket you was after! The stories – they'd get more and more wild as they drank more and more Scotch, and, believe me, the dockers generally had plenty of that.

But not everyone was a potential customer for purveyors of 'dodgy' goods. Just as there was condemnation of big businesses suspected of indulging in profiteering at the expense of an already hard-pressed population, so there was – ostensibly at any rate – widespread disapproval of the small-time spivs and crooks seen to be getting rich on the backs of the suffering of others.

Another thing that happened was that lowlifes in the docks would steal the rations from the lifeboats on the ships. You can't get lower than that, can you?

The so-called spivs were just arseholes who'd avoided getting called up, but who were somehow well enough to work the black market at the expense of the rest of us.

The black market went on an awful lot. The wide boys were all at it and words cannot explain what I thought of them. They would steal ration books [from people] or break into the food offices to steal them and sell them on at a great profit. They made so much money illegally, while our boys were risking their lives to bring food and stuff into the country.

They were all right flashing their poge about in the pubs. We'd come home on leave and see them at it. Flash bastards, the lot of them. Buying the girls drinks and promising how they'd get them all kinds of gear if they were 'nice' to them.

Prostitutes did good business with lonely servicemen and even prisoners of war, just as they will always do when there are men longing for temporary female company. The less professional among them, however, like their more unfortunate civilian counterparts, had to resort in increasing numbers to the ministrations of the back-street abortionist. This growth in illegal terminations, along with the rise in venereal diseases, was of sufficient statistical significance to alarm the authorities into producing what must have seemed shockingly explicit information campaigns.

Prostitution, robbery and the black market were difficult enough to control, but preventing looting could be even harder. When a whole area was in chaos, with the emergency services more concerned about saving lives than catching sneak thieves, it became something of a free-for-all. Despite notices being posted to warn that looting was 'punishable by death or penal servitude for life', it remained a problem and personal belongings in houses, as well as goods in bombed business premises and shops, had to be closely guarded.

My dad was away most of the time, digging up half-alive or half-dead victims of the Blitz, which meant that Mum had to deal with things on her own [in the shop]. Queues around the block for their fags and tobacco were no challenge to her, and she swiftly dispensed with their requirements and settlements. Much more important to her was the possibility of burglars of the stock. I remember listening to the efforts of my mum and sister in barricading the front door with lemonade crates, while the back door was blown off its hinges from the force of a bomb blast, allowing any burglar to have his way.

Businesses that stocked goods in limited supply were an obvious target for black marketeers. But it was said, many times over, that poorer families couldn't have afforded to buy stolen property even if they'd wanted to. And I was given the same reason for why they didn't have to worry about having their possessions stolen during the blackout or when they were in the shelter.

Why should we be worried about the likes of them? We had nothing to nick. Potless. I tell you what, we was one of them families who the burglar would have felt sorry for, and would have left something for us that he'd nicked from somewhere else!

. . . not many people had anything worth stealing. We had no televisions, videos, radios, computers or similar items. We were all in the same boat: skint.

*

Our family certainly wasn't afraid of burglars, because we had nothing to steal. We had very little money and couldn't afford any stuff on the black market.

But quite paltry items *were* looted by opportunists, and from families who definitely couldn't have afforded to replace them – even assuming they could find somewhere to buy them from other than the spiv on a street corner trying to sell them back their own possessions out of a suitcase.

Of course there was crime about. There were the villains . . . pick-pocketing and shoplifting went on. But there was also the stealing and looting from homes that had been bombed, I think that was despicable. I don't think you could have got any lower than that.

We were a family of eleven children, and didn't even notice the shortages, but we did lose quite a bit from people pinching from the house, [including] the pictures and statues, which my mother had loved.

Knowing that children, accustomed to pre-war poverty, were used to going without didn't make the situation any more acceptable and helps to explain – if not necessarily condone – why not all offences were committed by professional thieves, greedy, selfish adults or corporate profiteers.

Us kids would nick a few potatoes and a bit of rhubarb from the railway embankment where the signalman grew it, and the occasional apple from the greengrocer's.

In 1942, the authorities cleared a bomb site in Old Bethnal Green Road, and they stacked up all the wood – the remains of the bombed-out houses. There were floorboards, doors and even lots of lavatory seats! It was all fenced off, for obvious reasons – a huge pile of firewood would have vanished overnight. During the school holidays I decided to get some firewood for my gran, so over the fence I went. I gathered the small items – bearing in mind they were all made of wood – such as the lavatory seats. After a couple of forays, I got really confident, but then one day I climbed back over the fence and a gloved hand felt my collar. This big tall policeman said, 'Right, feller-me-lad, back it all goes, and I don't want to see you again!'

Greengrocers would shout, 'Stop, thief!' and throw rotten apples at you. On cold and frosty mornings, the local bobby would creep up on me and whack my cold ears with the tips of his gloves. A trick the milkman would use was to let you think he hadn't seen you bending down behind his cart with your hand in, then, zoom, you would be transported into space with his size-twelve up your jacksy. The caretaker of our flats acted like a stormtrooper. He would twist your arm up your back with one hand and grab your ear with the other. He'd then frogmarch me back to our flat, where our mum would plead with him to screw me arm back on. Then she would take me in – after several slaps around the head – and she would put her face up close to mine, red with rage, spittle spraying from her mouth, and say, 'What have you been up to now, you little bugger?' After several beatings with a leather strap, I was sent to live with my grandmother, whom I loved dearly, [but] I was sent back home when the Blitz stopped – back to the battle in the flat between my mum and dad.

One of my best friends was a boy named T–, who lived opposite. He was a well-liked young man, but one of the biggest thieves I have ever met. Wherever we went he would try to steal things.

With schooling disrupted, fathers away in the forces and mothers busy with their paid work, domestic responsibilities and civil defence duties, young people were often without adult supervision, and convictions for youth crime and delinquency soared.

Thing was, there was opportunities – plenty of them – and what can you expect when you was allowed to run riot? We was kids, not vicars at some tea party. But we wasn't bad kids – no matter how it sounds. We knew how far to go, what was right and what wasn't.

But it wasn't shortages, opportunism or even the sometimes chaotic lack of order that led certain people into crime. Instead, it was fear, cowardice or maybe other less understandable reasons that resulted in another wartime crime – this one committed by young men who had been called up.

We kept chickens in the war – Gert and Daisy. They were a bit of a dead loss. They didn't seem to have many eggs, but we kept them. My mother and I were at breakfast one morning after Daddy was killed [by a bomb] when, suddenly, scrambling over our wall, came a man who took no notice of us. My mother went out very bravely and started to swear at him. He unhooked the fence – the wire netting where the chickens were kept – and scrambled up on our wall and ran along it and, evidently, hid in the church. He was closely followed by a policeman and a detective, but they were both quite elderly, I suppose because of the war – the younger men were all away. [They] scrambled through our house and over the garden after him and caught him in the church. He was a deserter.

I had a half-brother who was in the navy. I thought the world of him and looked up to him as my hero. One day the police came round and we feared the worst – that my brother had been killed. But we were wrong. He had deserted and the police were looking for him. They caught him and took him back to his ship, but only for him to desert again. What happened to my hero? I think I understand now, but not then.

Then there were those who, for a range of motives, refused to be conscripted in the first place – the people who made the decision to become conscientious objectors.

As children we were warned not to talk to conscientious objectors.

In a word, I thought conscientious objectors were disgusting.

Despite a prevailing view that the fight against the Nazi occupation of Europe and the spread of fascism was a justifiable war, there were those who, because of their pacifist, religious or political beliefs, did not want to join that fight. Provision had been made under the Military Training Act of May 1939 for those who sought permission not to be involved in combatant duties or military service, although individuals were required, under that act, to go before a tribunal to make their case. On the whole, objectors were treated far better this time round than they had been in the First World War, but they were still not always successful, and the manner in which they were dealt with varied considerably, largely depending on the composition of the tribunal. Failure rates to persuade tribunals ranged from 6 per cent to over 40 per cent.

A considerable amount of public hostility remained. 'Conchie' was definitely not a term of endearment and the Peace Pledge Union, which supported objectors, was frequently admonished for both its own pacifism and encouraging it in others. By 1945 approximately 5,000 men and 500 women were charged with offences relating to conscientious objection, with the majority being sent to prison. An additional 1,000 or so individuals were court-martialled and given custodial sentences for failure to obey military orders.

Those who were successful at their tribunals carried out a variety of non-military jobs.

At the time the war started, I was working for a Canadian company. They immediately closed the office and went back to Canada, so I was out of a job and registered at the Labour Exchange. The first job I was offered was with a local firm who were making something to do with armaments. I refused to go for this job. The next offer was with the War Office. Again I refused. I explained that I was a pacifist and wouldn't work for the war effort. I was told that I would have to appear before a committee who would decide whether I could continue to receive the 'dole'. I turned up at the time and place. What I didn't know at the time was that my mother-in-law was a member of the committee. When my turn came round, the chairman said, 'The next person on the list is named [surname]. I suppose she's no relation of yours.' Ma asked him what my first name was, and, on being told, explained I was her daughter-in-law. She asked why I was there. The chairman said, 'She says she's a pacifist. She's refused two jobs on the grounds that she won't help the war effort.'

Ma said, 'She is a pacifist.'

So the Chairman said, 'I'm afraid you can't sit on this case.' And Ma had to go out of the room whilst my case was being discussed. They decided I could not get any more dole. Fortunately, I found myself a job with Lloyds bank in St James's Square in the West End. L– [her husband] was, at this time, still working in a stockbroker's office in the City. He had registered as a conscientious objector but had yet to be called up.

We were now members of the Pacifist Service Unit,* attached to a group home in Ring House, on the Highway. We spent two nights a week working with the unit and were on call for emergencies. The

* PSUs were relief projects set up in major cities by the Peace Pledge Union.

local authority had provided shelters for people, but, when the bombing started, things began to break down. The shelters needed cleaning and the loos needed to be emptied.* So a group of pacifist students from Cambridge University came to take on these tasks. They did the hard work during the day, and when L– and I came on duty it was to take refreshments round the shelters, or to join the first-aid teams who dealt with minor injuries and illnesses. Each shelter in the areas was visited every night, or it might be that we stayed in one, keeping an eye on things. One such occasion was when incendiary bombs were dropping on St George's-in-the-East. These caused the bell to fall through the roof and land up in the crypt. We had to move all the people out into another shelter under the railway – L– kept them all singing until the all clear went hours later.

Fire-fighting was another one of the things the chaps did, and L– was on the roof of Ring House one night when it was set alight by incendiaries. He had, by this time, been before his own tribunal. They decided that he was a genuine pacifist and that he must do social work in the community. It was in about May 1941 that the Rev. Alexander [Lex] Miller asked us if we'd be prepared to run a hostel for old people, as a lot of them had been bombed out of their homes and were in reception centres. Some had been sent to the country but had returned; some had refused to be sent out of London. They were blocking up the centres and the local authority was trying to set up a hostel for them. The vicar of [a church] had left the vicarage in Commercial Road to go to the country with some of his flock. So Lex Miller organized the house for use as a hostel, where we were able to cater for sixteen old people. In June 1941, L– and I moved in as wardens.

The old people were an interesting lot. One was Mrs S–. It was a rule of the hostel that everybody bathed on a regular basis and a

* There are stomach-churningly graphic descriptions from people who had to endure the squalor of some public shelters, most notoriously, perhaps, the so-called Tilbury shelter in Stepney.

roster was drawn up. Mrs S– refused to bathe – she had been shipwrecked in the Red Sea in her early teens and she'd seen enough water to last her all her lifetime. We had to get the district nurse to come and supervise her! Another was Mr F–. He was a bachelor who had been engaged but his fiancée left him for the driver of a horse-bus who was earning more money than him – 2s 6d! He was very helpful and always brought the dirty dishes from the dining room to the kitchen. His one trouble was that he suffered from wind, and he made his own accompaniment, and as he went upstairs to the common room he would let rip on every stair.

One day I had to go into the men's dorm and I heard funny noises coming from under one of the beds. When I looked, there were about four dozen chicks in boxes. One of the old boys had been trading every Sunday morning on Club Row!

One very old lady wore the most wonderful undergarments. Her drawers were like two drainpipes of beautiful embroidered cotton. You put each leg on separately and tied them round your waist. She also had a collection of lovely bonnets. She knew I was interested and said I could have them when she died. Unfortunately, I never had a look in. Although she hadn't had a single visitor whilst she was in the hostel, the minute she was dead they arrived and were gone with her things before you could say, 'They would have done her in for her hatpin, let alone her hat.'

I worked at the hostel all day, and in the evenings at a club run for the local youngsters. I taught them how to make their clothing coupons go further by making skirts out of old trousers and blouses from old shirts. I also helped with the netball team. At first, when we went on the buses to away matches, I was very embarrassed by their language and tried to pretend I wasn't with them. I soon learned it was better to hide in the middle of them! They were a smashing lot of girls.

We stayed at the hostel until I became pregnant with my first child. We left towards the end of 1943. I had registered with the East End Maternity Hospital, known locally as the 'lying-in-home'. The day came for me to get the hospital coach to take me to Newport Pagnell, where the baby was going to be born. And, my God, did I get a send-off. All the windows of the hostel were open and filled with people, and one of the PSU boys was there giving me a noisy saxophone farewell. The work had been quite hard, and at times very dangerous, but I look back with great pleasure. We were accepted as 'conchies' and we met some really lovely people.

Others had to settle for duties which involved working with non-combatant units within the forces.

I was called up in September 1940 after a conscientious objector's tribunal and an appeal against their decision . . . [I was] persuaded by my family that the right thing to do was to go into the non-combatant corps, which I was required to do, and see whether my then so funny conscience would accept it. This I did and, after training . . . [I went] to a company which were doing various tasks. My main post was to be an army porter in a hospital, dealing with everything from holding people on operating tables to holding them on post-mortem tables. This was morally a very acceptable job.

There were those who never got as far as the tribunal stage, being unable to cope with the thought of the disapproval that would be directed towards them. But they wouldn't automatically have faced condemnation. One East Ender told me how he was glad to be called up, as the world needed all the strength it could muster to 'defeat the evils of Nazism', and yet, despite risking his own life and losing members of his family in the Holocaust, he still had the heart to say the following:

If my beliefs were to be meaningful, they [conscientious objectors] had to have their rights, though I had difficulty in understanding their beliefs in those dire circumstances.

And another interviewee could also see the logic.

Personally, I didn't blame the conscientious objectors, because who could be a brave hero, knowing you could be killed and have to leave your beloved family for ever?

But such was the general contempt in which conscientious objectors were held that even some individuals in reserved occupations worried about being viewed in the same light.

My dad joined the Royal Marines. He was actually a special constable before being called up and didn't need to go in the forces at all, but he was afraid he would be branded a conscientious objector and a coward, so he went in. Apparently he had heard some women talking with contempt about men who didn't want to go and fight like everyone else.

. . . my dad worked for the post office and could have been exempt from national service, but, not wishing to be called a 'conchie', he joined up. He said that he could pick which job he could train for in the army, but Mum said it was because I was such a miserable baby, especially at night, that he joined up to get some peace.

According to the people I spoke to, there was widespread doubt as to the motives of some of the conscientious objectors.

To my mind, I think that there were two sorts of conscientious objectors. The genuine ones, who were willing to go into non-combatant positions such as in the Medical Corps, work on the land or in coal mines, those people I had a lot of time for, because they had a principle but were willing to do their bit without having to handle weapons. But then there were some who just wanted to skive and duck out of doing anything to help the war effort, and I just think that they were the scum of the earth.

That there were individuals who claimed to be conscientious objectors as a means of skiving was doubtless true. I met people who preferred not to have their stories told but were prepared to talk to me privately about how they actively sought ways to 'get out of it', although not always through conscientious objection.

But whether you were sincere or faking it, conscientious objection was not necessarily a cushy option or lacking in danger.

I had leave [from the non-combatant] corps in December 1940 and, my home being in Ilford, I took a train [from where I'd been working in Cambridge] and was very, very cross when the air-raid warning sounded and we stopped under Bishopsgate Station, where we stayed for four or five hours, a mere 500 yards, I suppose, from Liverpool Street Station, and [a few] miles from home. But there we stopped . . . Flickering on the walls opposite above Shoreditch Station, I imagined, were lights, much too bright for anything permissible when bombs were falling, and this went on for hour after hour. I did not know then that this was the Moor Lane [now Barbican] area of London on its first intensive bombing. Finally, the all clear went and we staggered into Liverpool Street Station, and at an even later time I got home and had my leave. As soon as I got back to Cambridge, we were under orders to move to Islington, [where] we were employed clearing this Moor Lane area, which was flattened almost completely, except for jagged, broken teeth sticking in the air, one church tower and one school building. Everywhere the jagged corners of buildings stuck up, safes could be seen sticking out on high floors, built into the brickwork. Our job was to make these places [secure] with the aid of the professional – more professional – Royal Engineers, to remove rubble [and] to find safes and report them, and any other documents that might not be destroyed, but nothing that was not in a safe . . . could have survived. So we worked as labourers . . . but not for very long, because one evening several of us were feeling rather

32. Damage to Spiller's Flour Mills, Royal Victoria Dock, following the first mass daylight raid on London on 7 September 1940. Spiller's was part of the largest complex of grain mills outside Canada.

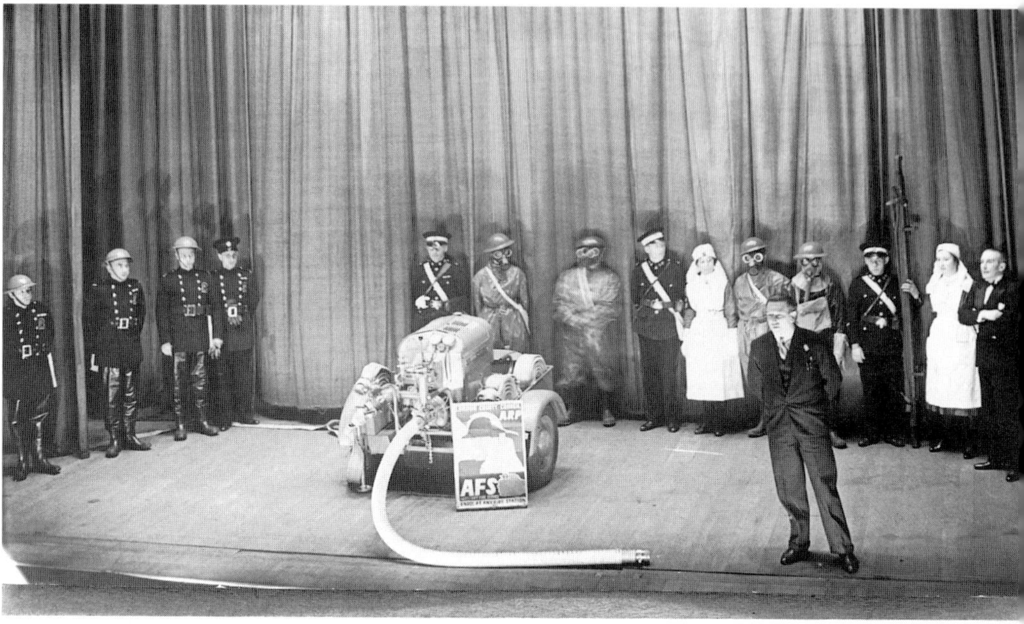

33. (*Above*) A 1939 appeal for civil defence volunteers from the stage of the 'Ipp' – the Poplar Hippodrome, East India Dock Road.

34. (*Right*) Protecting the docks, November 1941. A detachment of the Port of London's Home Guard, originally known as Local Defence Volunteers, march with fixed bayonets.

35. Tin hats, buckets and stirrup pumps were the somewhat limited tools and protection used by fire watchers such as these men on duty on the roof of the Troxy Cinema, Commercial Road.

36. The London Fire Brigade battles with blazing warehouses in the Eastern Basin, St Katharine Dock, 8 September 1940.

37. (*Right*) Salvaging what was left of the tens of thousands of tons of sugar that went up in flames in the West India Dock, 8 September 1940. With little confectionery available, the resulting 'toffee' was collected – by some daring individuals – as a sweet treat.

38. (*Below*) Members of the Women's Legion preparing cheese rolls for London dockers. The Legion operated mobile canteens, distributing drinks and snacks throughout the docks, so that the men could be sustained without unnecessary interruption to their vital handling of cargo.

39–40. Enjoying their work – women showing off newly found skills on the railways and the factory floor. Note Phyllis's boiler suit and her patriotic 'Victory Roll' hairstyle. Like the railway ladies' berets, it kept her hair safely tucked away from any machinery.

41. Taking care of homeless East End youngsters. The gummed paper on the windows was to prevent the glass shattering in the event of a blast.

42. A rather more elaborate use of gummed paper to protect the window of the Victoria Wine Company in East India Dock Road, the scene even including four miniature, paper barrage balloons.

43. These London families settle down to enjoy their Sunday dinner, despite being in the lean-to shelter at the back of their houses where they were forced to live after their homes were blitzed.

44. And these Londoners enjoy their special day, despite the sandbags, tin helmets and gas masks, and the lack of a traditional wedding gown.

45. Even 'down the shelter' – in this case a section of uncompleted Underground line between Liverpool Street and Bethnal Green – Londoners could still enjoy a knees-up.

46. (*Left*) King George V Dock, March 1946. The war is over and young Peter Stewart, wearing his siren suit despite the air-raid warnings having long been silenced, is somewhat dubious as he inspects tins of honey and dried fruits. The goods were sent from Australia aboard the SS *Moraybank*.

47. (*Below*) It's 1946, and yes, we have some bananas! A stall in Bethnal Green proudly displays the much-missed fruit and also has beetroot for sale at 5d a pound. But it would be a few years yet before there was enough of everything – from meat to housing – to go round …

queer and a lot went to bed without a meal . . . Nearly 100 people reported sick that evening out of our unit of some 300. The temperatures were so high that they were stretcher cases for hospital. Mine was 99.8 and I was put down as needing to go to hospital, but I was carrying stretchers on to the . . . Green Line buses that were converted into ambulances. Finally I went to hospital and got to bed, and the next morning mine was the highest temperature of all at 104 . . . It was influenza.

For the conscientious objectors genuinely committed to their beliefs, being sent to prison was a price they were prepared to pay.

We were put on to making roads [in] known shell dumps . . . The dumps were in half-buried corrugated-iron huts, smaller than normal Nissen huts, open at the ends. It was not collusion [but our] whole section refused to make the roads – we'd made roads elsewhere – on the grounds that this was for the purposes of getting munitions out. We also had the suspicion that they were poison gas shells, but that was not the point. It was munitions. We were formally warned and marched back to camp, where the major decided that as we were largely Christians in the unit, he would get the support of a Christian and produced the bishop . . . [He] lectured us on the iniquities of disobeying legal, lawful orders and the theory that Christians should take part in the war, and the result was that all except six of us went back on duty. But the six were adamant, me, poor fool, being one [of them]. I was under arrest for weeks.

The way combatants regarded non-combatants when they were working within the same unit varied considerably. Some referred to them as 'colleagues', seeing them as skilled people doing useful jobs, but others held them to be almost as despicable as the enemy, or simply not very able. But the work they did was of real importance to the war effort. Producing home-grown timber, for instance, made a vital contribution to the country's stock of raw materials. This was particularly important when the Merchant Marine, which brought stocks in from abroad during peacetime, was either carrying other vital cargoes or being blockaded and attacked by U-boats.

And yet, as I found in so many people's stories of wartime, despite the seriousness of the situation, there were still diversions to be enjoyed even if you were a 'conchie'.

We had some characters, communists and Jehovah's Witnesses, and as always, in the middle, poor Anglicans like me. I had trouble at one point when I was working on an army depot and said to this corporal, 'If you tell me to move barbed wire I shall refuse,' and this alarmed them. They didn't know what to do with me, so it gradually went up the ranks, until the colonel came down and lectured us. He said, 'Stand forward the man who refused orders.' Nothing happened, so I was ordered to stand forward, and I said, 'I have only said that if you order me, I shall refuse it. I have not refused an order.' They just collapsed.

The forestry unit [I was put with] was made up of professional timber workers [and] forestry workers of various sorts. They were a Royal Engineers company of 100 men, amongst whom there were two saw doctors, who could make and mend saws in a way that was quite miraculous. We were employed both to work the sawmill and fell trees. I had experience of using a felling axe [and] was quickly on to that work. [It] was very interesting working with these professionals and very satisfying in its way. On one occasion – remember, we conscientious objectors were working with combatants – one of the Royal Engineers sergeants told a man called G–, 'Clear the pit of sawdust,' and G–, being a communist and a trade union man, replied, 'Not my job, Sergeant.'

'Doesn't matter,' said the sergeant. 'You do it.'

'Well, I've been working all day. [It's] that chap's job, I'm not doing it.'

Two sergeants and a corporal were called [and] the sergeant ordered [him] again, and G– said, 'No,' and they put him on a charge. He was given twenty-eight days' military imprisonment [at] Shepton Mallet. Being a conscientious objector – although a communist – he had the right to refuse to handle arms in any form, and the army were required not to require him. He came back as a first-class Bren gunner, and when the major in charge enquired as to why he had done this when he knew very well his rights, he said, 'It'll come in so useful when it comes to the revolution,' and, turning to the sergeant major, he said, 'And you know who the first person I'll use a Bren gun on will be, don't you?'

[13] *Leisure Time*

> Uncle Bill used to play the accordion in the street and we all used to dance!

In pre-war British society, life was, on the whole, predictable and sheltered for young working-class men and women. You married a local boy or girl, were found a couple of rooms along the street from your mum and dad and the rest of the family, and settled down to have kids of your own. The wife looked after the home and domestic matters, while the husband went out to work and 'brought home the bacon'.

Paradoxically, the war – a time of fear, danger, anxiety, austerity and restriction – would, in some cases, prove to be a liberating experience. There were more new people to meet and more new things to try than ever before, and a surprisingly good time could be had. Thanks to the sense of urgency that came from not knowing what might be waiting for you just around the corner, it was, in the words of the old song, a case of 'Enjoy yourself, it's later than you think . . .'

But initially, at the outbreak of war, it wasn't that easy to have fun. The government feared that enemy bombers would seek out places of public entertainment, deliberately targeting areas where large numbers of civilians were gathered together, with the intention of causing maximum casualties and widespread panic. As a result, there was an immediate closing down of all popular venues – from speedway tracks to cinemas, dog-racing stadiums to London Zoo.

In the beginning of the war, as we were settling down to that dreadful fact, we were not allowed to meet in large numbers, so it was no school, cinemas, churches, sports meetings . . .

For a short while at least, if you wanted to be entertained it was very much a case of having to make your own fun. One person I spoke to enthusiastically remembered 'courting was [a good way] to pass the time, as was going for walks with your sweetheart!' Less romantic, but equally fondly recalled, were the stories about musical entertainments. People described varying levels of accomplishment in singing and dancing, high standards of piano playing and maybe less impressive – but still engaging – efforts on the comb and paper. Then there were the turns that sounded as if they owed their origins to the music hall.

Dad was not only a dab hand on the accordion, but he used to upturn a dinner plate over a burning candle until it had all turned black and then draw pictures on it with a match stick.

Grandad was like a sort of magician. He didn't do tricks exactly but, to amuse us, he could sort of fiddle with a pack of cards and turn it into a beautiful fan, shaped like the inside of one of those big twisting sea shells, and he could roll up a newspaper, rip off a few apparently random bits and pieces, do a bit of pulling and fluffing, and he'd have made a ladder or a palm tree from it, really tall and strong. As good as the turns you saw on the stage. His card tricks used to have us all guessing, but we never figured them out. And he could pull a penny from right out of your ear. We loved that, especially if we got to keep the money!

A frequent visitor to our house was an old friend of my mother, accompanied by her two children . . . her husband served in the NFS [National Fire Service] as part of the heavy rescue team . . . he had seen some terrible sights and relayed these to his wife . . . a wonderful storyteller [who] in turn would spin stories from these awful events and convey them to anyone who would listen. And they were always much better drama than anything the radio had to offer. My mother and I were avid fans and would listen attentively to the next episode.

We had several parties at the flat, where all the relations would come over for knees-ups. We didn't have record players, just a piano and other musical instruments with which we made our own entertainment. The dancing would be very boisterous and I remember the wooden floor of the flat bouncing up and down when we were all doing 'Knees up, Mother Brown' . . . The old boys downstairs must have thought the Germans were there with their land mines.

Singing has always been a morale booster. Like whistling in the dark, it helps keep a good face on things, even when you're confronted with the 'bogeyman', and it draws people together, making them feel part of something bigger than themselves – so important at times of crisis or distress. Many of the songs people remembered singing have lasted in popular memory for sixty years or so. Be they silly novelty ditties which urged us to hang out our washing on the Siegfried Line, dreamily romantic tales of nightingales singing in Berkeley Square or powerfully sentimental songs like 'We'll Meet Again', they all serve to show what Noël Coward meant when he described the potency of popular music.

We could always have a singsong. There were some lovely songs that came out in wartime, real lovely melodies, like the Vera Lynn songs and Glenn Miller – the sort of tunes you could dance to. But, as you know, at first they closed all the dance halls down.

It was quickly realized that there was a need for public diversion, and places of amusement and entertainment were soon opened up again – some within a week of their initial closure. But after reopening, it was interruption and disruption that would present problems for the next six years.

I was told an unverifiable but nonetheless amusing story about someone attending a football match at which, in a glorious moment of audience participation, members of the crowd were invited to take the place of favourite players who had been called up for national service – so long as they had the right-sized feet to fit the players' boots. The reason I think it's probably true is the many other football stories I came across of teams losing or winning with bizarrely high or low scores because of the unusual team make-up – the usual back line now being off somewhere on the front line.

Things got back to more or less normal – at least, as normal as possible. Places would stop open even in a raid, until the planes got close. Sometimes they would clear the place or inform you that it was dangerous, and then you made up your own mind.

If we tried to go to the pictures the siren would go off and we would leave, or we'd be on our way to a dance and, yes, the siren would go, and we'd try and make our way back home.

Regardless of the interruptions, people were still prepared to take their chance, as they craved distraction from the blackout, the rationing and separation from their loved ones. As can be seen from the vast amount of coverage in contemporary newspapers, cinema was one of the most popular diversions of all, a hugely popular way for the public to spend their free time, with people 'going to the flicks' as often as they could afford. Despite restrictions to programming and hours of opening, in the cinema you could escape into another world. Whether you opted for the dark cosiness of the luxuriously carpeted and curtained picture palace or the very basic facilities of the fleapit, you were now able to enjoy not only the main feature and the B film, but the all-important patriotically 'spun' newsreel, and the more overtly official, ministry-produced propaganda shorts. These brief films covered everything from slightly hectoring tips on how to recognize Nazi spies to cheery extollings of the virtues of fuel savings in the home.

There were certainly plenty of premises to choose from. They weren't as seemingly ubiquitous as the pubs that stood on just about every street corner, but there were more than enough to supply the most ardent filmgoer with entertainment. And with programmes showing everything from *The Wizard of Oz* to *Gone With the Wind* and with movie stars like Carmen Miranda and Betty Grable, Clark Gable and Bing Crosby, is it any wonder that cinema was so popular? Especially considering the added bonuses that came from spending your leisure time there: you used their fuel, thus saving your own precious supplies, and the picture house could double as an informal shelter during an air raid!

During a lull in the air raids my mother said to my sister, 'Why don't you go to the pictures?' It was only at the top of the road where I lived. So we said, 'All right.' And she said, 'I'll have the baby while you go.' So we were nicely sitting in the pictures, seeing a Bette Davies film, *Now Voyager*, and we was nice and comfortable, when all of a sudden it came on the screen – an air-raid warning.* Well, my sister turned to me and she said, 'Tell me what happens,' and she ran, and I said, 'All right.' I sat there, watching the film, and every so often there was a loud crash! Bang! Still I sat there. I was thinking, 'Ooh, I must see the end of it.' Looking sideways, there was no one either side of me at all and I thought [there must be] plenty of people

* It was usual practice to flash up a sign warning patrons. How many took notice varied considerably.

behind. The time went on and I was getting to a lovely part of the film, so nice, and I looked around and . . . there was about me and another two people in there, and I thought, 'Oh, God, I'd best go home now.' I still stayed for five minutes and then there's a great big loud resounding crash and I jumped up and that time I had to go home. As I came across Green Street . . . shrapnel was falling and everything – brick, pieces of brickwork and masonry – was all falling all around me. I was doing a little run and then going into a doorway, and running again until I finally got into my house and run down the air-raid shelter. My sister was sitting there with my mum and her little girl, and my sister said to me, 'What happened?' I said, 'I nearly got killed, that's what happened!' I never did see the end of the film . . .

. . . at the cinema, if an air raid started, it was up to you – you either stayed on watching the film, trying to hear what they were saying over the bomb blasts, or you left for the shelter. We didn't go much as money was short, but if we did, we stayed, because once you went out you weren't allowed back in unless you paid again. Also, the raids always seemed to come half an hour before the film ended, so you missed the end. The same applied to the music hall, which we all loved. During the raids the comics would come on and tell jokes with dust from the shaking building falling all over them and the stage. We were all encouraged to join in a singsong – gas masks at the ready. Many's the time 'There'll Always be an England' would drown out the noise of the bombs.

This evacuee and her companions still made the effort to haul themselves along to the flicks, despite the fact that they were all in the advanced stages of pregnancy.

The hospital where I was booked to have my baby was hit by a bomb, so I was asked to evacuate to have her. About twenty-six of us, all within three or four weeks of delivery, were sent to a nursing home in [Somerset]. We were all young and fairly good-looking. Sometimes we would go to the pictures in the afternoon. There would be soldiers there by the dozen. As we sat there, we could hear them saying, 'I'll have the blonde one,' or, 'I'll have the redhead.' We arranged it so that when the lights came on all we pregnant ladies stood up together. You should have seen the soldiers' looks of surprise! At least it was a good laugh for us.

Sadly, not all outings turned out to have such amusing conclusions. This story illustrates one of the particular cruelties of wartime: the arbitrary matter of who did or did not 'cop it' – the 'Why them and not us?' or the 'Why us and not them?' – that stays with people for the rest of their lives.

H– and I decided to go to the pictures one evening. I was always afraid, but said I would go anyway. As we were going in we met two friends in the foyer who told us the light warning that a raid was coming had been turned on. Like us, they were planning their wedding. We said cheerio and went in anyway – only to hear later that the block of flats where they had been going to had been bombed. She was one of the survivors, but her darling had been killed. What a wicked world.

It was the experience of living in that 'wicked world' that made people crave distraction from the reality of what was going on around them, and the wireless was then as much a part of people's lives as the television is today. There had been television broadcasts before the war but for most people in the East End TV sets were beyond their pocket. However, on Friday 1 September 1939, two days before the declaration of war, television output came to a halt, and would be off the air for the next seven years. So television was no longer an option – even for those who could have afforded it – and the next day, Saturday 2 September, all the national and regional radio services merged into a single BBC station, broadcasting daily from 7 a.m. to 12.15 a.m. Such a radical change to a medium of real mass importance must surely have marked the moment when even the most reluctant had to admit that something momentous was about to happen.

We listened to the wireless a lot, and there were quite a few comedy programmes on, but the most important programme was always the news on a Sunday evening. They played the national anthems of the different countries as they fell to Germany, and sadly there got to be so many that they only played the first line of them.

We enjoyed listening to *In Town Tonight*, all the big fights and *ITMA*.

ITMA was one of the most widely recalled radio shows, even if it wasn't everyone's favourite. It had an amazing weekly listening public of 16 million – at a time when the UK's population was just over 47.75 million.

ITMA stood for 'It's That Man Again' – an allusion to the way newspapers referred to Hitler when describing his latest actions. It was a comedy show which began in 1939 and was to be broadcast until the death of Tommy Handley, its star, ten years later. As with *The Goon Show, Monty Python's Flying Circus* and the more recent *Fast Show*, much of its success came from its repetition of catchphrases, its larger-than-life characters and its sly digs at the establishment, all of which captured the British imagination and rapidly entered into general currency. Colonel Chin-Strap was readily echoed as he encouraged refills for his glass with a cheery, 'Don't mind if I do'; Mrs Mopp's slightly saucy 'Can I do you now, sir?' was widely and knowingly mimicked; and anyone a bit shifty-looking was mocked as being like Funf – the not very threatening or convincing spy who carried out missions for the Nazis. One of the programme's pleasures was that it sent up the sometimes ludicrous machinations of ministerial bureaucracy – an all too familiar nuisance for those living through the war. The full extent of Handley's popularity and the dedication of his public can be gauged from a description of the adoring send-off that followed his sudden death from a cerebral haemorrhage. Not only was the full six-mile route of his funeral procession lined by many thousands of devoted fans, but his memory was celebrated and honoured at services in both St Paul's in London and Liverpool Cathedral.

Two other programmes that were more overtly morale-boosting – or perhaps that should be production-boosting – were also very popular. These were aimed at those in the workplace, busily producing for the war effort, but were as likely to be listened to in the home as the factory. *Workers' Playtime*, broadcast at lunchtime, toured variety and musical acts all around the country, visiting the canteens of factories involved in the war effort. And, from mid-1940, there was the twice-daily broadcast of *Music While You Work*. This show featured big-name bands playing orchestral versions of popular songs, and was intended to buck up workers as they sang along to the stirring tunes during the mid-morning and mid-afternoon broadcasts – traditionally periods which saw dips in production.

Youngsters were also catered for by the BBC's radio output with *Children's Hour*, but in those days before electronic games and computers, children were keen to find the means to amuse themselves in rather more 'hands on' ways – even if, or possibly because, those ways might not be to the taste of most adults.

For amusement on cold winter evenings we had cards, books or dominoes, with which we used to construct houses and, no doubt influenced by the war, we would fill with flies with their wings removed and proceed to bomb. Another favourite sport [when evacuated] was to catch flies and throw them into the webs of fat hedgerow spiders. Typical boys' fun? There was little radio [for children] and, of course, no TV.

Even during the war we used to rake the streets and get up to all kinds of business. Not like chavvies* today. But we had a good time, and learned one or two things about life. And what it felt like to graze your knees without going running to your mother telling tales and suing people 'cos you'd 'got a baddie'!†

This young lad had a rather more sophisticated experience of wartime entertainment, which he was able to enjoy with his father – well, most of the time.

Dad was always interested in the theatre, but Mum wasn't, so I used to go all over east London with him, seeing all the shows. Once at the Queen's in Poplar – practically in the docks – the bombs were dropping all around, but no one thought nothing of it, and the show carried on. The chorus girls were still dancing and the comedians still telling jokes. Two shows a week we'd see. We'd go and visit Nan first, and Dad would give her her shilling for a Guinness – she liked a drop of that – then we'd go to see the show. The Queen's, the Walthamstow Palace, East Ham Palace – by the station, where the old C&A used to be, Finsbury Park Empire. I liked the Queen's and the East Ham Palace best. Dad also used to go to the Windmill with his mates, but I was never allowed to go there. That's where they had the tableaux vivants – the nude shows, where, if the girls moved, it was breaking the law, but if they stood still they were all right. No, he never took me there!

Another favourite pastime that was best left to adults was going to the pub. While beer wasn't officially rationed, it was

* From 'chavy', a slang word for child.

† A childish or sarcastically 'wimpish' term for a wound or sore.

often in short supply, and when it *was* available it could prove to be a very watery affair when compared to the familiar brews of pre-war days. But the pub was still a haven. It was a place to relax, somewhere to share the warmth of the fireplace and to enjoy the benefit of the lighting, and it provided a break from what was going on outside those warm, fug-ridden walls. It gave you a chance to enjoy yourself for an hour or two, and all the while saving your own precious stocks of coal, gas and maybe even electricity, if your home was that stylish.

But when the alcohol shortages took hold, opening hours were shortened and what the landlord could 'allow' his customers was sometimes severely curtailed. Prices rose and drinking glasses became as precious as the bottles themselves.

Around the docks, one of the most dangerous places in the country for civilians, it could be particularly difficult to take a stroll down to your local, even if it did have supplies of booze or a few packets of your favourite cigarettes.

A lot of the publicans [round there] had buggered off, but if you happened to know anybody they'd say, 'Here, don't put it around, but so and so's opening tonight for two hours' – the Red Lion or the Connaught – 'But don't put it around, like. We don't want too many.'

You could usually get a drop of *something* to wet your whistle, but it'd be on the QT – someone'd tip you the wink and you'd be in there, fast as you like!

Despite all the problems, when pubs did open, they were as popular as ever.

The pubs did good business. It was a way of letting your hair down.

Other problems carried over from peacetime and, even with widespread shortages and reduced alcoholic strength, there were still those who couldn't handle the drink that was available.

Me and my mates witnessed a lot of fights outside pubs in those days.

They'd have a sniff of the barmaid's apron and that'd be it. All the jealousy about what had gone on at home, while they was away fighting for their country, would all come out and a fight'd start. So long as no one got too hurt, it was like free entertainment – you could have a few bob on the winner!

Of course, if you preferred, there were healthier ways to spend your leisure time. Within the grimy ruins of bomb-damaged London, there were the parks, the green lungs of the East End, to be enjoyed – although even they had been transformed by the war.

Places where people had once taken their almost pastoral ease were now doubling as utilitarian centres of salvage and wreckage dumps, ack-ack stations, sites of sties for communal pig clubs, centres in which locals could 'Dig For Victory' and locations for primitive, rain-sodden, trench-type shelters – all very far removed from their original purpose of being simple havens of fresh air, healthy exercise and refreshing relaxation. The importance of the parks as refuges of leisure was still recognized. Facilities were still provided for visitors, including free, ragged pre-war deck chairs in which to sunbathe and outdoor dances, which were well attended despite the lack of male partners.

These had been enthusiastically reinstated by the authorities, alongside the parallel reinstatement of bank holidays, as part of the 'Holiday at Home' drive, which was intended to save fuel and prevent road congestion by curbing unnecessary civilian movement around the country. Victoria Park, bordered by Bow and Hackney, had whole programmes of entertainment to

tempt locals to stay put. These ranged from full, professional performances by the Sadler's Wells ballet company to swimming galas in the now sadly demolished lido – what the Luftwaffe failed to destroy, 'progress' did instead.

But no matter what entertainment was put on for them on their doorsteps, some East Enders weren't impressed. After facing the relentless demands made on them in their bomb-ravaged streets, they were determined to find a way – whether legal or not – out of town and down to the seaside, looking for a chance to disport themselves on the beach between the coils of barbed wire intended to thwart potential invaders.

There was one legitimate reason, other than evacuation, for Cockneys to leave the capital and that was to go hop picking in Kent. Hopping was a much-relished opportunity to really get away from it all, even though hard work – and bombers – were involved. It offered a genuinely rural respite, because, regardless of the war, there were still hops to be picked, money to be earned from doing so and, best of all, a 'holiday' to be had away from the raids over the East End.

Come September we would go hop picking to Yalding in Kent. Our relation would take us down in his lorry, firstly rounding up all our goods and a piano on the back – and not forgetting all the family. There would be Grandpa and Grandma, aunties, cousins and all the children going to get paid to pick hops and enjoy having a holiday in the countryside on the strength of it. It seemed most of the men, including my dad, if not away at war, and all my docker uncles would come down on the weekend if they could. Those who did not sleep in the huts would sleep in the tents with us children. All and sundry would muck in with picking the hops. My gran was strict with all us children, saying she wouldn't stand for any slacking – later we were allowed time to play. The best time was when the family went to the pub to celebrate in the evening – several played the piano in the pub and they danced and sang till closing time. We just sat outside drinking our lemonade and listening, not missing anything the adults got up to. I believe the publican thought all East Enders were thieves, because he had cleared away anything not attached to the bar or the floor just in case it walked. Bare floorboards and a bench – what hospitality. Anyway, going back to the [farm] was hilarious: people singing in the blackest of nights, some falling into ditches, picking themselves up and laughing. Very sobering!

It was certainly a break from London, and a real treat in many ways, but not everyone had a totally relaxing time of it.

When the bombing started in 1940, Mum decided to take the younger ones of us to the hop fields in Kent. We went down by lorry, and it was very exciting as we had never been to the country before. We weren't accepted by the locals as – to them – we were running wild, scrumping for apples and pears and vegetables, but food was so much more plentiful in the country and so we were never hungry down there. [But] it wasn't long before the bombs started falling there too. We would all run to the fields to shelter or duck under the hop bin. You could see the planes coming in the distance. During those five weeks, all the children had jobs to do – finding wood, carrying water back to the hut, going shopping in the nearby village. But then it was all over and it was back to the Blitz. I can honestly say we never really had a childhood – we had to grow up fast.

'Home dwellers' was the name used by local people living around the hop farms to describe themselves, and they referred to the strangely behaved, peculiarly dressed and oddly accented Cockneys as 'foreigners'. But the lack of tolerance and gaps in understanding between these two groups – and there were many – were nothing compared to the shock felt when genuine foreigners arrived *en masse* from the United States of America.

The GIs were to have a huge impact on blacked-out, ration-weary, bomb-devastated Great Britain. They were healthy, well fed and handsome-looking in their sharp uniforms. And with their apparently limitless supplies of unrationed goodies from their PXs, with plenty of money in their pocket and speaking in accents only heard in Hollywood films, it's no wonder they turned heads. Their presence wasn't universally welcomed, however, and there were the famous comments made about them being 'overpaid, oversexed and over here', and that girls attracted to them – and their supply of otherwise elusive 'luxuries' – were said to be wearing the 'new Utility knickers – one yank and they're off'.

But, as more than one perfectly proper woman remarked when remembering the fun that the GIs had injected into an otherwise cheerless world.

They brought music and laughter back into our lives. And my goodness we'd missed having a good time. It was like a film I'd seen that went from black and white into colour.*

It is hardly surprising that lonely young women, hungry for fun and distraction, should have reacted with enthusiasm to the arrival of lonely, disoriented young men.

My elder sister used to go out and entertain the Yanks that were here then. I'm not saying she gave her favours away to them lot, but she certainly had a good time.

The GIs didn't only give us gum and candy bars, they gave us something else – the Jitterbug. This had only ever been seen before in the films. We were amazed when they came to the church dances and turned the floor into an acrobats' delight! The local girls soon picked it up, as did the kids. Never short of partners, the single girls – and some of the married ones – loved it, and the village [where we were evacuated] became Americanized almost overnight.

After Daddy died . . . we lived with my granny and my Aunt J–, who was probably only six years older than me. She was working and going out with an American. My granny said, 'You'll get your throat cut and be found in a ditch.' He was called, of course, Hank. She was

* She couldn't remember the film, but it was possibly *The Wizard of Oz*.

taken to Bushey Park, where the Americans were stationed, and she heard Glenn Miller's band, which she thought was marvellous. Well, we all did.

There were good, decent girls, and there were girls who were no better than they ought to have been. And the same went for the Yanks. But, Christ, they were handsome fellers!

To get yourself one of those good-looking fellers, you needed to look good yourself, which wasn't always easy, and considerable effort was required if, in the words of the song, you wanted to 'keep young and beautiful'.

I very often spent spare time searching out chemist's where I could get some make-up – it was very scarce.

It was ironic how, parallel to that scarcity, there was a new affluence for women as they took on relatively well-paid war work, and, thanks to images from Hollywood films and magazines, they were living through a period that displayed a growing acceptance of women wearing make-up.

It wasn't only cosmetics that were scarce. Metal hairgrips and curlers had all but disappeared from the shops and improvisation in home hairdressing called for rags and pipe cleaners to be used in their place. The 'Victory Roll' was very popular, as it required nothing more than wrapping your hair around a scarf or a sausage of rags circling the back of your head. It was practical too for factory workers using machinery, and was actively encouraged as a safe alternative to the draped, peek-a-boo look of movie stars such as Veronica Lake.

But it wasn't all do-it-yourself and improvisation. Professional hairdressers, as sole traders, were allowed to continue with their businesses, and in the drab world of blackouts and bomb sites, when even soap was a luxury – a particular problem with London's hard water – they provided a popular treat to be indulged in by women starved of feminine indulgences.

My first perm was in 1940, at a local hairdresser's, where I sat under a contraption with wires hanging down from the ceiling above my head. These were attached, one by one, to sections of my hair. That was OK – until the warning went! I was given the choice – stay, or get unplugged and go to the shelter. I stayed, and finished with a great perm.

My sister-in-law was a party girl, very good-looking, with blonde hair, and she would saunter down the street holding the arm of two American officers. She said she only dated officers! She almost married a Canadian, but her mother stepped in and said she wasn't to – they didn't disobey their mothers in those days. She said that the war years were the best years of her life – dancing and dining 'up West' most nights. Her name was Gladys but she called herself [a glamorous film star's name]. She and her equally good-looking sister did all the hair-dyeing and hair-curling and had fights over who wore what clothes.

Less worldly-wise girls needed to exercise a measure of caution when dealing with the glamorous young Americans.

My friend Ivy and I met two Yanks, who invited us to the West End for a meal. When we got there, they began looking for a hotel. It was only then we realized that their intentions were far from honourable. As we walked by Oxford Street tube station, we told them we needed to look for a toilet. We went down one entrance, came up the other side, and did a runner all the way back to Bethnal Green!

Even during those six long years, a different kind of beauty could still be found among the horror and the fear, if only by those who chose to see it. This woman recalls her childhood spent close to the river.

[We'd been] singing songs round the piano . . . having a good time. It was a beautiful June night and we came back across in a boat, and Daddy went and tied it up. I can remember it was still, and hearing the clink and the water and the oars. It was lovely, and Mum and I sat on the edge of what was sort of a flood wall in the arch, which would have been about – what? – three feet up to stop the flood water coming in, and listened to him. He came back, and the tune they'd played was 'Always' and my mother always remembered it afterwards. We walked down to the rails and there was all this red light in the sky as you looked down the river. [It was] London burning.

[14] *The Aftermath: It's All Over, or is It?*

I can remember the first civilian plane that went over after the war. We all rushed out into the garden to watch it.

This is part of a poem written during the war by Lilian Ainger, one of the people who contributed their personal testimony to this book.

One day the war will be over,
And the lights will shine again,
And the boys will come home,
And the bells will chime,
And London will rise from the ashes,
And there will be peace again.

And we must make sure that that peace will last,
We mustn't repeat our fathers' mistakes,
Our children must never see London burn,
As I saw her burn last night.

And the following is a skipping rhyme from the 1940s, commemorating the landslide general election success of the Labour Party in 1945. To my personal knowledge, the verse was still current in the East End at the end of the 1950s, even though we had a queen rather than a king by then and Churchill had been voted back to power in 1951 and then out again in 1955. I can remember chanting it with a whole line of girls as we bounced up and down, while two of our friends turned the long skipping rope that stretched right across the street. At that time, because of the 'rude' word it contains, it definitely wouldn't have been used within adult earshot.

> Vote, vote, vote for dear old Attlee,
> Punch old Churchill in the eye.
> If it wasn't for the king,
> We would do the bastard in,
> And we wouldn't go voting any more!

The first post-war election wasn't held until July, two months after the end of hostilities – enough of a gap for the euphoria to dispel and for discontent to have had a chance to sink in. Before then, Churchill had experienced a very different public response as he was cheered, glorified and fêted as part of the country's celebration of VE Day – Tuesday 8 May 1945 – the holiday that marked the end of the war in Europe.

> The one thing that really stands out in my memory was the end of hostilities in Europe, with the lights on all over the place, and we could sleep safely in our beds, knowing that soon we would be home and making new lives together. It was good when the war in Japan ended as well, but it didn't make such an impact on me as VE Day had done.

Drab little debris-cluttered, bomb-damaged East End turnings, with jagged bits of shattered houses sticking out like broken teeth in an already dull smile, were gloriously transformed for street parties, using the same Cockney ingenuity that had helped see the residents through the travails of war. Cheap bunting in red, white and blue – made available off ration especially for the occasion – was draped from window to window and across the road and back again; garlands were threaded to decorate anything that didn't have bunting hanging off it; and banners were painted with messages declaring allegiance to king and country, and words of loving welcome in anticipation of the home-coming of family and friends in the forces. Tables, chairs and even pianos were hauled outside – despite the streets still being rain-slicked from the storms that had soaked the country in the early hours of the morning, in a somewhat uncanny echoing of the weather on the day war had been declared. Tablecloths were spread and covered with enough food and drink to keep the whole street going till the last neighbour standing finally surrendered and went to bed. Fancy-dress parades were held for the younger ones, races and games for the older children, and singing and dancing – the traditional Cockney knees-ups – for everyone and anyone who wanted to join in.

The blackout had already been partially lifted in the autumn of 1944 and had been ended completely in April 1945, so the East End was used to having its lights burning again, but the fireworks and bonfires that blazed on the evening of 8 May were to light up London in a way that – ironically – hadn't been seen since the worst of the Blitz. Bomb sites were plundered for any bits of timber that could be carted away, and the wood was built into tall wigwams, many of which were topped with gruesome effigies of Hitler ready for burning in place of the customary Guy.

I won't forget the street party at the end of the war. Bread and jam, and paste sandwiches, cakes and jelly. We had not seen so much food for years and years. Where did the mums find it all? After we all had a good feed, the dancing and singing started, and in the evening we had a big fire and the adults had beer to drink and the children ginger beer. Our bonfire got out of control and the fire engines were called. That was exciting for the kids, but the mums and dads got told off by the fire brigade!

*

One good memory I have is of a young woman, a perfect stranger, coming up to me, picking me up and twisting me round and round with tears in her eyes, saying, 'It's over, sonny Jim, the war's all over!'

Many of those who were to spend the evening in their street with those closest to them had already been celebrating in the West End – often with complete strangers, not behaviour usually associated with the reserved British public – whooping it up in Piccadilly, calling for Churchill in Downing Street, and cheering for the king in the Mall.

The day war in Europe ended, news came down to us in the incomplete tube tunnel, which [our firm] had taken over as a factory. We all stopped work and went up. It was such a relief. There were tears. Everybody was hugging and kissing one another. I went with some friends to the West End to celebrate. I say to my grandchildren, when they show pictures on the television of the celebrations in London, 'Your grandmother was amongst that crowd celebrating in Piccadilly Circus.' What a night that was.

I want to tell you about a brave East End girl. She lived in East Ham and was a WAAF officer [who] worked in the War Room bunker with Winston Churchill. She [wasn't] able to tell her story until later years because of the secrecy act, [then] she wrote her story and gave the family one each and one to me. I feel so privileged to have it . . . [as] she has now died. This is how she shared the end of hostilities: '8th of May 1945, VE day and London went mad. My watch managed to get to the office in the morning and there we were: stuck. We got through the crowds to Charing Cross station and managed to get to New Scotland Yard. From where I was escorted through a maze of tunnels, which ran through Westminster, including the Palace, parts of which form sewers, others formed passages built years ago to enable Royalty and Government to get through London to the Thames in case Britain fell. I went through some of these tunnels right down Whitehall and came up at King Charles Street. These tunnels were in constant use during the war and allowed the Prime Minister and members of the War Cabinet to travel from place to place unseen. All day and all night, Whitehall and St James Park were a solid mass of people, every nationality was represented, many had escaped from occupied countries and continued the fight in this country, now they could perhaps return to their homes and families. We were still busy with the Japanese war and many communiqués were pouring in from Germany, France and all the other countries now freed from the yoke of Nazism. But we were able to open our steel shutters and it was wonderful to let in the sunshine and fresh air. It was an experience to be in London at that time, the church bells would ring again, and not as a warning of the invasion of Britain by the Nazis, but as a symbol of hope. Everyone was tired after six years of hard work and sleepless nights with air raids; they were thankful the war was over, but sad at its cost in life and homes. Tears and laughter were close companions. The night of VE day was clear [and] warm, which was fortunate for the tens of thousands in the park. Just after midnight I went out and stood on the steps to the office to capture the atmosphere. It was indescribable. At last we could sleep in our beds, no more air raids, no more rockets, no more lives thrown away. The very air was electric. Suddenly I felt the presence of someone standing behind me – I thought it was one of the guards, but when I turned it was the P.M. He stood looking across the park to the palace, listening to the chanting of the crowds: "We want the King, we want the King!" interspersed with "We want Winnie!" He had spent a good part of the day acknowledging the cheers from the crowds both from the windows of the Home Office and at the Palace with the Royal family. He looked absolutely spent. The P.M. rested his hand on my shoulder and said, "M–, we have done a great job, but then we had a secret weapon that no other nation in the world has – we had a sense of humour. I hope I never see the day when you lose yours." As he turned to go back into the office, he added, "Don't stay too long and get chilled. You and I have a lot more work to do." It was this kind of thinking which made him so loved by those who worked with him. It was never "I" but "you and I" or "we".'

The end of hostilities was remembered with a mixture of joy and regret. Joy that peace had been declared at last, but regret that there were those who could not be there that night to enjoy the street parties with their friends and families, and, of course, that there were those who would never be there to share in the fun again. As M– put it so eloquently, at the end of the war 'tears and laughter were close companions'.

Like most people, we lost many friends in that awful war. I had a cousin, Charlie, who was presumed dead; my auntie even received the ministry notice. We did not know till the end of the war [that he was alive] when he was released with all the other prisoners after years in a stalag in Germany. Happiness at last and flags streaming from every home to welcome home our boys, our heroes, and a tear and a prayer for everyone who didn't return.

I was eight years old when the war ended, and I can remember Mum saying that Daddy was coming home. So, every day, I was asking, 'Is he coming home today?' We were staying with my aunt and uncle. Uncle T– worked at a textile factory as a manager and had use of a phone. One day, just before Christmas, he took my brother and me to work with him. The phone rang and Uncle T– said, 'Come and sit on my lap and talk on the phone.' I'd never had any dealings with phones before, but I was curious. He held the phone to my ear and said, 'Say hello,' which I did, and a voice said, 'Hello, darling, this is your daddy.' I couldn't understand why his voice was coming out of the phone and thought he was hiding. I jumped up and ran around looking behind the bales of materials to find him. Dad had actually phoned from the station to say he was on his way home. He was one of the lucky ones who made it. So many of them didn't.

Understandably, at a time when emotions were so heightened and when experiences had been so intense, there were to be other regrets.

The war was over. I was torn between two loves. I loved Westbury [where she had been evacuated], but I loved my father as well. I returned to him, after many tears at leaving Westbury and my family there, to more tears on my reunion [with her father]. I remember him to this day with love. I remember his face, full of tears, full of joy, at having me home again. This man who had lived through two world wars, still tall and upright, very proud of the young woman I was becoming, [and] I am proud to call him my father.

Despite the celebrations, life wasn't suddenly transformed into a wonderful Technicolor dream. Austerity is a word that was used not only when people were talking about wartime but also, frequently, when they described their experience of living through the years immediately after. Regardless of politicians' promises, and the possibilities presented by the Marshall Plan, life in our street was just as tough as, if not tougher than, it had been in the 1930s.

There were also more personal difficulties to be faced by men and women who had been changed by those six years and who would never be able to readjust. I was told of men who had fought and suffered only to return to their pre-war jobs, where they were expected to accept the same low wages that they had earned six years previously. Then there were the men who would never come home; marriages that wouldn't survive the years of separation; rationing that was in some instances more stringent than during the war; and housing shortages and worsening slums to face.

The following is a description of a post-war wedding which wasn't a lot different from those marriages solemnized during the height of hostilities.

I didn't get married until 1947, but it was still a Utility wedding. Firstly, we were married on 15 February. Now that winter was the coldest since records were started, and the 15th was the coldest day of the lot. That was for starters. Electricity was on ration, and it was off that afternoon, so there was no heating in the church. Fortunately, I had decided to be married in a suit to save on the coupons. It was really expensive, bought in D. H. Evans in Oxford Street. I wore it with navy-blue accessories. The reason I say 'fortunately' is because, when the photographer came to us, he told us that he had had to go back to the home of the previous bride, because she was in white, and it was too cold for her to stand outside. When we next saw the photographer, he told us that he could not take any photos, because the bride was in hospital with hypothermia.

But as one woman put it so stoically, 'I'm still here, thousands are not,' and she was right. At least the war was over and uniforms were being swapped for demob suits.

Yet not everyone was in a rush to return to the peace of the old days, a time when there had been little excitement, fun or danger to add an edge to an otherwise mundane life.

I missed my mates and I missed the exotic places I'd been lucky enough to see. Admittedly not in the best of circumstances, but it gave me a taste for travelling – for seeing something other than what blokes like me were expected to put up with for the rest of your life. I couldn't wait to get on a ship and get going again.

In fairness to him, post-war east London could hardly be described as either exotic or alluring, and it certainly wasn't remembered as such.

The East End of London in those days seemed to be full of smoke and fumes and other smells from working factories and railways.

*

Shabby is the word I'd use. Tatty. Like everywhere needed a good wash and brush-up and a coat of paint to spruce it up. But it needed more than that. A lot of it was in ruins for years. Disgrace really. But then that's the way round here's always been treated.

With the massive amount of damage, London would never look the same again, but if you did decide to stay put after being demobbed, the housing shortage – just as after the First World War – was a major issue to contend with. Apart from the state of the already cramped and antiquated housing stock, there had been a virtual halt to new building during the war, and when the severe curtailing of repairs, save those designated as absolute emergencies, was added to the equation, it is no wonder that overcrowding and slum conditions continued for many years – right into the present day, many would argue. Gradually, however, new schemes were put into place. Much of the remaining Georgian and Victorian street plan was replaced by a bold new vision of flats and high-rises, but it was a vision that was ultimately to fail, though no one admitted this for an indecently long time. Some people were moved into 'prefabs' – a supposedly temporary measure, despite some still being occupied over fifty years later – others moved out to the new estates and others just stayed away.

Down our street [Grove Road, Bow], there were two large debris or bomb sites where buildings had been bombed . . . They were used as short cuts and a very good path was worn across, and the boys used to 'play over the debris' – at what, I never knew. I can well remember walking across there to call for my friend to go to school – Coborn School in Mile End Road. My friend lived in a prefab in Antill Road [that] had been put up on part of the bomb site – originally for people whose homes had been knocked down.

*

The other members of my family – sisters, cousins and their kids – all went straight back [from evacuation in the country] to the East End after the war, but I stayed down there for a few more years as it was so hard to get a house back in London after all the bombing.

For those who did return to the East End, the changes could be quite shocking after spending years away from home.

I do not remember how we came back to London. It must have been by train. The first thing I recall is walking along a main road through the East End with Mum and some of my sisters and brother. I was holding a large bundle of coats in my arms and was enthralled at the large buildings all around me. I was looking up at these huge buildings and walked straight into an iron lamppost. These were non-existent in the village, so I had never seen one before. That really hurt and I had a lump come up on my forehead the size of a tennis ball. There were trams, lorries, cars, people walking about, thousands of them, and, of course, horses and carts – at least some of them were civilized. The bustle and noise was new to me. Half of the buildings were in ruins, smashed by the bombs, and there were large gaps in the terraced houses where the homes had been completely wrecked. Where these gaps had been left there were deep holes in the ground, partly filled with the broken bricks and timbers left over from the house. They had erected small brick walls alongside the pavement to stop people falling into the hole. Some of the houses that remained were propped up with wooden stays at the side to hold them up and were obviously unstable. In some of the larger gaps, where several houses had been demolished, they had erected temporary housing known as prefabs, for those who had been bombed out of their homes. These consisted of square prefabricated concrete buildings that had bathrooms, kitchens, living rooms and bedrooms. They were very comfortable and, although meant as a stopgap, were lived in for many years after the war. B–'s sister lived in one, as did B–'s mum and dad.

As well as the physical damage, the shortages, the continued rationing and the housing problems, there was a general economic malaise that exacerbated the doom-laden feeling induced by austerity. This had resulted from the end of the USA's Lend-Lease deal, which had been struck with the UK in 1941. Under this arrangement, America supplied Britain with goods on a lease basis, and then, come the end of the war, Britain – supposedly in a better economic position – would pay for them. But the ending of the agreement in August 1945, immediately following victory in Japan, resulted in even more difficulties for a battered and shell-shocked United Kingdom.

When women spoke about life after 1945, their memories were usually far more personal and often concerned the dissatisfaction they felt with a society that expected them to return to exactly the same social and economic position they had been in before the war. But, to paraphrase a current cliché, the Jeannie was out of the bottle . . .

> [Life] had been interesting because you'd got away from your ordinary work, but when the war was finished and the men started to come back, some of the women were leaving, because their husbands were coming home and they wanted maybe to have children and to do things . . . The chief clerk asked me if I would like to go upstairs, where all the ladies were working on a typewriting job. I did go up there but because I couldn't type, I hated it. One day I went to him and said, 'I loathe it up there. I think I'll have to leave.' And he said, 'Don't do that. I'll get you downstairs again.' I was happy then . . . the docks [had become] such a large part of my life.

Of course, women felt torn – especially those who were fortunate enough not to have lost their husbands, fiancés or boyfriends, and felt they should be grateful rather than discontented.

. . . there was a lot to celebrate at the end, but there was also an awful lot of sadness. [For us lucky ones] our menfolk returned and we had to get adjusted to married life, the men to find jobs, and us to take on our wifely duties. We all missed the good money we had been earning, but thanked God that we had been reunited with our loved ones.

But not everyone who might have been judged fortunate in these terms appreciated their situation, and some had to endure almost unbearable family difficulties. As has been well documented, some women were not ready or prepared to welcome their men home with open arms. They had tasted the hard but welcome freedom of the workplace, with its financial rewards, companionship and the opportunity to contribute to life in the wider world, and were not pleased by the prospect of having to return to domesticity. There were those who simply refused to accept being quietly shunted back into the home. I was told of how fed up some women felt at having men getting under their feet, of no longer being able to go to bed when they felt like it, and having to cook, clean and provide food for another adult – an adult who might as well have been a stranger to their children.

The presence of children could cause other problems, particularly if they were embarrassing little newcomers to the household who couldn't be explained away – it was difficult to lie about the paternity of a baby conceived at a time when the husband could not possibly be the father. While probably not exactly a common occurrence, it was, according to stories I was told and to – admittedly patchy – statistics, something that happened often enough to be remarked upon. And as adoption was being increasingly formalized during that period, it wasn't something a woman could easily conceal unless she made private, informal arrangements.

This poor girl I worked with, she disappeared, and then the next thing we knew was she had a new little 'brother' – and her mum must have been knocking fifty. We all knew what had really happened. Shame she had to pretend like that. But they were different times. Sad when you think of it. But she went on to get quite a good job, working for a dentist, so perhaps it was for the best.

Unwanted pregnancies had some young women opting for illegal, and therefore unregulated, and dangerous abortions. Several people had stories similar to the following memory, which was related to me by a woman whose family had lived in West Ham.

My mother was well known for helping people, whether it was laying out the dead, nursing a girl through her labour and delivering the baby, or, you know, helping her in other ways if she couldn't go through with having it. And there were these powders you could take, but I don't know if they really did any good or if they would make you ill. Girls who were desperate would try anything.

It wasn't only women who were scared or resentful about situations over which they had no control. Like the man who wanted to continue travelling and seeing the world, there were plenty of others who weren't able to settle back down in peacetime. They too missed the companionship and even the excitement of the past six years, but they also had terrible memories and loss to deal with on their return to the routine of everyday life. This discontent was to take its toll and 1945 saw a massive 150 per cent increase in divorce rates over those for 1938.

Children, on the other hand, seemed to prove to be more resilient – as they so often do – and, like this young lad and his pal Tommy, were to make the most of their situation, although maybe not always in a manner that would impress adults, particularly if those adults were their parents.

We spent a lot of our time playing in derelict and bombed-out houses. Most of them just had the walls and roof left, and the insides were just bare rafters. We would walk along the wooden joists and climb into the old bedrooms and ceiling areas. If my parents knew what I was doing they would have had a fit. If any walls that were remaining looked unstable, we would knock them down and generally complete the damage the Germans had started. We would also make our own toys and games, mainly from the floorboards of the bombed houses. This was a good strong plank of wood. We made scooters with the aid of ball bearings for wheels and metal bolts for axles. We also made go-carts from old pram wheels we found thrown away on bomb sites. The base and cockpit were made from the same floorboards. Thank goodness there was not much traffic on the roads, as we would race around them like madmen, with no brakes to stop the things. In the winter we made sledges from the boards. The metal runners underneath were made from thin slats taken from old beds – also found on the bomb sites. We made bows and arrows from wood we got from trees in the local churchyard and [along the] railway lines. Our favourite weapon was the catapult. These were made from a forked piece of wood that had to be carefully selected from the trees or bushes. The rubbers were obtained from strips of old cycle inner tubes, and the leather missile holders were made from the tongues of old shoes we also found. I do admit that on more than one occasion I managed to knock out a streetlight with a well-aimed stone. We were able to play cricket in the streets as well because there was not much traffic . . . We used oilcans or a lamppost for wickets, the bats were shaped from the good old floorboards and that bad boy Tommy nicked the balls . . . We could also have gone swimming in the local baths, where we had our weekly scrub-down, but that cost money. Instead, we used to go to the many canals that ran through the East End. They still had towpaths alongside the water and I often saw large carthorses towing barges laden with goods along the canal bank . . . The lads would jump or dive off the road bridges. Tommy and I had several ways of making money. We would chop up wood from the bombed houses, make them into small bundles and sell them as kindling for the fires. Just about every house needed this, as nobody had central heating, just open coal fires. We gave our own families 10 per cent off – only kidding. These coal fires caused thick black smoke to belch from every chimney, and we suffered the most horrendous thick smogs. You could literally not see a hand in front of your face sometimes, and I can still see the conductors walking in front of the buses to show the driver the edge of the road. There was a small coal merchant's in our street and when the call went out that he had received a delivery of coal, I had to queue up for my mum to get some. We could only get 28 lb at a time. We had to make it go a long way . . . Many a floorboard from the bombed houses went up in smoke in our house. Another method of earning money was not so pleasant. When the local council started moving the old people from the houses into new flats, they were not allowed to take any animals with them. Usually they were elderly ladies who kept cats. We would offer to take the cats down to the RSPCA for a shilling a time, where they would be put to sleep. We would put the cats in an old sack in case they tried to escape and run away.

The 'excitement' of the war might have been over, but there were still plenty of other thrills to take its place.

Every Saturday morning, we kids would go to the local cinema in Roman Road, known as the Bug Hutch or Flea Pit. The films put on were especially for kids, and our heroes were Flash Gordon, Laurel and Hardy, Abbott and Costello, Old Mother Riley, Roy Rogers and his horse Trigger, Hopalong Cassidy and many others. Flash Gordon was a space traveller, and every week, at the end of the episode, he would be left in a perilous position, where his life was in danger. It seemed impossible for him to escape, and we would be left in suspense until the next week, when, guess what, he survived. At other times, when adult films were showing and we couldn't get in, or could not afford the ticket money, [we] would bunk in. The method we used was to go to the exit door at the side of the cinema and, by using a bent piece of strong wire, push it through the gap between the double doors. We would then manoeuvre it around until it caught behind the fire escape release bar inside the door, give it a yank and the doors would come open. It usually took a number of tries to get it right, but that was only the beginning. We then had to go to the seating area where they had a curtain across the exit passage because of the light behind. We would get on our hands and knees and crawl under the curtain, across the aisle and squeeze into any empty seats. If the usherette didn't catch us and throw us out, we would sit there in fear of the manager coming round to ask us for our ticket stubs. Sometimes we would spend a long time trying to get through the doors and, because the management were aware of what we were doing, they would wait behind the doors and grab us, not too gently, and throw us out on to the street.

There were more organized, legal pleasures for children – pleasures that were doubly relished after the long years of restricted travel.

We'd go by train from Stepney East, and go past our own house and garden, looking down on it as if we were flying over. We'd stick our heads out of the windows in the tunnels and get soot in our eyes. My mum and Aunt Rose would get us singing: 'I do like to be beside the seaside'. We'd pack sandwiches – enough to keep Mafeking going for a month – some of which got eaten before we'd even got as far as Plaistow. When we got to Southend, the tide had always gone out about fifty miles, and wasn't due back in till Wednesday week, and the people who had bought a ticket for a boat trip around the pier sat glumly in the Skylark and waited. We'd splodge about in the smelly, grey-blue mud, up to our knees, catch crabs, eat all the sandwiches, have cups of tea from 'A Tray for the Beach', and, if the budget ran to it, we got a spill of candy floss, and even a Kiss Me Quick hat. If we didn't go by train we went on a chara. That always involved a stop halfway – that's all of fifteen miles – so that people could 'water the horse', 'strain the greens', 'spend a penny', then top up with a drink or two and give the kids a run. We even went to Margate by steamer from Dover Pier. It was so out of the ordinary, so exciting, you'd have thought we were emigrating.

The effects of the war were to linger for many more than the six years of conflict. As we have seen, its official ending didn't mean the end of having to go without. Clothes were rationed until 1949, and food only came entirely off ration in 1954, when the purchase of meat was finally deregulated – a quite astonishing nine years after the end of the war. And even as late as the 1950s, when I was a child in the East End, our games on the bomb site, clambering among the debris, still included playing 'war', and ducking down to take cover at the sight of the occasional plane going overhead. But by then the time was approaching when we would be told that we had 'Never had it so good!' and the so-called slum clearances were to result in the destruction of much of the old Cockney way of life. Refurbishment of the older housing stock was not considered an option back then. Instead, rather than putting in decent plumbing and leaving people with some choice about where they lived, there was the wholesale destruction of row after row of houses that had once been their homes. Families, neighbourhoods and eventually whole communities were split up, as people were moved out to the tower blocks and to estates like those in Dagenham and Harold Hill. Then came the final blow for great swathes of the East End – the closure of the docks and the beginning of what would become Docklands.

But all that, of course, is quite another story . . .

*

I will leave the final words to two of the people who contributed their testimonies to this book.

What a waste of life and time it all was, but, looking back, it might have shaped us into something worthwhile. I hope so.

I came to realize that not only was I lucky to survive, but also in not losing any of my relatives to the war, having not only my father but uncles and cousins in every branch of the armed forces. Two cousins in the RAF, one a flight engineer on Halifaxes and another who flew Typhoons in the 2nd TAF [Tactical Air Force], an uncle who was torpedoed in the Mediterranean, they all survived. They were to become my storytellers when they all returned home, and what stories they were! They were better than any *Boys' Own Annual* tales of derring-do. I was to relive the victorious 'Beginning of the End' Battle of Alamein, through the Normandy landings on D-Day, to the disappointment of 'A Bridge Too Far' at Arnhem. I felt that I knew what it was like to be freezing cold at 20,000 feet at night in a bomber over Germany and to launch rockets from a fighter-bomber in a 400 mph dive at the very V1 and V2 sites that were trying to destroy us at home. Now they are all gone and I find myself the storyteller for my own children and grandchildren. Unlike me they were born into more peaceful times and have been taught to regard war as the abomination that it really is, but they still like the stories.

Chronology

The following is certainly not an exhaustive chronology of the Second World War, nor is it meant to be patronizing to those who are only all too familiar with most of the events it outlines. Rather, it is intended to provide a reference framework of dates that are significant to quotes and comments made in the book, which, because of the nature of the material, was organized thematically, not chronologically.

1918

11 November First World War ends with the defeat of Germany

1919

28 June Treaty of Versailles peace treaty is finally signed by Germany and the Allies, creating the Covenant of the League of Nations and setting out the requirements for Germany's reparations, disarmament and ceding of its territories.

1921

29 July Hitler elected leader of the National Socialist Party

1930

August British unemployment over 2 million
September increasing economic crisis in Germany
15 September Nazi party has surprise election successes

1933

30 January in an economically and socially chaotic Germany, Hitler is appointed Chancellor

March escalating Nazi persecution of Jews; opening of the first concentration camps

1934

2 August President Hindenburg dies and Hitler announces he is to take the title Führer

1935

Germany breaks the terms of the Treaty of Versailles when Hitler demands the right to increase his armed forces by conscription and begins a huge rearmament programme

1936

July civil war begins in Spain

October Jarrow protest march begins to draw attention to the almost 70 per cent unemployment in the region

1937

April National defence provision is included in the British budget

27 April in support of Franco, Hitler sends the Condor Legion of the Luftwaffe to Guernica, in Spain's Basque region, to try out the new Nazi military tactic of blanket bombing a civilian population and over 1,600 people are killed

12 May coronation of King George VI and Queen Elizabeth five months after the abdication crisis

1938

January government announces that all schoolchildren will be issued with gas masks and will practise emergency drill

March Germany announces union with Austria (*Anschluss*); British car production is given over to aircraft part manufacture; major increase in Britain's defence budget as rearmament continues

29–30 September Hitler is 'appeased' when the Munich Agreement hands over the Czechoslovakian territory of the Sudetenland to Germany; Neville Chamberlain returns to Britain waving a paper signed by Hitler, which the Prime Minister claims will assure 'peace for our time'

November Sir John Anderson is given responsibility for ARP and evacuation planning

9 November *Kristallnacht*: an orchestrated night of terror against Germany's Jewish population

1939

Over 1 million unpaid civilians volunteer for civil defence duties

Unemployment continues to be a very real and debilitating problem in the many depressed regions of Britain

National Registration Act creates a register of the whole population as a precursor to the issuing of identity cards, which will happen in September

January IRA bombing campaign in London and other parts of British mainland, which continues into 1940

15 March Germany marches into Czechoslovakia, in direct contravention of the Munich Agreement

March–April Britain continues to rearm and the government introduces the compulsory conscription of men aged twenty and twenty-one

April announcement of plans to evacuate up to 3 million children if war breaks out

May Germany signs the 'Pact of Steel' with Italy

July anti-terrorism legislation is rushed through in efforts to halt IRA activities on the mainland

23 August in a surprise move, Germany signs a non-aggression pact with the Soviet Union

24 August Parliament introduces legislation making provision for emergency powers, covering matters including security, public safety, industry and the requisitioning of land and property

25 August IRA bomb kills five people in Coventry; Mutual Assistance Treaty signed between Britain and Poland

28 August 900 schools in London take part in a nationwide evacuation rehearsal

29 August Home Office declares that, as part of their air-raid precaution plans, places of public entertainment will be closed if war breaks out; speedway motorcyclists volunteer to act as dispatch riders for the London Fire Brigade if war is declared

30 August government tells people not to panic-buy as there is plenty of food available; plans revealed for the setting up of Citizens' Advice Bureaux in London and other major cities to assist people with problems in the event of war

September National Services (Armed Forces) Act extends conscription to males up to forty-one years of age; raising of the school leaving age is suspended; President Roosevelt of the United States makes declarations proclaiming his country's neutrality

1 September Germany invades Poland; in Britain the blackout is enforced and evacuation of children, pregnant women and visually handicapped people begins; hospitals in London and other strategic locations are cleared by discharging all but the most sick patients – with those remaining transferred to the countryside – to make space for the high numbers of predicted casualties from bomb and gas attacks

3 September 11 a.m. Britain declares war on Germany – as will France, Australia, Canada and New Zealand; British

Expeditionary Force is sent to France; places of public entertainment are closed and the BBC is reduced to the single Home Service station; people are obliged to carry their gas masks at all times

4 September on the home front, the beginning of the so-called Phoney or Bore War; German bombs are not causing problems, but the blackout most definitely is

10 September Canada declares war on Germany

17 September Soviet Union invades Poland

October early grumblings about food retailers profiteering begin to be heard

November Germany and Soviet Union formalize their dividing up of Poland; failed assassination attempt on Hitler; Soviet Union attacks Finland; more IRA bomb atrocities in central London

1940

Nearly half the number of evacuated children and the majority of mothers return to their homes; shortages in armed forces sees conscription age range widened again; exceptionally cold and stormy winter with fuel shortages adding to the discomfort

8 January rationing of food begins in Britain

February government launches one of its many poster campaigns, this one concerned with gossip, including slogans which entered everyday language, such as, 'Walls Have Ears' and 'Careless Talk Costs Lives'

3 April Lord Woolton is made Minister of Food

9 April Germany invades Denmark and Norway

10 May Germany invades France, Belgium, Luxembourg, the Netherlands; Churchill replaces Neville Chamberlain as Prime Minister

14 May Anthony Eden makes appeal for Local Defence Volunteers, later to be renamed the Home Guard

15 May Dutch surrender

19 May in France, the British Expeditionary Force withdraws to the Channel coast, where they are trapped under fire

22 May an extension of the Emergency Powers Act of the previous August is rushed through, giving the government unprecedented authority over the British population and its property

26 May–4 June Operation Dynamo, the evacuation of Allied forces from Dunkirk: approximately 338,000 British, French and Belgian troops are rescued by the navy and a supporting armada of civilian vessels

June appeal goes out from the Ministry of Aircraft Production for scrap metal, as workers in the industry do a seventy-hour, seven-day week

28 June Charles de Gaulle recognized by Britain as leader of the Free French

July U-boats attack merchant ships in the Atlantic; timber in very short supply – women urged to wear lower heels to help conserve stocks

10 July–31 October Royal Air Force fights the Battle of Britain

13 August south-east England bombarded by the Luftwaffe

15 August daylight raids and air battles over Britain

17 August Germany declares a blockade of Britain

23–24 August all-night air raids on central London

3 September Operation Sealion, Germany's plans for invasion of Britain, is set for 21 September

7 September the Blitz begins and the East End is the target as the docks are set ablaze in a second Great Fire of London; lacking adequate shelters, Londoners take refuge in underground stations – despite government concerns about health and safety and civilian morale

15 September massive air raids on London, Bristol, Cardiff, Southampton, Manchester and Liverpool; survey shows that two-thirds of Londoners are getting fewer than four hours' sleep a night because of the raids, and the majority of them still have no official provision for sheltering

12 October Operation Sealion postponed until spring 1941 as Germany's focus turns to the Soviet Union

4 November London experiences first night without bombing raids since 7 September

9 December Britain begins western desert offensive against Italy in North Africa

1941

22 January Tobruk, North Africa, captured by the British and Australians

March succession of calls from Ministry of Labour for women to 'do their bit' for the war effort; essential work order requires all skilled workers to register and move to more essential work as instructed

11 March US Congress passes the Lend-Lease Act, allowing Britain to be supplied with equipment for which it would not have to pay until after the war

April National Service Act allows for all citizens to be liable for national service, military or civilian

10–11 May that night massive bombing raids over London, damaging the Houses of Parliament, Westminster Abbey, St Paul's Cathedral, the Tower of London and the Royal Mint

24 May HMS *Hood* is sunk by the *Bismarck*

27 May Royal Navy sinks the *Bismarck*

June clothes rationing introduced

14 June USA freezes German and Italian assets

22 June launch of Germany's Operation Barbarossa, attacking the Soviet Union

12 July Britain and Soviet Union sign pact of Mutual Assistance

December increasing shortages of goods sees 'points' scheme introduced to supplement rationing
7 December Japanese attack the American Pacific Fleet at Pearl Harbor
8 December Britain and United States declare war on Japan
9 December conscription age for men raised to fifty; call-up introduced for single women aged between twenty and thirty, with the National Service Act now making war work compulsory; lifting of the marriage bar to allow women to enter the labour force

1942

Steep rise in incidence of venereal disease causes increasing official concern
January the first GIs arrive in Britain at a time of escalating scarcity
20 January SS leader Heydrich runs the Wannsee Conference on the implementation of the 'Final Solution' for the so-called 'Jewish Question'
February soap rationed to a single 3oz bar per month; lines painted in baths to indicate acceptable depth of hot water as fuel shortages take grip
23 April bombing of historic British cathedral cities
June domestic crockery no longer to be available in decorated, fancy designs, but only plain, white and functional
21 June Rommel takes Tobruk
July British 8th Army holds the German offensive at El Alamein in Egypt; sweet rationing introduced
August furniture rationing introduced, with the Utility scheme restricting the quality and design to twenty-two basic items; Montgomery takes command of the 8th Army in North Africa
October–November Battle of El Alamein; the Germans were

finally forced to retreat and, on 15 November, church bells were rung all over Britain in celebration of the victory in Egypt – famously dubbed by Churchill as '. . . not the end . . . not even the beginning of the end . . . But . . . perhaps, the end of the beginning'

2 December in Chicago, Professor Enrico Fermi creates the first controlled nuclear chain reaction

17 December Anthony Eden, the Foreign Secretary, makes statement in the House of Commons about the Nazis' mass extermination of Jewish people

1943

January unemployment now almost non-existent, but austerity is an increasing problem

18 January resumption of Luftwaffe raids on London

2 February last of the German army surrender at Stalingrad, their first major defeat

3 March Bethnal Green tube disaster

May all women aged between eighteen and forty-five are now expected to be involved in some form of war work

16–17 May that night Guy Gibson leads the Dambusters raid

9 July Allies invade German-occupied Sicily

3 September Allies invade Italy

13 October Italy declares war on Germany

18 November RAF launches intensive raid on Berlin

1944

Suspension of the three-year 'cooling off' period to facilitate quieter divorces for people married during wartime

Following a series of miners' strikes, inciting or causing stoppages of essential work is made an offence

Civil Employment Act compels all employers of those on national service to give them back their former jobs after demobilization

21 January–8 April Londoners experience the 'Little Blitz'
March RAF using increased bombing power in its continuing raids on German cities
12 May Germans surrender in Crimea
4 June Allies enter Rome
6 June D-Day landings by Allied forces in Normandy
12–13 June that night first V1 flying bomb hits London
July evacuation from London again under way
25 August liberation of Paris
September Allied troops continue to push forward through France and Belgium
8 September first attack by a V2 rocket in Britain
17 September blackout replaced by far less stringent 'dim-out'
20 October surrender at Aachen sees the first German town in Allied hands
December Home Guard is 'stood down' and will be officially disbanded one year later; plans revealed for post-war London, including new towns, a green belt and ring roads
16 December Battle of the Bulge begins in the Ardennes

1945
27 January Auschwitz liberated
28 January Battle of the Bulge ends
4–12 February Churchill, Roosevelt and Stalin meet at Yalta, in the Crimea, to discuss how they will deal with Germany and Japan in the post-war world
13 February RAF razes Dresden, with estimated deaths of up to 250,000 people
27 March last V2 launched at Britain
29 March last V1 launched at Britain
13 April Belsen and Buchenwald liberated
28 April Mussolini captured and hanged by Italian partisans
29 April Dachau liberated

30 April Hitler commits suicide
2 May German troops in Italy surrender to the Allies
4 May Britain captures Rangoon in Burma
7 May unconditional surrender of all German forces at Rheims
8 May Victory in Europe – VE – Day celebrated
28 May Lord Haw-Haw (William Joyce) captured at Flensburg
26 July following the results of the general election on 5 July, Labour takes power as a landslide sees Attlee succeed Churchill as Prime Minister
6 August US Air Force drops the first atomic bomb on Hiroshima
9 August US Air Force drops the second atomic bomb on Nagasaki
14 August Japan agrees to unconditional surrender
15 August Victory over Japan – VJ – Day

Acknowledgements

My sincere thanks to all the people who wrote to me – some with stories for the book, some just to reminisce, others with poems written during the war and in later life when thinking back – to those I met and interviewed, to those I spoke to on the telephone and to those who sent me e-mails.

There were a few people – those I met in bookshops who were kind enough to give me their telephone numbers so that we could meet up and discuss their experiences – who, sadly, I was unable to contact due to a file lost after my computer was infected with a virus. I hope we have the chance to meet again, as I'd love to speak to you.

As promised to those who contributed their stories, I have kept their identity anonymous. Occasionally, for clarity or because I was requested to do so, I have included names or places, but, I hope, not in any way that will compromise anyone's confidentiality.

Roy Abbott
Walter Ablett
Lilian Ainger
Laura Anderson
Bob Aspinall (Museum in Docklands)
Harry Atterbury
Reg Baker
C. H. Barnes
Patricia Bennett
Irene Bishop
Stanley Brand
Heather Brown

Fred Burman
Carpenters Estate History Group: Mary Bushell, Evelyn Collings, Nicky James Collings, Molly Coutts, Maureen Elly, Jean Ferrett, Nancy Goodyear, Joan Halford, Donna Keizar, Vera Le Masurier, Alice Lloyd, Clara Marney, Frances Nash, Joan Shield, Violet Sloan, Roy Thomas, Vic Turner Jnr, Vic Turner Snr, Sue Ward, Sue Wooldridge
Mrs Q. Champness
John Copley
Eric Cropper
Thomas Daniels
Joan Dann
Julia Deeks
Bill Dykes (now living in the USA. I have tried to contact you several times, Bill, but failed. I do hope you get to see the book)
Ethel Edwards
Joan English
Jack Fearon
Jean Fenn
the late Ken Fletcher
Dick Flockhart
Charles E. Foster
Eileen Gadd
Doreen Gibbs (Edmunds)
Pat Gordon
Pat Gray
Anne Griffiths
Tom Griffiths
Coralie Grogan
Mrs Audrey Guy
L. G. Guy
Mrs J. Hall
Freda Hammerton

Connie Hardcastle
Henry Harrington
Bessie Harris
Harry
Dawn Hawes and the stories of Shirley and Lenny Bradford
Mrs J. L. Hawkins
Derek Houghton
Ron Ingram
Doris Jackson
Estelle Jenkins
Mrs F. Johnson
Thomas Keyworth
Grace Knight (Westfallen)
Gus Krayer
Warren Lakin
M. Leach
H. E. Lilley
Chris Lloyd (Tower Hamlets Local History Archive)
Dorothy Lloyd
Ada Marshall
Roy H. Matthews
Len Mellon
Catherine Merrett
Alan Miller
Elsie Miller
Georgina Murphy
Jeff Nicholls
Ernie Oakley
Frank Osborne
M. Oughton
Marjorie Oxley
Winifred Parker
Lesley Pavitt
the late Rosina Pavitt

Vera Penman (whose sisters, Rene and Gladys, are two of the 'cover girls' on *My East End*)
Emma Piquemal, the Media Trust, and all the members of the Carpenters Estate History Group
Mrs D. Pountney
Bob Putt
Hazel Prentice
Phyllis Pryor
Paddy Rehithven
Lavinia Richardson and for stories and memories of her friend Betty and her late friend Margot, known as 'Peg'
Harry Roberts
Stanley Rose
Grace Rowse
David Sawyer
Violet Shaves
George Shaw
Joan Shaw
Wally Shea
Vi Sloan
Sylvia Small
Doreen Smith
H. L. Smith
Joan Smith
Olive Smith
Mrs Y. Smith
Len Spinks
Alan Still
Mary Josephine and Robert Tachauer
Don Taylor
James (Jim) Taylor
Pat Taylor
Pat Thompson
Richard Tidiman (editor, *East London Advertiser*)

Stanley Tooth
Ellen Turner
Leonard J. Turner
Barry Wade and his father, Albert
Enid Walsh
G. A. Ware
May White
Oriel Williams of the Museum in Docklands for her help and kindness in obtaining permission for me to use quotes from the museum's oral testimony archive – the names of the interviewees appear in this list
Ivy Wilson
Mrs M. L. Wood
Ivy Woodhead
Reginald Wright
Betty Yates
And, of course, those who chose to remain anonymous, and those who will not see their stories in print because of their untimely deaths; I hope their families can take some little comfort in my heartfelt efforts to do justice to their memories.

Sources of Information and Suggestions for Further Reading

Bethnal Green Museum of Childhood
Bishopsgate Institute
British Library and the Colindale Newspaper Library
Guildhall Library
Imperial War Museum
Internet (Information posted on the Internet needs to be treated very carefully, and additional sources should be used to verify data, but official sites, such as that of the Royal Air Force, can be very useful. The RAF site, for instance, covers the Battle of Britain, including daily reports for the whole period from 10 July to 31 October 1940.)
Mass-Observation Archive, University of Sussex (This is a good source for getting the flavour of the period, but, and I am not alone in this, I found much of the material distractingly condescending, as though it had been written by 'them' about 'us'. It might be a useful place to begin researching class attitudes in the 1940s.)
Museum in Docklands
Museum of London
Newham Local History Archive
Peace Pledge Union
Public Record Office
Tower Hamlets Local History Archive
Zoological Society of London

Addison, Paul, *The Road to 1945: British Politics and the Second World War* (1994)

Briggs, Susan, *Keep Smiling Through* (1975)

Calder, Angus, *The People's War* (1969)
– *The Myth of the Blitz* (1992)
Croall, Jonathan, *Don't You Know There's a War On?* (1989)
Demarne, Cyril, *The London Blitz: A Fireman's Tale* (1991)
Hylton, Stuart, *Their Darkest Hour* (2001)
Longmate, Norman, *How We Lived Then* (1971)
Mack, Joanna, and Steve Humphries, *London at War: The Making of Modern London* (1985)
Marwick, Arthur, *The Home Front* (1976)
Minns, Raynes, *Bombers and Mash* (1980)
Morton, James, *East End Gangland* (2000)
O'Neill, Gilda, *Pull No More Bines: An Oral History of East London Women Hop Pickers* (1990)
Samways, R., *We Think You Ought to Go: Account of the Evacuation of Children from London during the Second World War* (1995)
Smithies, Edward, *Crime in War Time* (1984)
Thorpe, Andrew, *Britain in the Era of the Two World Wars 1914–45* (1994)
Ziegler, Philip, *London at War 1939–1945* (2000)